H23 662 756 5

FRANKLIN, J.

Navy board ship models 1650 - 1750

Navy Board Ship Models 1650-1750

JOHN FRANKLIN

CONWAY
MARITIME PRESS

© John Franklin 1989

First published in Great Britain in 1989 by
Conway Maritime Press Ltd
24 Bride Lane, Fleet Street
London EC4Y 8DR

British Library Cataloguing in Publication Data
Franklin, John
  Navy Board ship models 1650–1750.
  1. Sailing warships, 1400–1860
  I. Title
  623.8'225'0903
  ISBN 0-85177-454-7

Designed by John Mitchell
Typeset by Lasertext Ltd, Stretford, Manchester
Printed and bound in Great Britain by
The Bath Press Ltd

Frontispiece
This model of the Third Rate Royal Oak
(c1741) is one of the finest examples of eighteenth-century craftsmanship. NMM

Contents

Acknowledgements

The preparation of this book has depended to a large extent on the cooperation of a considerable number of museums, institutions and private individuals. Information and a great deal of other help has been given freely and often far in excess of that requested, without which it would not have been possible. To all of the following, I would like to express my very sincere and grateful thanks.

The Trustees of the National Maritime Museum, and Dr A P McGowan, Chief Curator, in particular, for allowing the models to be removed from their cases for study and photography; Stephen Riley, David Tull, and especially Simon Stephens of the Department of Ships at the National Maritime Museum; David White and the Staff of the Draught Room at the National Maritime Museum; Mr Schuyler Jones, Curator of the Pitt-Rivers Museum, Oxford, for allowing me to study and photograph the models there; Linda Mowat, Research Assistant at the same museum for her generous assistance; Trinity House, London, for permission to see their collection of ship models, and to reproduce photographs of the *Bredah*; the Master and Fellows of Magdalene College, Cambridge, for permission to reproduce Anthony Deane's draughts; the Editor of *The Mariner's Mirror* for permission to quote from the Society for Nautical Research Occasional Publication No 6, *A Treatise on Shipbuilding* 1620–1625, edited by W Salisbury and R C Anderson; the Navy Records Society for permission to publish extracts from *The Autobiography of Phineas Pett*, Vol 51, and *Samuel Pepys' Naval Minutes,* Vol 60; Bell and Hyman Ltd for allowing the publication of extracts from the *Diary of Samuel Pepys*; the Hakluyt Society, for the quotation from *The Travels of Peter Munday;* the Staff of the Public Record Office, Kew, and of the Guildhall Library, London.

Arthur McGregor, Assistant Keeper at the Ashmolean Museum, Oxford, for his kindness in providing extensive information on the models at the Pitt-Rivers Museum; Dr Richard Luckett, Pepys Librarian, for his great help with the scales of Matthew Baker and Anthony Deane; Brian Lavery, for bringing to my notice the letters about the model for the Admiralty Boardroom and help in other ways; the Earl Cawdor for information on the model of the *Victory* in his possession; the Earl of Pembroke for allowing me to study and photograph the model at Wilton House; Mr V Montagu for welcoming me into his home to examine his collection of models; John Armstrong for his friendship and assistance.

My special thanks are extended to Mr and Mrs Roman H Kriegstein, Henry J Kriegstein and Arnold R Kriegstein for their hospitality, generosity and unfailing kindness in providing many of the photographs in this book, and much information on their extensive collection of ship models.

Finally, I would like to thank Robert Gardiner of Conway Maritime Press, not only for accepting my book in the first place, but for his patience and understanding in awaiting my long overdue manuscript.

Photographs taken by the Author are reproduced, where applicable, by courtesy of the following: the National Maritime Museum, Greenwich, London; Mr Roman H Kriegstein, New York; the Earl of Pembroke, Wilton House, nr Salisbury, Wiltshire; Trinity House, London; and the Pitt-Rivers Museum, Oxford.

I
Historical Background

Although the story of English models of ships of war begins in the late sixteenth century with those known to have been built by the shipwright Phineas Pett, this book commences at around 1650, being the earliest time from which models survive in any numbers. It is terminated in 1750, not so much because later models are of less interest—there are many fine examples from the second half of the eighteenth century—but to confine it to a reasonable length of time. This one hundred years was the classic period of the Navy Board models, which were made in large numbers, as miniature replicas of the sailing warships, at the same time as the ships themselves were built. They are also often referred to as Admiralty or Dockyard models. These are all modern terms which may or may not be entirely accurate descriptions, and are usually given to mean the highly detailed and unplanked models, although they could be applied equally to the simple block models of the eighteenth century, for example. However, as Navy Board is the name by which they are generally and popularly known, I have used it exclusively to distinguish the detailed models, whether planked or not, from other types.

Apart from mentioning some of the techniques which may have been employed by the early craftsmen, this book is not concerned with instruction on how to build a Navy Board model, nor with the construction of the ships themselves, although it has been found necessary to touch on this subject at times to illustrate a point and make a comparison. The intention is rather to bring to wider notice certain aspects of models which are not readily apparent from observing them enclosed in glass cases, or from the necessarily limited descriptions on their labels. There was also felt to be a need for illustrating important models in private hands which are otherwise practically unknown. In this respect, I have had the privilege of examining the extensive collection of fine models formed by the Kriegstein family, a superb seventeenth-century Third Rate in the possession of the Earl of Pembroke, several very interesting and important examples belonging to Mr V Montagu, and others at Trinity House. I have also been very fortunate in having had the opportunity to take off the dimensions and make a close study of many models, and at the National Maritime Museum, the use of fibre optics was made available as an aid to examining the interiors.

This proved to be of very great value, and revealed details of the internal construction which, to myself at least, were not entirely expected, but with delight none the less. Constructional details in the holds such as footwales or sleepers, floor riders, pillars,

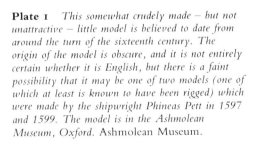

Plate 1   This somewhat crudely made – but not unattractive – little model is believed to date from around the turn of the sixteenth century. The origin of the model is obscure, and it is not entirely certain whether it is English, but there is a faint possibility that it may be one of two models (one of which at least is known to have been rigged) which were made by the shipwright Phineas Pett in 1597 and 1599. The model is in the Ashmolean Museum, Oxford. Ashmolean Museum.

breast hooks and transom knees are often fitted. 'Pointers' have been noted on two eighteenth-century models—a Third Rate of about 1712, belonging to Mr Montagu, and a Second Rate of about 1740 at the National Maritime Museum. These were pairs of diagonal braces spaced along the length of the hull in the hold and are well known in seventeenth-century shipbuilding, but not so much for the later period, although the use of them can be confirmed from the Establishment list of 1719. Buried below decks are finely made capstans, working whipstaffs and rope steering gear in meticulous detail, some of which may not have been seen since the models were first built. It is rather an eerie experience to see the work of a long-dead craftsman, such as a capstan on the lower deck of a seventeenth-century model, untouched and still covered with the dust accumulated over a period of more than three hundred years.

The Navy Board models are unique and quite extraordinary objects, not only for their great historical interest in illustrating the form, structure and decoration of ships from an earlier age in such perfect detail, but also for their beautiful appearance and the remarkable execution of the work in making them. Because they are in three dimensions, a very great deal can be learnt from models which cannot be obtained from any other source, such as documentary material, pictures and draughts, and it can be taken for granted that most of the constructional work follows very closely the practice in full-size shipbuilding. That they are unique is simply because nothing else exists which so vividly illustrates in miniature the industrial technology of anything — other than ships — which was produced in the seventeenth and eighteenth centuries. It is doubtful, too, whether anything else has ever been made from so many thousands of tiny and intricately shaped pieces of wood.

In the field of naval architecture, seventeenth-century models are of course highly important for their hull design, and for students of the subject and modelmakers it would be of enormous interest if the lines could be taken off some of them. As far as I know, only two models have had their lines taken off—the First Rate *Prince*, 1670, at the Science Museum, and the Fourth Rate *St Albans*, 1687, at Trinity House, draughts of which can be obtained respectively from the National Maritime Museum and the Science Museum. Very few contemporary draughts exist for the period prior to about 1700, and for the modeller wishing to make one of a seventeenth-century ship, the choice is very limited. One advantage of the models being in frame is that the hull shape can be followed infinitely better than on a fully planked example, and it is clear that there are very many interesting variations for ships of all Rates, particularly for the lines at bow and stern.

Origin and purpose

For the most part, the origin and history of Navy Board models is shrouded in mystery, and hardly anything is known of those who made them, which ship they are intended to represent, and not least, the purpose for which they were made. The widespread opinion is that they were made as preliminary designs for approval by the Navy Board (and, in the seventeenth century, the King) before the ship was begun, and so that members of the Board unfamiliar with the subject could better understand the proposed construction. This is sometimes proclaimed as an established fact when there appears to be no real evidence to support the supposition. The idea is an attractive one, but is it really true? What evidence there is suggests the contrary in general. It is very difficult to believe that an incredibly detailed model would be prepared as a preliminary design, and looking at it from a purely practical point of view, the time factor in building them alone would preclude it. Superbly detailed models are suggested as being preliminary designs for a group of ships, such as the Third Rate 70s of the 1719 Establishment, for example, in which case they would be of no particular ship. But it seems hardly feasible that one would be prepared as a design for ships which, after all, had only a small increase in dimensions and were very little different in appearance, general features and fittings from their immediate predecessors. We know that in the seventeenth century, Phineas Pett made a framed model of the famous *Royal Sovereign,* 1637, as a design before the ship was begun, and it is possible that some of the earliest framed models that exist may have been preliminary designs also,

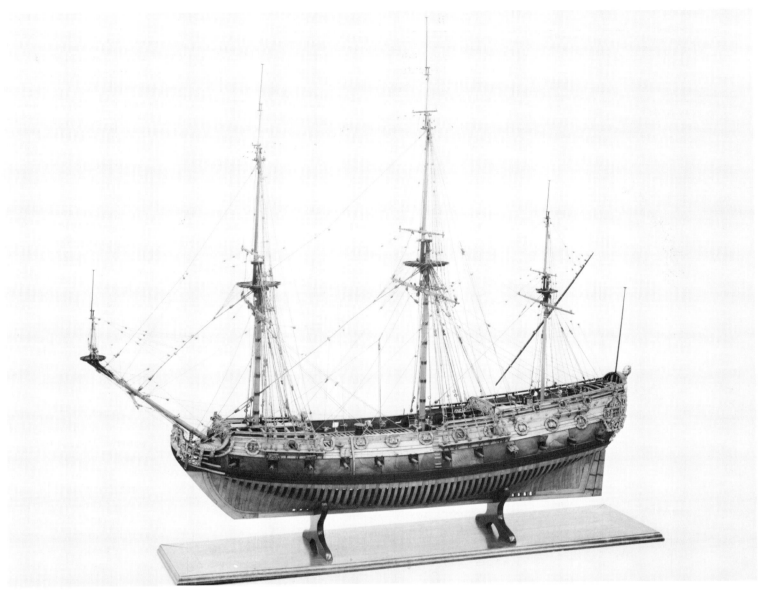

Plate 2 *A typical unidentified seventeenth-century Navy Board model of a Fourth Rate of about 1695. The model was once in the collection of King William IV. The rigging is of recent origin. NMM.*

★ It is not always certain whether this was actually intended to mean a model in three dimensions or a draught, considering the ambiguity of the term in the seventeenth century.

but it is hard to accept that the superbly made and detailed ones dating from after around 1670 come into that category. As an example, the well known model of the Second Rate *St Michael*, 1669, can be cited, which is one of the earliest of the detailed models. If the model had been a design for the *St Michael*, it would have been made at some time in the mid-1660s. She was a prestige ship, and we can be sure that if the model was presented at the Admiralty for approval by the King, the Duke of York and members of the Navy Board, the industrious Mr Pepys, Clerk of the Acts, would no doubt have mentioned this important event in his famous Diary, probably at some length. Pepys had an insatiable interest in anything beautifully made or of a curious nature and was clearly fascinated by ship models, but although there are frequent references to them in the Diary, there is not one word to connect them with the design process.

Models *were* certainly made as designs, and there are official orders requesting shipwrights to do so, but they are not entirely specific as to the form they should take. In an order dated 1645, for example, shipbuilders were required to present 'moddles' before they 'proceed in building'.[1] This could have meant anything.★ In a Navy Board order of 1716, the Master Shipwrights were requested to submit a 'solid' as a design, and this was almost certainly intended to mean a simple block model, not a detailed one (see Appendix I on block models). A painted block model was all that was really necessary as a design (to show the shape of the hull,

Plate 3 *Documentary evidence relating to eighteenth-century models is extremely rare, especially when it specifically refers to a known model. This entry (headed by a small drawing of a ship) in the Ashmolean Museum Book of Benefactors records a model made in the Queen Anne period by William Lee for Dr George Clarke. Clarke presented the model to the Ashmolean at some time before his death in 1735, and it is now in the Pitt-Rivers Museum, Oxford. A translation of the Latin is given in the description of Model No 18. Ashmolean Museum.*

the gun port arrangement and other external features) to meet the requirements of the order. Block models were clearly made in fairly large numbers from soon after the turn of the eighteenth century, but it is quite likely that they were made for design purposes long before, and the fact that they have not survived is perhaps because they were not considered worth keeping. Although it can only be speculation, there may be another reason for the disappearance of block models if they were indeed made in the seventeenth century. It is quite possible that after perfecting the shape of the hull, the models were sliced up at the stations to prove the lines, or even that the sections were actually used to draw the finished body plan. Ways can be found of building a Navy Board framed hull so that it can be dismantled at the station lines and reassembled, and the earliest examples of these, too, may have been used for the same purpose.

As to the purpose for which the detailed Navy Board models were made, several suggestions can be offered. Several eighteenth-century models are known with certainty to have been specially made as commissions. A very fine rigged Third Rate from the Queen Anne period at the Pitt-Rivers Museum, Oxford, was made as a commission by William Lee from a Dr George Clarke. The records of the model are not specific, but this was almost certainly Master Shipwright Lee of Woolwich, and although Clarke held high positions at the Admiralty, the model was clearly made for him in a private capacity, and had no connection with the Navy Board (see Model No 18). Another one is the Fourth Rate *Centurion*, 1732, which was made in around 1747 for Lord Anson. That some models are known to have been made as a commission at all suggests in turn that it must have been a fairly common practice throughout the period, and others would no doubt have been specially made as gifts for important persons. The *St Michael*, 1669, for example, was apparently once owned by Rear Admiral Sir Robert Holmes[2], and being Commander of that ship, it was probably made specially for him.

Another suggestion is that many models may have been begun at the same time as the ship itself, and while they might not have been completed in every detail of decoration until many years later, the hull was built in stages corresponding to the work on the ship. Perhaps the Surveyor of the Navy visited the dockyards periodically to inspect the work, and the proposed internal layout, for instance, could have been demonstrated to him directly from the model. This might explain the small alterations which are sometimes seen on models, which were clearly carried out at the time they were made. Gun ports are seen to be blocked up, and bitts are shifted from one side of a beam to another, with the original holes so carefully filled in they are practically invisible. On a rigged Fourth Rate of about 1695, at the National Maritime Museum, the mizzen mast was shifted aft about a scale 4ft 0in, and the old holes in the decks repaired. All this may have been done due to a change of mind while the ship was being built. Experiments may have been carried out on models while they were being made, which would account for the presence of some of the detailed work below decks that can be seen on the completed model only with great difficulty. This is suggested by an unidentified Second Rate, about 1702, at the National Maritime Museum, which is fitted with the earliest known example of steering worked by rope, and is one of the very few where the rope itself is actually in position. The arrangement of ropes is somewhat different from the usual practice of later years, and it may have been done as an experiment to demonstrate the new-fangled steering system on the model while the ship it represents was building. If this was the case, it would not have mattered if the work was covered up afterwards and not easy to see.

It appears that those involved in modelmaking were mainly shipwrights and no doubt a number of models were made by these men purely as a pastime to celebrate the full-sized ships they had built. For instance, a very beautiful and highly detailed rigged Third Rate in the possession of the Earl of Pembroke can be deduced (but not certainly) from initials on the cradles to have been made by John Shish. The cradles also bear the date 1692, but the last Third Rate built by Shish was thirteen years earlier in 1679. There are reasons for believing that it is indeed one of the ships built by Shish, and we can imagine that he spent many years lovingly and patiently making and rigging this elaborate model, and finally, in 1692, put on it the date of completion. Young shipwrights may have made models as well—not as designs but as an aid to learning the art of shipbuilding.

As so little is known about the real purpose behind Navy Board models, nothing absolutely certain can be said about it. But the weight of evidence (particularly the time factor) strongly suggests that they were not preliminary designs, with the qualification that some of the earliest models may have been, and perhaps some of the other less detailed ones of the seventeenth century.

The hallmark of the Navy Board model is, of course, the very distinctive framing of the hull. The basic principle of construction remained unchanged for over one hundred years except for variations in building up the deadwoods, and it may have been in use for modelmaking long before the date of the earliest surviving models. The hulls are generally supposed to be left unplanked below the wales so that the interior could be examined, but I find it hard to believe that this was the real purpose, for two main reasons. Firstly, the internal work in the hold can only be seen by placing an eye close to the small gaps between the futtocks and stern transoms, and then only with difficulty and in a strong light. Secondly, although the construction in the hold is of great value to us today, it is all normal shipbuilding practice, which would be of no particular interest to anyone at around the time the model was built. To build a model so that all the decks and other internal details could be fitted, it was necessary to construct a framed hull. The early modelmakers obviously took enormous pride in their hull construction, and there would have been little point in covering it all up with plank. Furthermore, it saved them a great deal of work! But whatever the reason, we can be thankful that models were left unplanked, otherwise much of the interest in Navy Board hulls would be lost.

The model builders

The consumate craftsmen who built these beautiful models are shadowy figures—a few names only are about the sum total of our knowledge. Some of them can be deduced from initials on cradles or sterns to be known shipwrights, but only a handful of actual names are known with any certainty, and then only for those men who were working in the eighteenth century. The two earliest are the aforementioned William Lee, and William Hammond, a young shipwright from Portsmouth Dockyard who is recorded as having made the Third Rate *Captain*, 1708. This model is at the Science Museum, London. No names appear to be known from then until 1744, when James Edwards, John Mitchell and Adam Cooper were seconded from Deptford to Woolwich Dockyard to assist in the completion of a model for the Admiralty Boardroom. These men were shipwrights, but it is probable that for much of the time they were employed in the building and rigging of models. In 1747, Benjamin Slade of Plymouth Dockyard made a model of the Fourth Rate *Centurion*, 1732, for the former Commander of that ship, Lord Anson. A Third Rate of about 1745 is recorded as being made by John Hancock of Deptford Dockyard. This model is unidentified, but being made at Deptford suggests a connection with a few Third Rates built there in the 1740s. Hancock also made a model of the Sixth Rate *Dolphin*, 1731, as she was after being converted to a fireship in 1747. The last three models are at the National Maritime Museum[3]. Although nothing is known of the models he built, mention must be made of Prince George of Denmark, husband of Queen Anne and Lord High Admiral of the Navy, who had small workshops for that purpose at St James Palace.[4] This is quite intriguing. The models made by Prince George may have been simple ones, but on the other hand it is feasible that he was a competent craftsman and built them in the typical fashion of the time. We may wonder whether any examples of his work survive.

In the case of a model known to have been made by a certain person, or when

Plate 4 *The bow of the* Royal William *showing the superbly carved equestrian figurehead. Although he died 17 years earlier, King William III is allegorically depicted as riding roughshod over his enemies who are symbolised by a manacled figure. NMM.*

initials suggest a known shipwright, the name could be taken in general as being that of the principal craftsman involved in the work. This can only be assumed, however, for it is probable that in some cases initials or a name on a model were just put there out of courtesy to the Master Shipwright of the Dockyard where it was made. The Third Rate *Boyne*, 1692, for instance, has enscribed on the break of the poop 'Ye Boyne Bt by Mr Harding', which means that Fisher Harding built the ship herself, and he may not have had any hand in building the model. Another model, which has the date 1698 and initials FH on the cradles, appears to be of a quite different style of craftsmanship from the *Boyne*, although it probably represents another of Harding's ships.

There would have been a number of other men engaged in making a model, as well as those employed in the actual shipwrights' work. Carvers, artists, specialists in miniature metal work and others would all be involved. On the best eighteenth-century models, details such as tiny hinges on bulkhead doors, and filigree work sometimes seen on stern galleries (perhaps made from silver), are of such superb quality it suggests that jewellers, or perhaps watchmakers, were brought in from outside the Yard to assist in the work. Detail work on different models can often be detected as being apparently made by the same hand. An example of this is seen on the Third Rate of 1692 at Wilton House which probably originated from Deptford Dockyard, as did the *Boyne* of the same date, and on both models the distinctive design and manufacture of the port lid straps are so exactly similar that they were almost certainly made by the same man.

Although there are some slightly inferior models, the quality of workmanship in general was of a consistently high standard throughout the period. But this same quality is relative to the period in which a model was made. The craftsmanship of the Second Rate *Coronation*, 1685, for instance, does not compare with the best work carried out in the eighteenth century, but it is a superb example for the time when it was made. The change came about quite suddenly, and it appears as though a completely new school of modelmakers emerged in a fairly short period at around the turn of the eighteenth century, roughly corresponding to the accession of Queen Anne. I suppose it depends on one's preference, but in my opinion the quality of seventeenth-century models is far more attractive than the more precise nature of the work in later years. The seventeenth-century modelmaker was certainly more concerned with actual joints in construction, and many finely fitted examples can be found of various kinds from scarphs to dovetails. Sometimes joints can only be detected when the glue has failed, such as on a particularly well made Fourth Rate of about 1691 at the National Maritime Museum, where the cross piece of the fore jeer bitts is loose. Instead of a simple slot as might be thought, the cross piece itself is scored and fitted with a form of bridle joint let into housings each side of the bitts. This was a much stronger joint, and it was no doubt done simply because it was the proper one, although it would have entailed more work and be impossible to see after it was put together. It is minor details like this which are one of the fascinations of Navy Board models, and it well illustrates the lengths gone to by men who were unconcerned with extra work and to whom time was of little consequence. Everything was of course made entirely by hand with sharp cutting tools and scrapers, giving that indefinable quality to the work which is almost impossible to achieve by the use of machines and glasspaper. Between them, the hullmakers, carvers, painters and metal workers created a true work of art, albeit one of a severely technical nature.

Modern restoration

In the earlier years of this century — or perhaps even before — a great deal of 'restoration' was carried out, and many models are not all they appear to be. Damaged hulks with much of their decoration missing were repaired, rigged, sometimes altered, and transformed into highly finished models with added details such as anchors. These models are full of anachronisms. No doubt the intentions were good and the work may have been well done, but in consequence they have completely lost any value they once had as historical records. The worst of this was carried out on models in America, but to a lesser extent it was prevalent in England as well, which is sometimes unsuspected. This is very difficult to detect due to replaced carvings, repairs and overpainting having attained some sort of age in their own right. But 'restoration' can be obvious, as on an attractive little model of a galley-frigate at the Pitt-Rivers Museum where much of the black work, including the capstan etc, is overpainted with a rather lurid purplish colour, which detracts from its appearance to say the least. Fortunately, responsible restoration is mostly limited to cleaning today. A fine William III Fourth Rate in the Kriegstein collection, for instance, has recently been carefully cleaned back to the original finish, and removal of the offending gold paint applied to the carved decoration revealed the original fine gold leaf in all its glory.

Before leaving the subject of restoration, it is relevant to mention an interesting case concerning two almost identical models of a certain seventeenth-century Fourth Rate, one believed to be original, the other a copy. The 'copy' was sold in 1944 at a well known London auction house for the large sum in those days of

Plate 5 *The stern of the First Rate* Royal William, *1719. The fine detail and craftsmanship is typical of the best quality models made in the first half of the eighteenth century. The upper quarter figure represents the Greek mythological goddess Athene who is accompanied with her attribute of a small owl symbolising wisdom. NMM.*

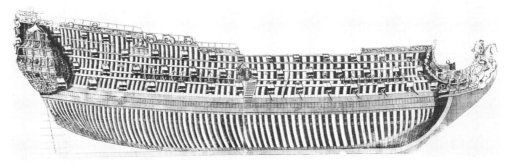

Plate 6 *Contemporary engraving believed to be of the First Rate* Britannia, *1682. The framing of the ship, with single futtocks, is much the same as a Navy Board model, but it is certain that a three-decker of this period would be framed with two, or probably three, futtocks. NMM.*

£275. The model was described in the catalogue of the sale as being of a seventeenth-century Royal Barge. On being pressed by the purchaser after the sale, the vendor insisted that the model was original but much restored, although he knew very well that the other one — now known as the 'original' — was still in his own possession. Having examined both models, I would not like to say with any certainty that either is entirely original, or entirely a copy: and they would need to be compared directly together to arrive at a more positive conclusion.

Although a considerable number of models have survived, there were certainly more in existence at one time which are now lost. From the writings of Phineas Pett and Samuel Pepys we know that there were once models of important ships such as the *Prince Royal*, 1610, the famous *Royal Sovereign*, 1637, and the *Richard*, 1658 (renamed *Royal James* at the Restoration in 1660), but nothing has been heard of them since. Apart from these, there must have been many other models made in the seventeenth century of which nothing is known and which have since disappeared without trace. But however tragic it is that models have been lost, particularly the named ones of the early seventeenth century, we have to be grateful that so many of these fragile objects have survived — often in a perfect and undamaged original condition — and also, of course, that they were ever made in the first place.

Footnotes

1. *The Mariner's Mirror*, Vol 14, p 282.
2. Frank Fox, *Great Ships* (1980) p 101.
3. A H Waite, *National Maritime Museum Catalogue of Ship Models*, Part 1.
4. David Greene, *Queen Anne* (1970) p 202.

II
Hull Framing

Origin of the Navy Board framed hull

The well known and singular nature of the hull framing, with the single futtocks overlapping the floors and top timbers, is the hallmark of the Navy Board ship model. When framed models were first built is not exactly known, but it was certainly at some time early in the seventeenth century. The earliest known written record of one is the model prepared by Master Shipwright Phineas Pett in 1634 as a preliminary design for the *Royal Sovereign*, 1637, which was described by a contemporary writer as 'soe contrived that every timber in her might be seen and left open and unplanked for that purpose, very neat and delightsome'. Nothing is known about the disposition of the timbers in Pett's model, but there is little reason to believe that it was any different in principle from those of a later date.

From the evidence of the earliest examples that still exist, it is clear that by the mid-seventeenth century, the practice of building framed and unplanked models was firmly established. Much doubt has often been expressed as to whether the Navy Board style of framing represents full-sized shipbuilding practice, and it is often described as 'stylised', or a simplified modelmaker's convention. This is true to a certain extent, as there is no comparison at all with eighteenth-century shipbuilding, or even with the framing of ships in the second half of the seventeenth, although at that time the general principles were much the same.

But perhaps we should look back to an even earlier period, to about the time when models were first built. A very clear description of hull construction at that time can be found in the valuable work known as the *Treatise on Shipbuilding*, believed to have been written about 1625. In the section on the parts of a ship's frame are three relevant passages, the first concerning the floors:

> The floor timbers are properly a certain number of timbers both afore and abaft the midship bend, flat the whole breadth of the floor and from thence rounding up to the wrong heads (floor heads) which is as high as the first sweep.

The floors were spaced according to the 'timber and room', with the spaces, or 'rooms', between the floors being entirely filled with the lower ends of the futtocks, thus forming a solid fore and aft band of timber up to the floor heads, as in Fig 1A. The second passage describes the futtocks:

> The futtocks or ribs of a ship are certain round pieces of compass timber swept out according to the mould of every bend, scarphed to the wrong head below and to the naval timbers aloft. In *great ships* they are framed into parts called the upper and lower futtocks. [Author's italics]

At this point, it should be mentioned that the term 'scarph' in hull framing is used in the sense of one timber lying alongside another, not as a joint between two timbers in line as in a keel scarph, for example. When a futtock was specified to have scarph with a floor or top timber of say 7ft 0in, this meant that the ends of the two timbers overlapped by that amount. The mention of 'naval timbers' suggests that the heels of the top timbers were butted to the heads of the futtocks, with the naval timbers lying alongside and giving scarph to the butts as in the diagram Fig 1B.

The *Treatise* continues:

The naval timbers is properly that part of the bend which belongeth to the upper sweep, which is seldom framed apart but moulded into the upper part of the futtock and into the lower part of the top timber.

The way that this is worded clearly indicates that the naval timbers were not normally employed, and that the lower ends of the top timbers scarphed and overlapped with the upper ends of the futtocks, as did the lower ends of the futtocks with the floors, thus forming a solid band of timber at the breadth as in

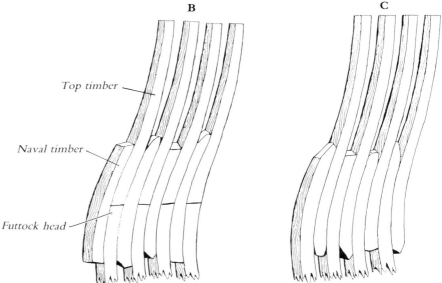

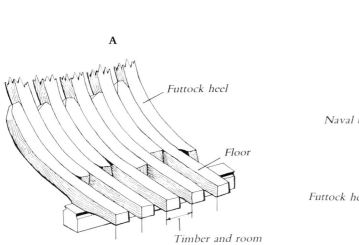

Fig 1 *Reconstruction of early seventeenth-century framing with single futtocks, based on the* Treatise on Shipbuilding *of about 1625.*

A *This illustrates the solid band of timber in the lower part of the hull caused by the scarphing, or overlapping of the futtocks with the floors. The heels of the futtocks normally terminated a foot or so from the keel. Also shown are the individual divisions of the 'timber and room'.*

B *The top timbers are butted to the futtocks, with 'naval timbers' giving scarph to the butts. The* Treatise *mentions naval timbers, but indicates that they were not normally employed.*

C *The top timbers are scarphed to the futtocks in the usual manner, which forms the solid band of timber at the breadth.*

Fig 1C. The interpretation of this can only mean that 'great ships', perhaps with a breadth in excess of about 30ft 0in, were framed with two futtocks, and lesser ships with only one, which is of course the same as the framing of a model, and almost certainly the origin of it. For well over a hundred years there were only minor variations in the framing of a Navy Board model, with a few notable exceptions, although during the same period significant changes were made in the framing of an actual ship. It would seem that once the particular technique in building the frame had developed and become widespread, modelmakers were reluctant to abandon the established method, and continued to build them as they always had been, perhaps because it was found to be the easiest and quickest way of doing it.

It can be argued that the solid work in the area of the scarphs on a model does not show any space between the timbers for air, or any reduction in the siding of the frames as they rise up towards the top of the side. But again we have to look back to the earlier period, as according to contracts of the time there were no spaces allowed until towards the end of the seventeenth century, and then only between the timbers at the breadth, and most of the reduction in the siding was in the top timbers. With respect to the lower scarph, all through the seventeenth century and well into the eighteenth, the siding of one floor and one futtock was equal to the timber and room except for a tiny tolerance of an inch or less, and there were certainly no spaces in the lower part of the hull. With regard to the scarphs at the breadth, a typical contract would specify 'to have scarph of 6ft 0in and the rooms to be filled with timber'.[1] The 'rooms' in this case are the spaces between the upper ends of the futtocks. Whether this meant that the lower ends of the top timbers were to be left thick enough to fill the rooms, or that packing pieces were inserted is uncertain. But the important thing is that the timbering of the hull at the breadth was intended to be solid, as on a model.

By the 1690s, the scarphs at the breadth are sometimes specified as 'scarph 6ft 0in, and 1½in space between each timber for aire'. This is only the equivalent of $\frac{1}{32}$in at a scale of 1/48, and it would be unreasonable to expect this small gap to be shown on a model, as it would severely complicate the building of it. There was not a great deal of difference in the framing of a model and normal full-sized construction in the second half of the seventeenth century — it was just that ships were framed with more futtocks. Two became usual for the smallest ships, and three or four in the larger Rates, all erected individually timber by timber, and alternately overlapping each other. Due to this method of building, it was not possible to connect the futtocks together with fore and aft fastenings as in later years, when it became the practice to make up double frames on the ground before erection. It was the massive fore and aft strakes that held everything together. Once the internal footwales (or sleepers), middle bands, clamps, spirketting, and the external mainwales were in place, all lying across the scarphs and bolted or treenailed through the frame timbers, fastenings between the timbers themselves were not necessary.

Fig 2 *Although this is a Dutch ship, dating from around the mid-seventeenth century, the framing is in most respects strikingly similar to that of an English Navy Board model. However, the ends of the timbers that appear above the bottom planking seem to be too high for the floor heads, and it is possible that they are in fact naval timbers uniting the futtocks with the floors. Apart from this, the only real difference is that the ends of the timbers are not trimmed off to a fair line as on a model, which would not be expected in full-sized shipbuilding construction.*
Scheepvaart Museum, Amsterdam.

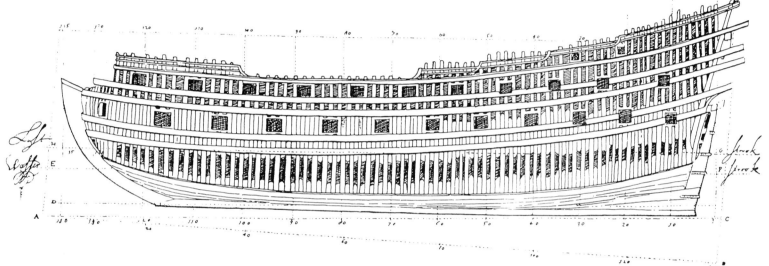

Types of model framing

The frame illustrated in Fig 3 shows the standard arrangement of timbers in midships of the great majority of Navy Board models. Only a few minor variations on this type occur. Sometimes the floors are let down into shallow scores, but this is uncommon, and on most models the floors rest directly on top of the keel as shown. On a few seventeenth-century models, the heels of the futtocks meet on the keel, but this was not normal shipbuilding practice of the period, as at that time the bilge water drained through limber holes cut in the lower edge of the floors each side of the keel, and it was necessary for the futtocks to terminate a foot or so from the keel. At least two seventeenth-century models show that the floor heads are cut off horizontally instead of square. Whether this was commonly done is not known, but it is illustrated very clearly in longitudinal section of a three-decker of about 1680, drawn by Edmund Dummer, Surveyor to the Navy at that time. The horizontal ends would certainly considerably reduce the scantling of timber necessary to get out the floors for a ship, but perhaps it was only done on the models to facilitate the trimming of the floor heads due to the grain direction of the wood. Although the upper ends of the futtocks are shown trimmed off to a fair line in the diagram, this does not seem to have been done on models where the top sides are covered with planking, as they are generally very uneven, and no attempt was made to level them up.

The framing of the *Boyne*, 1692, (Model No 11) illustrated in Fig 4 is basically the same as the standard type, but with every other floor, futtock and top timber omitted, except in midships where only the floor and top timber is left out. A model of the Fourth Rate *St Albans*, 1687, at Trinity House is the only other example noted with the same open framing as the *Boyne*, and there may be a tenuous connection between the two models, as both ships were built by Master Shipwright Fisher Harding at Deptford. This frame is one of the very few seventeenth-century examples where the futtocks meet on the keel. The top timbers are unusual in that the heels of them do not extend down below the wales as on the majority of models.

The unusual framing illustrated in Fig 5 is from the very fine Third Rate of about 1705 (Model No 18). No other frame of this type has been seen, and it is possibly unique. The framing upwards of the breadth is conjectural as it is concealed by the top side plank, and it may be that the ends of the timbers protruding below the wales are those of the top timbers as on the standard type. But on the other

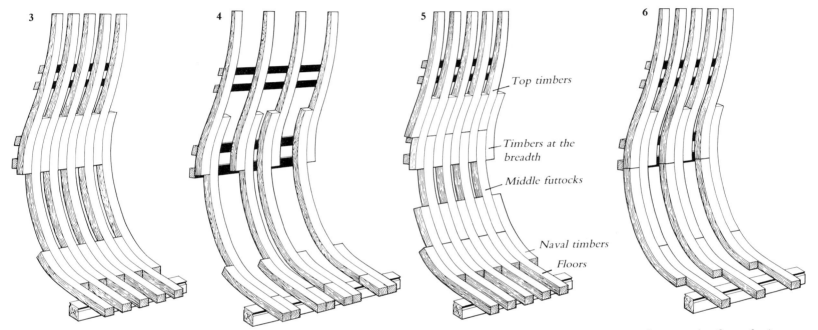

Fig 3 *The disposition of the timbers in a normal Navy Board hull. The great majority of models of all periods are built with this standard type of framing, with only a few small variations.*

Fig 4 *The framing in midships of the* Boyne *1692 (Model No 11). The construction is the same as the standard type, except that every other floor, futtock and top timber is omitted.*

Fig 5 *Midships framing of a Third Rate of about 1705 (Model No 18). It is possible that this frame represents a type of construction in use at around the turn of the eighteenth century. The parts of the frame are named according to the terms commonly in use at that time.*

Fig 6 *Framing in midships of an early Fourth or Fifth Rate, dating from about the middle of the seventeenth century (Model No 2).*

hand, it is possible that the method of scarphing the top timbers to the futtocks is just as likely to be the same as the arrangement in the lower part of the hull. If so, it is possible that the frame is a fairly accurate representation of full-sized construction at around the turn of the eighteenth century. At that time, the timbers of the frame were often not termed first, second or third futtocks. A typical contract for a Third Rate would specify and name the timbers in order upwards of the keel as 'floors', 'naval timbers', 'middle futtocks', 'timbers at the breadth' and 'toptimbers'.[2] From the length of floor in midships, and the lengths of the various scarphs that are given in the contract, it would appear that at least some of the timbers could not butt together. A possible interpretation of this system of framing is that the floors, middle futtocks and top timbers were in line and butted together, with the naval timbers and the timbers at the breadth lying alongside and giving scarph to the butts (see Fig 7). This leaves a gap of about 5ft 0in between the ends of the naval timbers and the timbers at the breadth, very similar to that shown on the model.

The interesting frame illustrated in Fig 6 is from a model of a Fourth or Fifth Rate of unknown date, but possibly as early as the 1650s (Model No 2). The use of widely spaced double frames constructed with two futtocks butted together, and the arrangement of the top timbers is surprising, and does not seem to conform to the normal practice in shipbuilding at that time, but the evidence of it certainly suggests that it may have been a variation. Intermediate top timbers are fitted between those extending up from the main frames. These are shown in the diagram as being closely fayed to the sides of the second futtocks, but on the model many of them have no connection at all, and appear to be held in position only by fastenings through the main- and chainwales. Another model with similar framing to this was a large scale three-decker of about 1670, formerly at Trinity House until it was sadly destroyed by a bomb during the last war.

The types of framing at the bow and stern of models, particularly in respect of the aft deadwoods, are far too numerous to describe. Instead, a number of examples of widely differing dates are given in the illustrations with a brief comment on each one. Cant frames appear on some models after about 1715, as they did on ships, and show a sophisticated technique in construction, but they are few and far between, and this type of bow and stern framing never apparently became popular with modelmakers.

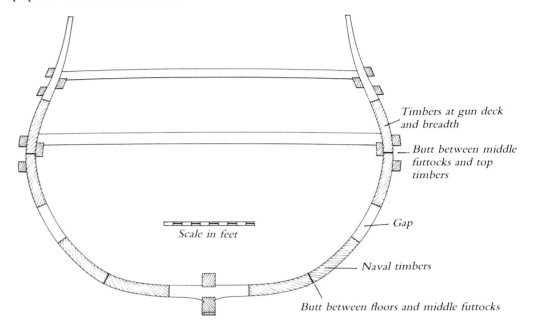

Fig 7 *Midship section of a Third Rate, based on the dimensions given in the contract-specification for the Newark, 1695 (breadth 41ft 4in, depth 18ft 0in). The arrangement of the timbers is conjectural, and based on the length of floors in midships at 23ft 0in, and the lengths of scarphs given in the contract: 6ft 9in for the naval timbers, 6ft 6in for the middle futtocks, and 6ft 0in for the timbers at the breadth. The hatched areas indicate the naval timbers, and the timbers at the breadth, and how they overlap and give scarph to the butts between the floors, middle futtocks and top timbers, therefore leaving a gap of about 5ft 0in as shown. Compare with the frame of the model illustrated in Fig 5.*

Timbers at gun deck and breadth

Butt between middle futtocks and top timbers

Gap

Scale in feet

Naval timbers

Butt between floors and middle futtocks

Construction of the model hull framing

The building of a Navy Board type hull is always of particular interest to modelmakers, and much speculation has been made as to how it was actually done. Unfortunately, the methods of the early craftsmen are completely lost, and nothing certain is known of how this apparently difficult and precise work was achieved.

A normal hull frame is built up from several hundred small pieces of wood, all of complex curvature and bevelling, and with the ends of the floors and top timbers perfectly trimmed off to provide the beautifully fair fore and aft rising lines. At first sight, it would seem that the many pieces of wood were all individually shaped, then assembled one by one to form the hull as in full-sized practice; but this is hard to accept, as it is certainly a long, tedious and difficult process, demanding much complicated setting out, and numerous problems arise in supporting the frame as it is being erected.

The primary purpose was to construct a hull in the most economical manner possible, and to achieve this, the early modelmakers *must* have perfected a method that produced a satisfactory result, but which at the same time was quick and fairly simple. The craftsmen who made these models were obviously ingenious and highly skilled, and it is possible that by employing certain techniques an experienced modelmaker and perhaps an assistant would have built the frame of a large model fairly quickly. There may have been several methods in use, at least in the initial stages of building the hull, but from a close examination of numerous models, it seems that in all cases, the spaces between the futtocks and top timbers were cut out *after* the hull was built up, shaped and smoothed to a final finish.

There are several reasons for suggesting this. Firstly, on many models it can be seen from tool marks that the shaping of the hull was achieved by working fore and aft across the grain of the wood. On some models, the interior of the hull is left with a finish produced by a fairly coarse rasp, and sometimes traces of this are evident on the outside as well. But in all these cases, the edges of the futtocks and top timbers are clean and sharp, which could not have been achieved unless the frame was entirely filled with timber. Secondly, it can sometimes be seen that the ends of the floors and top timbers were cut off to a still visible line drawn the whole length of the hull, which was obviously done after the final shaping of the hull. On one seventeenth-century model, the line for the heels of the top timbers was apparently drawn in error too close to the wales, and another line was then struck a little lower down, to which the timbers were trimmed.

Other clues can be found in the way the waste wood was removed from between the futtocks. Several models show that every one of the top timbers were trimmed off to the line below the wales by cutting about half way through, probably with a small sharp chisel, then snapping off the waste wood. Small frame

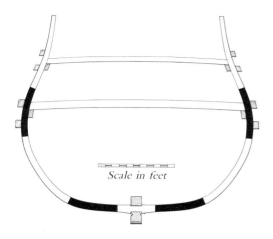

Fig 8 *Midships section showing the extent of the scarphs, or overlaps, of the timbers in the standard type of model framing. The lengths of floors in midships of a normal model range from about half to three-fifths of the main breadth.*

Plate 7 *A partly built model illustrating the probable initial stage of constructing a Navy Board framed hull. At a later stage, when the bow and stern had been completed, the lines for the ends of the timbers would be marked on the hull, and the waste wood removed from between the futtocks and top timbers. Author.*

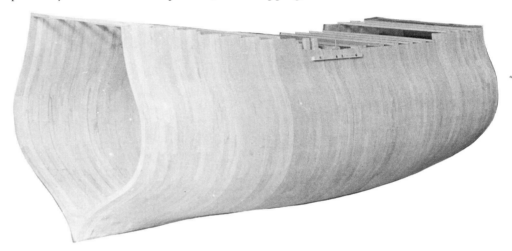

saws may also have been used to remove the waste wood, as traces of holes bored through the hull at the ends of the timbers are sometimes evident, almost certainly for the introduction of a thin saw blade. Where internal footwales are fitted, the upper one is usually precisely flush with the floor heads, and it is possible that in some cases, the ends of the timbers were trimmed off from inside the hull by using these fore and aft strakes as a guide.

On most models, there is evidence of much filing to perfect the trimming at the ends of the timbers, and it is clear that the craftsmen took great pride and care in doing this. Before cutting out the waste wood from between the futtocks and top timbers, we can imagine that a Navy Board hull in its initial stage would have looked like the partly built model illustrated in Plate 7. The framing of this particular model was not intended to be of the Navy Board type, but it shows the same general principle of building the hull up endways, with layers of wood

Fig 9 *Bow and stern framing of a Fourth or Fifth Rate, dating from about the mid-seventeenth century (Model No 2). No contemporary reference has been found for the series of vertical timbers between the transoms, but several other models are known with this construction of a date no later than 1702, and it was probably quite common in full-sized practice. Note the unusual scarph uniting the two parts of the aft deadwood.*

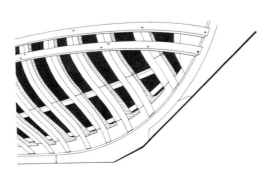

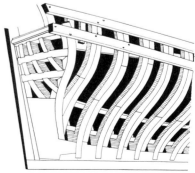

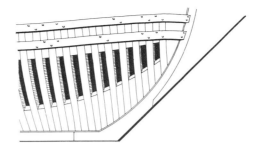

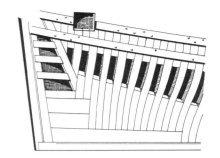

Fig 10 Bow and stern framing of a Fifth Rate of about 1670 (Model No 5). The built-up aft deadwood on this model is highly unusual.

Fig 11 Stern framing of a Second Rate of about 1675 (Model at the National Maritime Museum). This is an interesting example, with the deadwood curving up in a fair line to meet the heel of the fashion piece. It is possible that the deadwood was originally intended to follow the lower ends of the futtocks, as below this line the rising timbers are extended by finely fitted separate pieces of wood to fill the gap, as though it was an afterthought. Another oddity is that there must be a joint between a number of the timbers, which is concealed by the lower wale, as there is a clear difference in the wood above and below. There is an unusual zig-zag break in the line of the stern post rabbet, and a false post is fitted abaft the main post which extends down to the lower edge of the keel.

Fig 12 Bow and stern framing of a First Rate of about 1670 (Model No 4). The whole of the stern below the wales is fashioned from a single piece of thick timber, which has been fretted out to represent the transoms. The frame timbers are let down into shallow scores on the keel and at the stem, but not at the aft deadwood.

of such a thickness that two layers were equal to the timber and room. In a way, it can be thought of as a variation on the 'lift method' as it is known to modern modelmakers, but instead of the lifts being horizontal, they are vertical, and the shape of the hull is obtained from the body sections instead of the waterlines.

It can also be compared with the methods known to have been used by craftsmen in producing other difficult-shaped objects made of wood. Doors and panels of bombé commodes, serpentine-shaped drawer fronts, large wooden urns and vases, and other items of a compound curvature were all built up by laminating together roughly shaped small pieces of wood, and the whole then being shaped to its finished contours afterwards. So it probably was in the building of a Navy Board hull.

The hulls were probably begun in midships, with the layers of wood built up towards bow and stern, and the hull shaped down to patterns of the appropriate body section as each station line was reached. The layers would of course alternate, with one composed of futtocks, and the next of floors and top timbers, both of which would include some waste wood that would later be removed from between the timbers. Perhaps to facilitate the cutting out of the waste wood from between the futtocks, it may be that the layers of wood were glued together only at the areas of the upper and lower scarphs. The great advantage of building a hull in

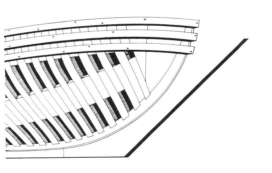

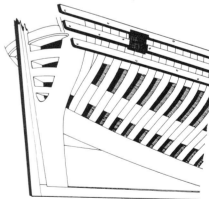

this way is that there are no loose parts, everything being held together as it is being built, and fashioned as a whole.

The thickness, or 'siding', of the timber was vital in building the hull. For instance, a model at a scale of 1/48, with a length on the gun deck of 150ft 0in and a timber and room of 2ft 6in, is built up of well over a hundred layers of timber. If each one of these layers is an average of only one hundredth of an inch too thick or thin, it follows that there will be an error in length of over 1in, or more than 4ft 0in on the scale. It is extraordinarily difficult to hand plane timber to such a thickness that when a hundred of those pieces are put together, it will agree to a predetermined length. But this was apparently done on the Navy Board hulls, whatever the method used to build them.

On the other hand, perhaps we should also bear in mind the possibility that not *all* models are as accurate in length as we would like to believe. The rising line of floor heads can be demonstrated as a diagonal on the body plan (see Fig 16) but this would not have been necessary if the line was marked directly on the hull, and it was probably obtained by the use of a spline, or perhaps a narrow strip of thick paper. If a straight strip of paper is temporarily pasted on the hull parallel to the keel in midships, and allowed to follow its natural curve toward bow and stern, it will generally provide a satisfactory rising line. The curve obtained by this method would be greatly affected by the shape of the body sections, particularly at bow and stern, and this might explain the considerable variations seen in the rising line on different models. The line of top timber heels varies almost as much

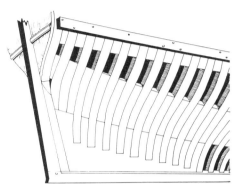

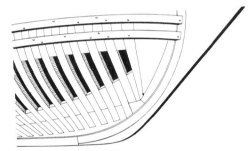

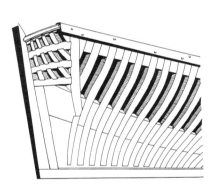

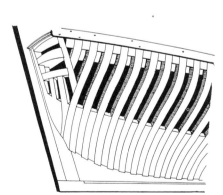

Fig 13 *Bow and stern framing of a Fourth Rate of about 1690, with a square tuck. The stern construction is very much simplified by the absence of transoms and the usual raking fashion pieces.*

Fig 14 *Bow and stern framing of a Third Rate of about 1702 (Model No 14). The long and shallow deadwood, and the deeply recessed timbers, are seldom seen at the bow of a model. Note how the small block of timber below the lowest transom has been carefully fitted to follow the lines of the ends of the hull timbers.*

Fig 15 *Bow and stern framing of the Third Rate Royal Oak (Model No 25). The rising line of floor heads is fairly high at the bow, but lower than normal at the stern. The timbers are let down into very shallow scores in the deadwoods, only about $\frac{1}{16}$ deep.*

as the rising line of floors. On most models, the line is parallel with the mainwales the whole length of the hull, but on others the line very often curves up sharply at the bow and disappears behind the wales, and sometimes this also occurs at the stern. Where the line is parallel, it may have been marked on after the wales were fitted by using them as a guide. In the other cases, the line must have been marked on the hull before the wales were fitted. This again suggests the use of a spline, as the shape of the hull just below the maximum breadth would cause it to curve up

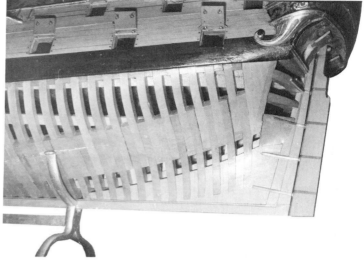

Plates 8 and 9 *Bow and stern framing of a Fourth Rate of about 1725 (model at the National Maritime Museum.) Although this model is at a fairly small scale of 1/64, the precision of the hull construction is remarkable. The usual block of filling timber at the bow appears to be solid, but on other examples it is seen to be in two halves and hollowed out to conform with the thickness of the frames. Note the neat joint of the stem with the knee of the head. Author.*

Plates 10 and 11 *Bow and stern framing of the Third Rate Bredah, 1692, 70 guns. None of the frame timbers are jointed to the stem or the aft deadwood, but the floors are let down on the keel about 1/16in. The waterline is unusually boldly painted on this model, which has a draught of 17ft 0in forward and 18ft 0in aft. The fore edge of the stem is indicated by a scribed line. A long scarph is marked on the stem, and also a shorter one on the cut-water. Author courtesy of Trinity House.*

at each end and create a line of greater sheer than the wales.

Once the hull framing was complete, the gun ports would be pierced. Little can be said about the many models which are completely planked internally and externally above the gun deck, but where it can be seen, there was obviously a great deal of work involved in framing the ports. The ports on the lower tier are simply cut through the solid timber at the scarph of the futtocks with the top timbers, and no lower or upper cills are fitted generally. On a few models, however, the length of scarph does not extend up past the ports, and in these cases, either small blocks of wood are inserted in the gaps between the top timbers or upper cills are fitted. The bulk of the work was in framing the upper deck ports, and those of the middle tier on three-deckers. Until around the mid-eighteenth century, the spacing of the hull timbers rarely agreed with the disposition of ports. On at least two early models, the upper deck ports are placed in the nearest available gaps between adjacent top timbers, and it seems that the modelmaker was not unduly concerned that this resulted in them being unequally spaced (see Model Nos 4 and 1). Apart from these, the ports above the lower tier on models are spaced at equal distances, which entailed cutting into the top timbers to a greater or lesser extent, and fitting filling pieces, chocks or spacers, and upper and

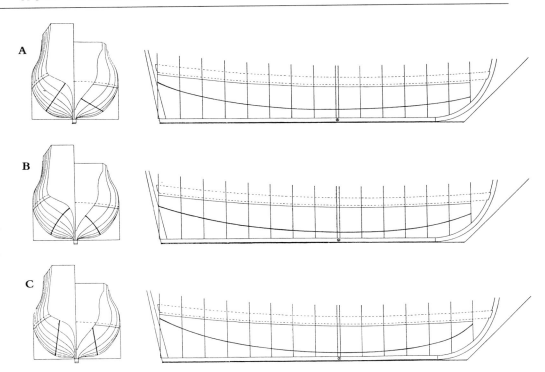

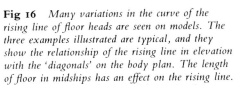

Fig 16 *Many variations in the curve of the rising line of floor heads are seen on models. The three examples illustrated are typical, and they show the relationship of the rising line in elevation with the 'diagonals' on the body plan. The length of floor in midships has an effect on the rising line.*

A *Floors are fairly long, and the angle of the diagonal in the fore body differs markedly from that in the aft body. In these cases, the rising line will always reconcile in midships, whatever the difference in angle of the diagonals.*

B *The floors are a little shorter, and the diagonals are of an equal angle, but slightly curved. In this type, which is very common, the diagonals generally cut the body sections at a right angle, suggesting that a spline was used to mark the rising line on the hull.*

C *The floors are shorter again, and the rising line curves up sharply at bow and stern, due to the almost vertical diagonals.*

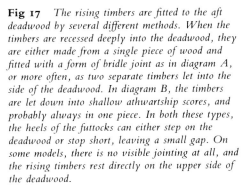

Fig 17 *The rising timbers are fitted to the aft deadwood by several different methods. When the timbers are recessed deeply into the deadwood, they are either made from a single piece of wood and fitted with a form of bridle joint as in diagram A, or more often, as two separate timbers let into the side of the deadwood. In diagram B, the timbers are let down into shallow athwartship scores, and probably always in one piece. In both these types, the heels of the futtocks can either step on the deadwood or stop short, leaving a small gap. On some models, there is no visible jointing at all, and the rising timbers rest directly on the upper side of the deadwood.*

lower cills are fitted, generally with well made angled joints to the vertical timbers.

The constructional work of the hull was completed with the fitting of the external main- and chainwales, and the internal deck clamps, footwales and keelson. On seventeenth-century models, these fore and aft strakes are invariably fastened with many hundreds of treenails in a staggered formation to every timber. In the case of a model built to a scale 1/48 and with a timber and room of 2ft 0in, for example, the fastenings are spaced at intervals of only $\frac{1}{4}$ in. This would have been similar to the fastenings employed in full-sized practice, but it is puzzling that it was found necessary in building a model, particularly with respect to the internal footwales where the holes are carefully stop-drilled, and not one instance has been noted where a treenail has come through the hull timbers. It may be that the modelmaker put in all these fastenings just because it was the proper way. On the

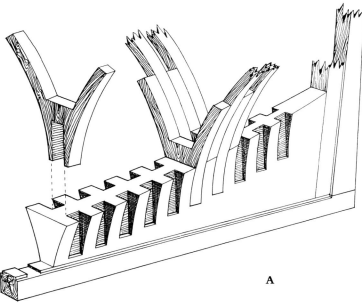

A

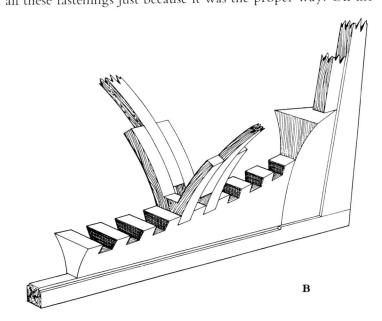

B

Fig 18 *A number of interesting types of keel/stem scarphs are seen on models. Although the scarphs are probably only half lapped, the external appearance in elevation no doubt represents the various joints in use by shipwrights.*

A *Fourth Rate of about 1715 (Model at the National Maritime Museum). Short scarph with rounded ends and many fastenings.*

B *Mordaunt, Fourth Rate, 1681 (Model No 7). The forward end of the keel curves up to form a long interlocked scarph with the stem.*

C *Bredah, Third Rate, 1692 (Model at Trinity House). Short plain scarph. This is a common type, and seen on most models of the eighteenth century.*

D *Third Rate of about 1705 (Model No 18). Short scarph with interlocked ends.*

E *Third Rate of about 1655 (Model No 1). Short plain scarph, with no visible fastenings.*

F *Second Rate of about 1702 (Model No 13). Short interlocked scarph. A false keel is fitted, but this is seldom shown on models.*

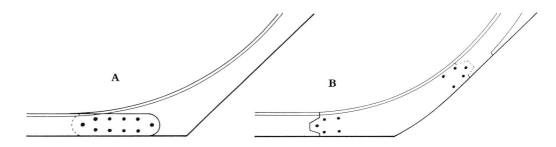

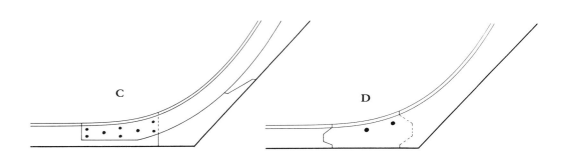

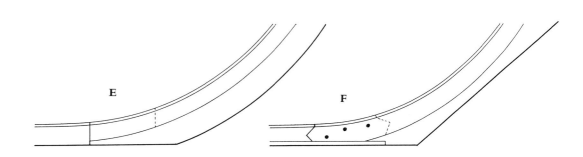

Fig 19 *Typical example of a floor rider. These athwartship strengthening timbers are commonly fitted to models, particularly those of the seventeenth century. Four or five are normally spaced along the length of the hull, and sometimes an extra broad one forms the main mast step. In length, the riders are generally the same as the floors, and they rest on the usual fore and aft footwales at the heads of the floors and heels of the futtocks. The thickened centre part is intended to make up for the weakening of the rider where it is scored down on the keelson. Square, stop-chamfered pillars are usually stepped on the riders to support the upper deck beams.*

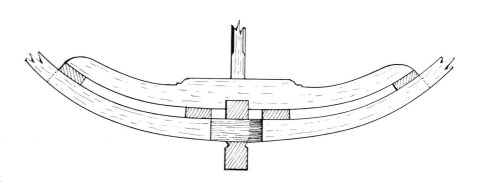

Fig 20 *Methods of framing gun ports. The examples illustrated are shown as pierced between adjacent top timbers, but on the great majority of models, there is no relationship between the spacing of the ports and the spacing of the timbers. In these cases, the ports are framed in many different ways, by cutting into the timbers more or less, and by the use of chocks and filling pieces.*

A *Upper deck port, framed with unjointed upper and lower cills (First Rate of about 1670).*

B *Circular quarterdeck port, pierced through a block fitted between the top timbers (First Rate of about 1670).*

C *Upper deck port, framed with upper and lower cills finely fitted with angled joints (Mordaunt, 1681).*

D *Lower deck port, with the lower cill formed by the timbers, and a separately fitted upper cill. This type is very common, and is sometimes also seen on the middle tier of three-deckers.*

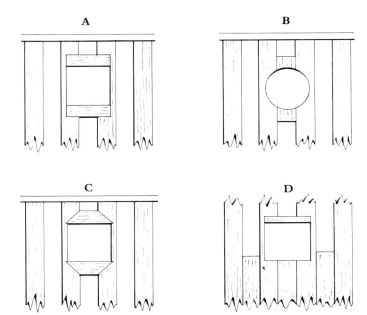

Footnotes

[1] Public Record Office, Adm. 106/3071. Contract-specification dated 1673 for four frigates. (These ships were not built).

[2] *Ibid.* Adm 106/3070. Contract-specification dated 1693 for the *Newark*, 1695, Third Rate of 80 guns on two decks.

other hand, it is possible there was a technique in use whereby the frame timbers were not glued and held together *only* by the fastenings in the fore and aft strakes, as in full-sized shipbuilding. But if that was the case, it is hard to explain how it was done.

Most models are fitted with two fore and aft strakes each side in the hold, with one at the floor heads and the other at the heels of the futtocks, but in a few instances there is a single broad plank equal in breadth to the length of scarph between the timbers. These represent the various very heavy timbers which gave strength to the scarph of the futtocks with the floors, and were known in the seventeenth century as 'footwales', 'sleepers', or sometimes 'footwaling sleepers'. These names are interesting examples of the change in terminology which often took place between the earlier and later periods. In the eighteenth century, the footwales became known as the 'thick stuff', and the term 'sleepers' was retained as meaning the curved timbers uniting the aftmost frames with the transoms, and the ordinary thinner plank in the hold was called the 'footwaling' or 'ceiling'.

Other interesting constructional work in the hold, when fitted, is mentioned in the model descriptions.

III
Construction
and Fittings

Deck framing

Unlike the basic hull framing of Navy Board models, which generally remained static and survived the number of changes that took place during the period, the framing of decks can always be taken as accurately reflecting full-sized shipbuilding practice at any particular time. Due to the nature of the construction, no short cuts or simplification was possible as in other features of early models, and the very many beams, carlings and ledges are all framed together in the correct manner. The amount of work involved in building decks is considerable on a model of a large ship. For example, on a three-decker the framing consists of approximately 110 beams, 300 carlings, 900 ledges and some 2000 tiny housed joints. In addition, numerous models of all dates and Rates show that the beams of each deck are let down to a greater or lesser extent into the upper edge of the deck clamps—another lot of joints.

Although contemporary evidence for letting the beams down on the clamps is scanty, it is found in some of the more detailed contracts of the late seventeenth century. The contract for the Sixth Rate *Penzance*,[1] 1695, specifies that 'every beam of the deck shall be dovetayled into the clamps', and it was probably standard practice in other periods for ships of all Rates. The beams are not seen to be dovetailed on models, but even so, it would have entailed a lot of work considering that they are hidden away beneath the deck plank in most cases.

The orlop deck is seldom evident on models, although the clamps are more frequently fitted. As far as can be seen, the First Rate *Prince*, 1670, is fitted with a full length orlop deck simply framed with beams and the carlings at the sides of the various hatches. The *Hampton Court* (Model No 6) is fitted with an orlop extending from about the position of the mizzen mast to the fore mast, again with only a skeleton framework of beams and carlings. The deck consists of nine or ten beams, which agrees with the number generally specified for a Third Rate in the second half of the seventeenth century.

Gun decks of two-deckers, and gun and middle decks of three-deckers are not easy to see on models, but they are evidently completely framed, and as detailed as the visible upper deck. Several models of the first half of the eighteenth century are designed to separate at the level of the lower gun deck, and illustrate the arrangement of beams, carlings and ledges in meticulous detail. The First Rate *Britannia*, 1719, at the National Maritime Museum is a particularly fine example of a take-apart model, and probably the only one of a three-decker, but it is unfortunately not displayed so that the decks can be examined.

The upper decks of most seventeenth-century models are distinctive for showing the pair of fore and aft beams forming the sides of the long tier of hatches and ventilation gratings in the waist. These are the 'long carlings', as they were termed, and distinct from the 'short carlings' of the outer tier, which were fitted between the main athwartship beams. The long carlings were of heavy scantling—up to 12in square on a Third Rate for example[2]—and are shown on models as partly let down on the beams, so that the upper part forms the coamings to the hatches and gratings, with the lower edge providing a support for the deck ledges. The long carlings were specified only for upper decks, and the evidence of models suggests that the practice was generally discontinued soon after the turn of the eighteenth century, when short flush carlings between the beams and separately fitted coamings became normal practice.

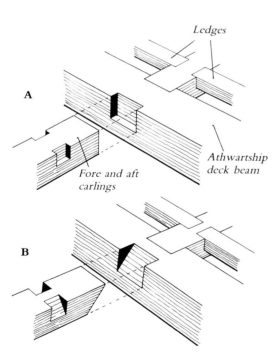

Ledges

Athwartship deck beam

Fore and aft carlings

A

B

Fig 21 *Deck framing joints*
A *Square ended carlings and ledges fitted into shallow scores. This is the normal joint, and seen throughout the period.*
B *Carlings and ledges fitted into angled scores. This joint occurs on the St Michael, 1669 (Model No 3).*

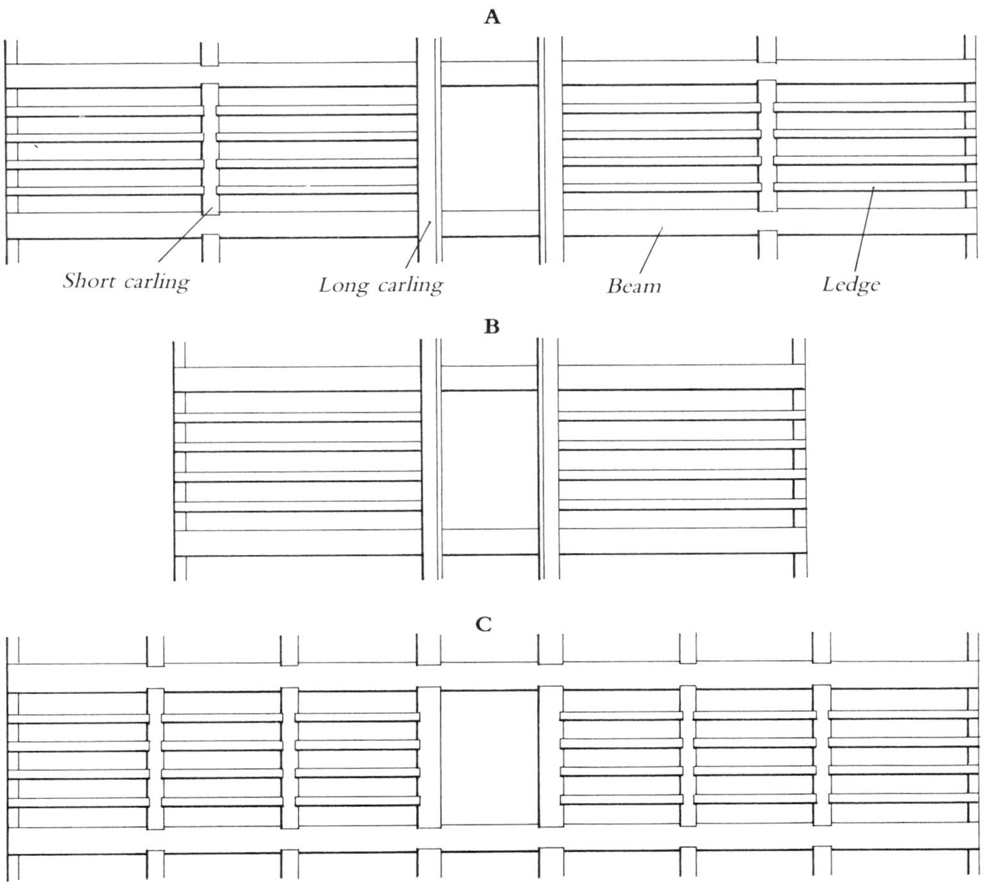

Fig 22 *Upper deck framing in midships (1650–1750). (The drawings are intended to illustrate the arrangement of carlings and ledges, and are not to scale.)*

A *Long carlings at the sides of the hatches, with a single outer tier of short carlings. This arrangement is seen on seventeenth- and early eighteenth-century models of all Rates except for small ships with a single deck. In the later period, a single outer tier of carlings is common on all Rates except for three-deckers, and the framing is the same as before, but with short carlings on the inner tier.*

B *Long carlings at the sides of the hatches, with no outer tier. This is normally seen only on seventeenth-century models of Sixth Rates with a single deck, and a few early Fourth and Fifth Rates. A highly unusual example of an upper deck with no outer tier of carlings on a large ship is seen on the 80 gun Boyne, 1692 (Model No 11).*

C *Three tiers of short carlings. This is seen on models of First and Second Rates from early in the eighteenth century, and Third Rates towards the end of the period. A combination of two and three tiers of carlings are sometimes seen on eighteenth-century models of large ships, with three for a short distance afore and abaft the main mast, and two on the remainder of the deck.*

A

Short carling   Long carling   Beam   Ledge

B

C

Fig 23 *Joints of ledges with long carlings (seventeenth-century models). When long carlings are let down on the upper deck beams so that they form both the coamings and support for the ledges various joints were used.*

A *This type is seen when the carlings are let down only on the beams the same thickness as the ledges.*

B *The carlings are let down deeper on the beams, and the angle of the joint is reversed.*

C *The ledges rest in a groove worked along the edge of the carling.*

D *The carling is rabbeted, and the ledges fit into shallow scores in the usual way.*

The number of carlings fitted each side on upper decks of models varies from one to three tiers according to the Rate and period. Typical arrangements are illustrated in Fig 21. The spacing of ledges also varies widely, but a rough guide— which determines the number of them between any two beams—is approximately twice their own width apart. Models of all periods show that carlings and ledges on upper decks normally terminate at about the position of the mizzen mast, with the remainder of the aft part of the deck framed with more closely spaced beams only, or sometimes with a long central carling and half beams.

From about 1670, the forecastle and quarterdecks on models of all Rates are lightly framed with beams spaced the equivalent of 2–3ft apart, and with carlings normally confined to openings in the decks such as companion ways and scuttles. An interesting exception to this is seen on the Fourth Rate of about 1691 (Model No 10), where the forecastle and quarterdecks are framed the same as its upper deck, with two tiers of carlings each side and a full quota of ledges.

Several models dating from before about 1670 suggest that the construction of

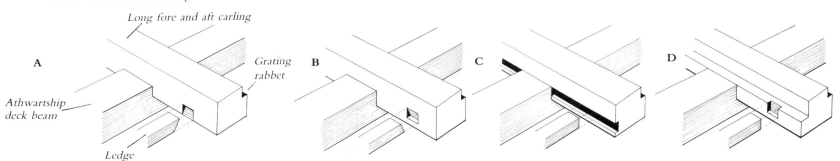

Long fore and aft carling

Grating rabbet

A

Athwartship deck beam

Ledge

B   **C**   **D**

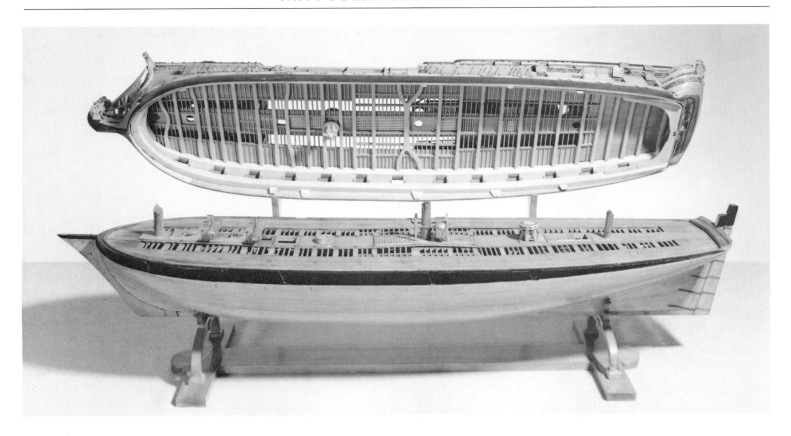

Plate 12 *A take-apart model of a Third Rate of about 1730. The underside of the upper deck shows that it is framed according to the 1719 Establishment, with three tiers of carlings each side in wake of the hatchways and main mast, and two tiers on the rest of the deck. An additional centre carling is worked in below the position of the fire hearth. The beams and ledges are let down flush with the clamps. It is surprising that this detailed model is not fitted with hanging and lodging knees at the beam ends. NMM.*

forecastle, quarter- and poop decks was much more substantial around the mid-seventeenth century than it was in later years. This applied to small and large ships, and an example of a forecastle deck on an early Fifth Rate is illustrated in Plate 13. The poop deck on this model is framed with beams spaced at little more than their own width apart. The forecastle deck of the Second Rate *St Michael*, 1669, is framed with a pair of full length carlings let down on the athwartship beams, and two or three closely spaced half beams between the main ones.

Beam knees

Plate 13 *Upper and forecastle decks of a Fifth Rate of about 1660. Both decks are framed with widely spaced main beams and long intermediate ledges. The quarterdeck is framed in the same manner, except that aft of the poop bulkhead, closely spaced beams only are fitted. Note the long carlings, with the ledges housed into the sides (Model No 2). NMM (Author).*

Where it has been possible to examine the interiors it seems that lodging and hanging knees were seldom fitted on models in the seventeenth century, and infrequently in the later period. The Third Rate *Royal Oak* (Model No 25) is fitted with a fine array of hanging knees, but no lodging knees, on each of the upper and quarterdeck beams, despite them being completely concealed by the wide strip of plank at the sides of the decks. On the Third Rate of about 1705 (Model No 18), the strip of plank at the sides is fairly narrow, and the ends of the athwartship arms of both lodging and hanging knees are visible on the upper deck, and hanging knees only are seen to be fitted on the quarterdeck beams.

'Standards', or vertical knees fitted above the decks, were specified throughout the second half of the seventeenth century, but these too are seldom evident on models. The interesting First Rate of about 1670 (Model No 4) is fitted with four or five standards each side on the gun and middle decks, and two or three on the upper deck in way of the bulkheads according to the practice in shipbuilding at that time. The standards on the model are very large, with the up and down arm reaching to the clamps of the deck above, and represent a thickness of about 1ft 6in.

The 1719 Establishment list specifies timber standards on gun decks, and iron ones on upper decks, but no model of this period has been noted with standards, at least on the more visible upper decks. By the mid-eighteenth century, however, timber standards appear on several models of two-deckers, a good example being the Fourth Rate of about 1740 (Model No 24), which is probably of a later date, where both the gun and upper decks are fitted with a standard between each of the gun ports.

When knees are fitted on models, there is usually a small chamfer worked round the edges or, as in the case of the *Royal Oak*, a small bead.

Pillars

The gun deck beams on models are commonly supported by a single tier of pillars stepped on the keelson, and on the floor riders when fitted. The pillars are represented as about 9in square, with stop-chamfered corners, and fitted either below every beam, or more often below every other one. The turned pillars below the beams of middle, upper and quarterdecks are generally in two tiers. Of noticeably slender proportions, and often tapered, the pillars are usually finely turned with mouldings of various designs at the lower and upper ends. Wood was the most commonly used material for turning pillars, but examples made from bone or ivory are seen on some eighteenth-century models.

Deck planking and wales

The extent of plank laid on decks varies from none at all on some of the earliest models, to others where one or more of the decks are completely planked. Between these two extremes, an average model is fitted with a strip of plank at the sides of all decks, a central strip on the forecastle, quarter- and poop decks, and in the eighteenth century, a central strip on the upper deck. This is a broad generalisation, and there are many different combinations, particularly in the seventeenth century. The *Coronation*, 1685 (Model No 9), for example, has a narrow strip laid at the sides of all the decks and no central plank at all, but part of the quarterdeck forward of the poop bulkhead is planked across its full width. On the upper decks of eighteenth-century models, a piece of plank is usually laid between two adjacent beams across the full width of the deck in way of the bulkheads, but this is not fitted in the earlier period, and the bulkheads just rest on the narrow strip of plank at the sides. The central strip of plank on any of the decks invariably narrows towards the stern. Decks in way of the aft accommodation are often completely planked, and sometimes laid with a veneer of diagonal black and white squares or other decorative material. The deck of the Captain's state room on the superb model of the First Rate *Royal George* at the National Maritime Museum is laid with thousands of minute wood blocks in a herring-bone pattern. During the first half of the eighteenth century, a fashion was emerging that became almost standard in later years, in that the forecastle and poop decks, and sometimes the quarterdeck, is more accurately described as fully planked, but with narrow openings each side. The openings are rather shorter than the deck itself, and terminate in shaped ends, usually a double ogee or a half round similar to an astragal mould. An example of this is shown in the illustration of the poop deck on the Second Rate of about 1740 (Model No 22).

Plate 14 *A Fourth Rate of about 1710 showing the typical light construction of the forecastle deck. The deck is not robust enough to take the upward strain of the fish davit, and the bolt of the span shackle just abaft the small ventilation hatch is taken down and fastened through an upper deck beam (Model No 19). Author.*

Throughout the period, the deck plank is of sheet wood about $\frac{1}{16}$in thick, and often marked out to represent the seams between individual strakes. The strakes are generally shown as a scale 12in to 18in broad. It is probable that if the modeller were to mark out the plank at all, he would do it according to the practice of the time, which would suggest that deck plank was laid in broader strakes than is generally supposed.

In the second half of the seventeenth century, models show that there was little change in the disposition of the wales. All Rates are fitted with a pair of projecting mainwales and — with the exception of small ships with a single deck — a pair of wales above the lower deck ports, which were usually known at that time as the chainwales. Singular departures from this standard arrangement are seen on the First Rate of about 1670 (Model No 4), which is fitted with triple mainwales, and the galley-frigate, 1702 (Model No 15) which has a single mainwale.

Fig 24 *The quarterdeck of a Third Rate of about 1655 as it would appear from below. The arrangement of full and half beams, and the pair of heavy carlings, extends from the break of the deck to just forward of the mizzen mast position, where the deck is at a raised level (Model No 1).*

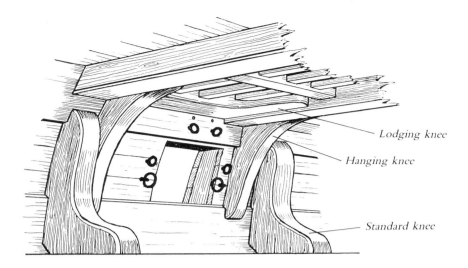

Fig 25 *Lodging, hanging and standard knees shown on a midships section of a Third Rate from around the mid-eighteenth century. Limber holes are cut in the standards at the angle of the deck with the side. The model, which is built to the large scale of 1/24, is at the Pitt-Rivers Museum.*

Lodging knee

Hanging knee

Standard knee

The only real change occurs in the wales above the middle deck ports of First and Second Rate three-deckers. The Second Rate *St Michael*, 1669, has no upper wales, but from the time of the First Rate *Prince*, 1670, models of three-deckers are fitted with a single upper wale, with the notable exception of the *Coronation*, 1685, which has a pair, and this became the general rule from about 1702 onwards.

From early in the eighteenth century, the chainwales above the lower deck ports on two- and three-deckers universally became known as the channel wales, and remained the same wales to which the chain plates were bolted, whether or not the channels themselves were at the same level. At least by the time of the 1719 Establishment, the upper wales above the middle deck ports of three-deckers became known as the sheer wales. It is sometimes believed that the sheer wales of three-deckers were those above the lower deck ports, and that the channel wales were above the middle deck ports, but according to the 1719 Establishment, it was the other way round. The Establishment lists and terms the wales in ascending order as mainwales, channel wales and sheer wales, and as the scantlings given for the sheer wales are considerably smaller than the channel wales, it is logical that the sheer wales were the highest of the two, and above the middle deck ports.

Mainwales in three, or sometimes four flush strakes begin to appear on models of two-deckers from about 1715, and on three-deckers from 1719, with flush channel wales following suit a few years later. The 1719 Establishment clearly specifies that both main- and channel wales were to be in flush strakes, but according to models the change was very gradual, particularly on two-deckers, and it is not until the 1740s that the old-fashioned paired wales finally disappear. Numerous examples show flush mainwales and paired channel wales, and sometimes vice-versa. Models dating from the 1730s and '40s often show a transitional type of mainwale in that the upper and lower strakes are broader and less thick than the earlier ones, and the middle strake is almost, but not quite, flush. This type is superficially similar to the projecting paired wales, due to the upper and lower strakes being black, while the middle strake is left in natural wood.

Channel wales are sometimes seen in a combination of paired and flush strakes. A Third Rate of about 1745 at the Science Museum is fitted with a pair of wales except in way of the fore and main chain plates, where the middle strake is flush. Another example is the First Rate *Victory*, 1737, at the National Maritime Museum, where the channel wales are in three flush strakes except for a short length at bow and stern, where they become paired.

A distinctive feature of seventeenth-century models is that the thinner strake between one or more of the paired wales is frequently not fitted. This always looks attractive in the case of either the chainwales or upper wales, where the

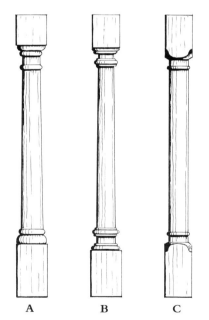

Fig 26 *Pillars*
A Boyne, *Third Rate, 1692. Painted red.*
B *Second Rate of about 1740. Turned from bone or ivory.*
C *Third Rate of about 1750. Natural wood.*

A   B   C

individual top timbers are left exposed.

Joints are often seen in the wales on models, either actually made or when the wales are laid on in a full length, scribed on. It is noticeable that when the wales are paired, the joints are shown as a simple scarph, and when flush, plain square butts are usual.

From about 1690, some models are fitted with a strake directly above the mainwales of an intermediate thickness between that of the wales and the ordinary top side plank. This was normal practice in shipbuilding, and was known in the eighteenth century as the 'black strake', but it is never commonly seen on models, although it is sometimes simulated by a band of paint, as on the *Coronation*, 1685.

Top side plank

The external plank on the top sides between the various wales and moulded rails is laid in one of two ways. In general, the plank on seventeenth-century models is of thin sheet wood, and in the eighteenth, separate strakes, both types occurring in a transitional period from about 1690 to 1715. Once the practice of laying the plank in separate strakes was established, it quickly became widespread after about 1705, and it is surprising that the technique was not adopted in earlier times. It is a case where an apparently simplified method was actually more difficult. In both types of planking, the wood has to be first prepared to thickness, and the additional work in cutting strips to the width of a plank would have been slight compared with the problems in laying it in one broad piece. As a typical example, we can take a look at the broad area of plank above the mainwales of the *St Michael*, 1669. The plank appears to be in a single length of well over 3ft, and obviously of a very hard wood about $\frac{1}{16}$ in thick. It is about $1\frac{1}{2}$ in broad, but because of the sheer of the wales, the plank would have to be taken from a piece at least twice as wide as that. The edges of the plank perfectly fit the long gentle curve of the wales. The plank is slightly curved across its width, and at the bow it twists and becomes flatter as it curves sharply round to meet the stem. The difficulty in the curve across the width can be seen in the numerous small brass brads only at the upper and lower edges of the plank, in addition to many treenails. The brads were probably put in before the treenails, and perhaps clinched on the inside to pull the plank down to the hull timbers. And then there are the thirteen ports. The openings in the plank are a little greater than the ports themselves, and form an even margin at the sides and lower edges of the ports to provide a rabbet for the lids. Whether this was done before or after fitting the plank is a matter for conjecture, but either way it would not be easy.

On numerous seventeenth-century models, the broad band of plank above the mainwales is of a quite different wood from the rest of the structure, and clearly of a softer and more flexible variety. In these cases, it seems probable that the choice of wood was influenced more by the ease with which the plank could be laid than by its decorative effect.

Fig 27 *Mainwales. The illustrations are to scale, and representative of wales on two- and three-deckers in the period 1650–1750. The planking above, between and below the wales is shown as fitted on the respective models.*

A *Third Rate of about 1655.*
B *St Michael, Second Rate, 1669.*
C *First Rate of about 1670. A unique example of triple mainwales.*
D *Third Rate, 1698.*
E *Fourth Rate, 1701.*
F *Royal Oak, Third Rate. Date uncertain, but probably early eighteenth century.*
G *Second Rate of about 1740.*
H *Yarmouth, Third Rate, 1748.*

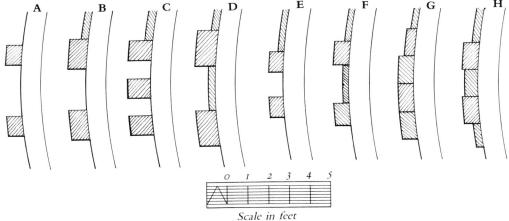

Scale in feet

The top side plank is often scribed to represent the seams between individual strakes, and sometimes also the butts. On some models the scribed seams are continued across the port lids. The quality of the scribing varies greatly. On some of the early models, the seams are somewhat wavy, often double where lines overlap, and there are many slips of the scribing tool. Even the well made *St Michael* suffers from careless work in this respect. In contrast, the seams on the *Royal Oak* (Model No 25) are marked with precision, and were it not that the grain of the wood suggests otherwise, it could be believed that the plank was laid in separate strakes. This was probably done before the plank was fitted on the model, perhaps with a small marking gauge. But it is clear that in at least some cases, the modeller made it more difficult for himself by scribing the plank when in position, which is evident from the seams frequently cutting across the heads of treenail fastenings. Seams are sometimes further defined in black ink, and are generally spaced to indicate strakes of about 12in broad.

Superb examples of planking in separate strakes are seen from the time the technique first appears, one of the earliest being the Fourth Rate of about 1691 (Model No 10). It would have been a much simpler method than the old one, as narrow planks readily bend edgeways to conform with the sheer of the wales, and the problem of the curve across the width of the plank and piercing the ports did not arise.

Internal plank

The extent of internal plank laid at the sides between the various decks is similar to deck planking in that it varied according to the period. As a general rule, the earlier the model the less the planking, with a few of the earliest ones having none at all. Apart from these, numerous models dating from before about 1700 show that it was common practice to plank only above the open decks. As a typical example, the Fourth Rate of about 1682 (Model No 8) is planked only above the upper deck in the waist between the forecastle and quarterdeck bulkheads, and above the quarterdeck forward of the poop bulkhead. The *Boyne*, 1692, and others of the late seventeenth century are entirely planked upwards of the upper deck, and from 1700 onwards many models, including three-deckers, are completely planked internally above the lowest gun deck. In full-sized construction, the internal fore and aft strakes consisted of the thick spirketting up to the level of the lower cills of the gun ports, with the space between there and the lower edge of the deck clamps shut in with thinner plank known in the eighteenth century as the quickwork, and in the earlier period simply as the plank between the ports. In the waist, a thick strake was fitted at the top of the side. This was originally the gunwale, which was generally called the string in the eighteenth century, and was in effect a continuation of the forecastle and quarterdeck clamps. On early models, the planking is simplified and laid in full width pieces of thin sheet wood, with the spirketting sometimes represented by a band of black paint. This was quite common until around the turn of the eighteenth century, but from about 1680 the practice of fitting the thicker spirketting and string in separate strakes became increasingly more frequent on the better quality models, and standard in the later period. The quickwork was sometimes scribed to indicate the seam between the two strakes of plank.

Fastenings

As fastenings in the construction of models are mostly confined to the fore and aft strakes and the three areas of planking, it is convenient to mention them at this point. Fastenings are of various types and prolific on all seventeenth-century models. But from the early 1700s—although they are still seen—the practice declined to a great extent, and on many models there are no visible fastenings at all. In these cases, of course, the use of glue was necessary, but it is probable that in earlier times the work was assembled dry and secured only by the fastenings. Treenails are by far the most common type of fastening. These little pegs of wood are invariably tightly fitted, and obviously employed in exactly the same way as in shipbuilding, by driving them into holes bored slightly smaller than the treenails themselves. But they are mostly oversized and seldom less than about $\frac{1}{16}$in in diameter, whereas about half that would more accurately represent a full-sized treenail on a model built to a scale of 1/48. Strangely enough, scale-sized treenails of $\frac{1}{32}$in or less always appear to be too small and insignificant on models, and actually look better if a little oversized.

An interesting example of the use of treenails as fastenings is seen on the *St Michael*, 1669. Many of those fastening the lower strake of the mainwales were never trimmed off internally, and protrude through the frames and deck clamps, as do others through the lower gun deck beams. They are pointed and appear to be tapered, and the heads of them vary slightly in diameter. Although it is not conclusive, this points to the possibility that the holes were bored with a very small tapered auger, and that the treenails were driven in until they tightened up, then the heads trimmed off flush.

Treenails are not generally the prominent and contrasting colour that is popular with modelmakers today, and which variety of wood they were made from is uncertain. Hard, tough and fine grained woods such as hawthorn and hornbeam may have been used, both of which withstand driving in with some force without breaking.

The use of fastenings made of brass, or perhaps copper in some cases, was also widespread, either exclusively throughout a model or in combination with treenails. Tiny round-headed nails and cut brads are often seen on seventeenth-century models, mostly in the edges of top side and deck plank. In a more refined form, brass was used in a similar manner to treenails, by hammering in short lengths of round brass or copper wire and filing the heads off perfectly flush with the surface of the wood. This type of fastening is frequently seen in wales and top side planking, and can be superficially mistaken for small dark treenails due to oxidisation of the metal.

Imitation fastenings are fairly common in top side planking. In each case they are indicated in the same way, by circles about $\frac{1}{16}$in in diameter sharply impressed into the wood of the plank. The markings are either bold, as on the *Royal Oak*, or barely discernible, such as on a First Rate of about 1675 at the National Maritime Museum. On this model, the simulated fastenings are shown as two in each strake of the scribed plank, with a line at the sides of the ports, and another half way between. In addition there is one treenail in each strake only at the sides of the ports, more or less corresponding to the marked ones.

Channels

In the eighteenth century, the broad horizontal planks carrying the deadeyes for the shrouds, and the wales to which the chain plates were bolted, were universally known by the respective terms 'channels' and 'channel wales'. During the earlier period, however, there was no distinction between the two, and both the channels and channel wales were more generally called 'chainwales', but for ease of reference it is convenient to describe them in eighteenth-century terminology. A typical example of chainwales meaning both channels and channel wales is found in a contract for four frigates dated 1673. The contract specifies:

> To have two wales for the convenience of the chain plates and both to go fore and aft, both to be 5in thick and 9in broad. To have fore, main and mizzen chainwales well bolted. To have one strake of 3in plank between the chainwales 10in broad.[3]

A possible reason for the same name being given to two apparently quite different things is that originally they were one and the same, and that the channels were merely a broadened part of the channel wale itself. This is suggested by the early Third Rate of about 1655 (Model No 1) where the main and fore channels are fastened directly to the hull timbers. It would have been easier to lay the

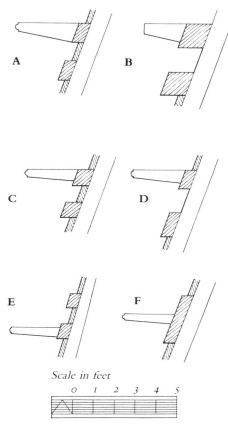

Scale in feet

0   1   2   3   4   5

Fig 28 *Main and fore channels. The channels are shown as on the channel wales above the lower deck ports, except for the example E, which is on the sheer wales above the middle deck ports. There is a great variation in the scantling of channels and channel wales on seventeenth-century models.*

A St Michael, *Second Rate, 1669.*
B *First Rate of about 1670.*
C Boyne, *Third Rate, 1692.*
D *Third Rate, 1692.*
E *Second Rate of about 1702.*
F Yarmouth, *Third Rate, 1748. On both the model and the draught of the* Yarmouth *the main and fore channels are shown on the middle of the channel wale instead of the normal position at the upper edge.*

channel wales first and fit the channels separately in the usual manner, but the man who made it carefully and deliberately fashioned them with projections each end which are scarphed to the wales proper.

Models are practically the only source for finding the breadth and thickness of seventeenth-century channels. Contracts generally specify the dimensions of the channel wales but not the channels, and they are not even mentioned in the extensive list of scantlings in Anthony Deane's *Doctrine of Naval Architecture*, 1670. Several representative examples of main and fore channels from models are illustrated in Fig 28, but there are many variations. The breadth ranges from about 2ft to a maximum of 3ft, and it is not always the smallest ships that have the narrowest channels. Mizzen channels are narrower in proportion. It is noticeable that the earlier the model the thicker the channels, and numerous models of different Rates prior to about 1680 show that the inner edges are the same in thickness as the breadth of the wale to which it is fastened, ie about 9in to 12in.

For the eighteenth century, the length, breadth and thickness of channels for all Rates can be found in the 1719 Establishment list, but the breadth was evidently not rigidly enforced, for it adds the qualification, 'But however sufficient to carry the shrouds clear of the Gunwale and Fiferails'. On any rigged model from the time of the Second Rate *St Michael*, 1669, to the Third Rate *Yarmouth*, 1748, it is clear that the degree of tumblehome of the ship's side above the channels is always *less* than the rake of the shrouds. In other words, the shrouds are closer to the side at the rails than they are at the level of the channels. Because of this, it is equally clear that the breadth of channels was not so much to increase the spreading of the shrouds by a very small amount, but that it was dictated by the necessity for the shrouds to clear the rails at the top of the side.

Models of three-decker First and Second Rates show that in the first few years of the eighteenth century, the main and fore channels were raised from their former position above the lower deck ports to above the middle deck ports. Although the purpose of this is obscure, it was almost certainly not because the channels in the earlier low position were vulnerable to damage, otherwise we would expect the channels on two-deckers to have been raised at the same time, and that did not happen until some 40 years later. In all probability, it was due to a small reduction in the tumblehome, and instead of increasing the breadth of the channels to allow the shrouds to clear the top of the side, they were raised to a higher level and remained about the same width as before.

The Third Rate *Yarmouth*, 1748, is one of the latest models of a two-decker to have the fore and main channels in the old position above the lower deck ports, and one of the earliest with the channels in the new position above the upper deck ports is the Third Rate *Devonshire*, 1745. At this time, the mizzen channels normally remained in the same position as before, and thus all three channels were at the same level, but the *Devonshire* is unusual in that the mizzen channels are also raised to above the quarterdeck ports. The original draught of the *Devonshire* was for a Third Rate of 80 guns on three decks, but she was completed as a two-decker, as were several other 80s including the *Culloden*, 1747, which was another early example with the channels above the upper deck ports. Although not perhaps particularly significant, all three channels on the model of the *Devonshire* are actually at the same level as on a normal three-decker of the time, and it may be that although the ship was cut down by one deck, the channels remained in the same position as they would have been on the ship as originally designed.

The loops of the deadeye straps for the chain plates to hook into are usually taken through small slots pierced near the edge of channels on models, but occasionally they are let into shallow scores cut in the edge where they are retained by a separate moulding planted on. The edges of channels are generally finished with an astragal mould, although some early examples are square edged. The moulding is taken round the shaped ends of channels except on the earlier thick type, where only the edges are moulded.

The main channels on late seventeenth-century First and Second Rates are usually extended forward to provide a landing at the entry ports.

Channel braces

The channels of seventeenth-century models are braced from above by timber spurs. In profile, the spurs are generally of an arched form, but occasionally they are more of an elongated S shape. Small projections are usually worked in at the upper and lower ends where they are fastened by brass pins or treenails. The outer

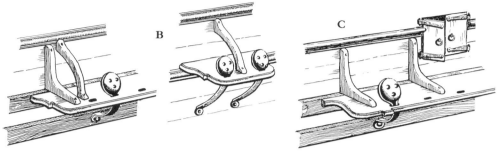

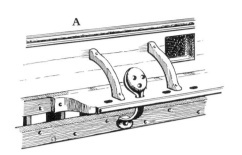

Fig 29 *Types of channel braces.*
A *Timber spurs. Main channel of a Fifth Rate of about 1670.*
B *Combined spurs and timber knees, or 'standards'. Main channel of a Fourth Rate of about 1715. The main backstay stool is also fitted with a single spur, but this is not often seen on stools.*
C *Standards only. Fore channel of a Fourth Rate of about 1710.*

edges are either rounded off, moulded with an astragal, or sometimes left square. The use of spurs gradually declined in the early years of the eighteenth century. From around 1700, vertical timber knees, or 'standards', appear and by about 1720 this type of brace superseded the old-fashioned spurs altogether. Several examples dating from the overlapping period are fitted with a combination of both spurs and knees on the same channel, notably one of the three models of the First Rate *Royal William*, 1719, at the National Maritime Museum. The edges of knees are finished in a similar manner to spurs, but small beads worked round the edges are not uncommon. An approximate guide to the numbers of spurs or knees fitted on any one channel is one at each end, and one each side of the ports on models of small ships. On the first three Rates, there is usually an additional one between the ports.

Chain plates

The earliest example of chain plates on models is probably on a Third Rate dating from about 1650 at the United States Naval Academy Museum, Annapolis. A photograph of the model before it was restored shows that the main chain plates are very long, slightly curved and double bolted to the side just above the mainwales. The fore chain plates are similar but single bolted, as are those at the mizzen. The rigging of the model before it was restored is believed to have been of eighteenth-century origin, and it is possible that the chain plates were added at that time,[4] bearing in mind the Third Rate of about 1655 (Model No 1), which is not fitted with either deadeyes or chain plates. On the other hand, some of the Van de Velde drawings of ships prior to around 1650 clearly illustrate long double bolted chain plates that are quite different from those of the second half of the seventeenth century.

During this long period of some 50 years, with the main and fore channels of two- and three-deckers on the upper strake of the pair of chainwales above the lower deck ports, the chain plates are very short and single bolted to the lower strake. Mizzen chain plates are similar but smaller and bolted directly to the side. The shape of this short type of chain plate in profile varies from straight to an almost full quarter circle.

According to the *Lizard*, 1697 (Model No 12) which is not fitted with chainwales and has the channels low on the side below the single tier of ports, the chain plates of seventeenth-century Sixth Rates were bolted to the upper strake of the pair of mainwales.

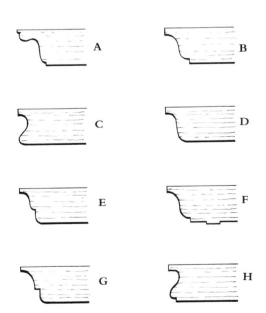

Fig 30 *Channel ends are finished with many different and attractive designs.*
A *Fourth or Fifth Rate of about 1660.*
B *Fifth Rate of about 1670.*
C *Third Rate of about 1702.*
D *Marlborough, Second Rate, 1706.*
E *Lion, Fourth Rate, 1738.*
F *Fourth Rate of about 1710.*
G *Fourth Rate of about 1725.*
H *Devonshire, Fourth Rate, 1745.*

The first major change is seen on First and Second Rate three-deckers in the first few years of the eighteenth century which have the channels in the raised position above the middle deck ports. The chain plates are much longer, often reaching down to the wales above the lower deck ports, and either double bolted or single bolted but with a separate preventer plate. In profile, this type is either straight, slightly curved or an elongated S shape.

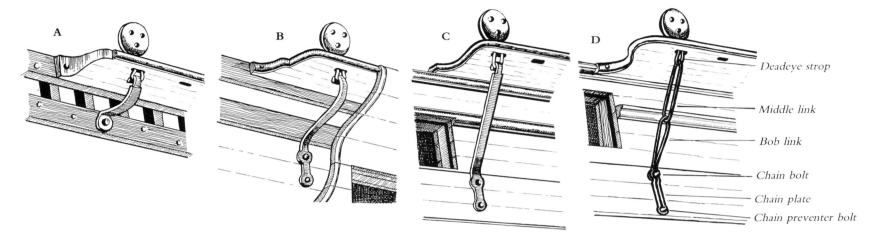

Deadeye strop

Middle link

Bob link

Chain bolt

Chain plate

Chain preventer bolt

Fig 31 *Types of chain plates.*
A *Short chain plate single bolted to the lower chainwale. Main channel of a Fifth Rate of about 1670.*
B *Longer chain plate double bolted to the side below the wale. Fore channel of the* Lion, *Fourth Rate, 1738. Note that the chain plate follows the same serpentine curve of the bill board of the anchor lining.*
C *The chain plate is again bolted to the wale, but much longer due to the channel being in the raised position above the upper deck ports. Fore channel of the* Devonshire, *Third Rate, 1745.*
D *Links of chain. Main channel of a late eighteenth-century Fourth Rate. The several different parts are named according to a list that accompanies the model. Note that the earlier term 'chain plate' now applies only to the lower part, which was normally the preventer plate. (For a further reference to this, see Model No 24).*

On two-deckers, the earlier type is still fitted until around 1715, when the chain plates on main and fore channels are longer and fastened to the side below the channel wales except for those that come in way of the gun ports. As on three-deckers, they are either double bolted or fitted with preventer plates, the former being the most common. In the first half of the eighteenth century, mizzen chain plates on all Rates are similar to those of the earlier period. The final change in the period 1650–1750 occurs with the introduction of chain links instead of the earlier chain plates made from solid bars. Models and draughts suggest that the new type first appeared in the 1740s on two-deckers, and coincided with the raising of the channels to above the upper deck ports, although an exception to this is seen on the Third Rate *Devonshire*, 1745, which has long straight chain plates (see Fig 31C).

Although chain plates are insignificant items, there was obviously a great deal of care taken in making them. Some of the early ones are a little crude, but those of the best quality are fine examples of miniature metal work. Not at all simply cut out from thin sheet metal, they are rather fashioned from solid-looking brass, with swellings in way of the bolts, and polished so that there is no trace of a tool mark. Sometimes the outer edges of chain plates are carefully bevelled, and in this respect it agrees with the 1719 Establishment specification, which gives one dimension for the thickness in the middle, and another lesser one for the edges. Some chain plates are painted black, and a few early ones are even gilded, but the majority are left with a natural brass finish. The fastening bolts usually have small round heads.

Gun port lids

The lids of gun ports are generally made from single pieces of wood, and shaped inside and out as necessary to conform with the slight curvature of the side. The lids at the bows are often of a compound shape, being curved both ways, and the foremost ones on the upper deck are also twisted due to the top sides flaring out at that point. The probable procedure was to cut the lids to size from thicker wood, shape the inner side, fit the lids in position and flush off the outer side level with the top side plank. The lids fit into small rabbets formed by the top side plank being set back from the edges of the timbers and cills framing the ports. In most cases the lids are thicker than the top side plank, and to allow them to lie

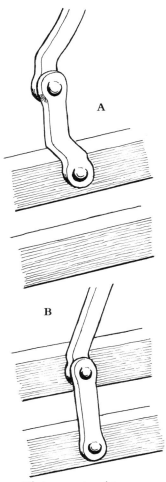

Fig 32 *Chain preventer plates.*
A *First Rate of about 1702.*
B *Second Rate of about 1702.*

Fig 33 *Port lid hinges.*
A *Prince, First Rate, 1670.*
B *Fourth Rate, 1682.*
C *Boyne, Third Rate, 1692.*
D *Third Rate of about 1702.*
E *Fourth Rate of about 1725.*
F *Fourth Rate of about 1730.*
G *Lion, Fourth Rate, 1738.*
H *Fourth Rate of about 1690.*

flush, either the rabbet is deepened into the port framing or a rabbet is worked round the lid as well. The latter method is seen on the First Rate *Prince*, 1670, and a few later models, but although it is not common, it more accurately represents a built-up lid made from two layers of plank.

Where the lower edges of ports cut into the mainwales towards the stern, it was the practice from around the mid-eighteenth century to fashion the lids so that the line of the wales remained unbroken. This was not done on the earlier models, however, although the line of the wales is sometimes continued across the lids with black paint. Where a lower deck port is pierced either wholly or partially in way of the anchor lining (if fitted), the lid is thickened accordingly to provide a flush surface with the lining.

The port lids are hung on a pair of 'hooks and hinges', as they were termed. The hooks are very simple: short pieces of wire pushed into holes bored in the hull planking above the ports, and bent at right angles for the hinges to pivot on. They are nearly always opposite-handed to retain the lids, and either face inwards or outwards. The hinges—mostly of brass—are seen to be made in two basic ways. In their simplest form, the hinges are plain and cut from thin sheet metal, with the ends bent round the hooks and the straps fastened to the lids with two or three crude rivets. Sometimes the ends of the straps are bent round the hooks and taken down to the first fastening. The joints are usually soldered. This type is seen on the galley-frigate, 1702 (Model No 15) and other not so well made models. In contrast, the hinges on most good quality models are superbly fashioned from what looks like solid brass, with the holes for the hooks bored out. In general, the fastenings of this type are countersunk rivets with the heads filed off perfectly flush so that they are almost invisible. Small round-headed rivets are also sometimes seen.

The upper deck port lids in way of the main and fore channels are often in two halves, and side hung similar to a pair of doors. This is more often seen on eighteenth-century models of all rates, but the First Rate *Prince*, 1670, and a few others of the earlier period are so fitted. The practice was obviously dictated by the shrouds in some way, but it is clear that although the shrouds are very close to the sides of the ports on rigged models, they do not obstruct the raising of a normal top hung lid. A possible explanation is that half lids were fitted on ships to facilitate the unshipping of them should the need arise. Unlike on models, it is

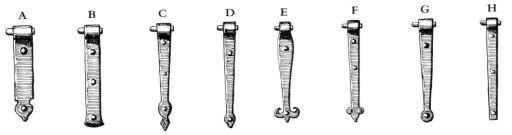

probable that in shipbuilding both hinge hooks faced the same way, and to unship a lid due to its thickness it would have to be raised considerably and slid off the hooks sideways by as much as 6in or more. This would not be easy in the case of a port with shrouds close to each side, however, which may explain why the lids are in two halves and side hung, as they would be readily unshipped by lifting them off their hooks.

Until the early years of the eighteenth century, ports are often pierced in the doors of the forecastle and quarterdeck bulkheads. The lids are hung in various ways, and typical arrangements are illustrated in Fig 34. The Third Rate *Boyne*, 1692, is notable for having two ports in the poop bulkhead—one in the single door at the port side and another pierced in the bulkhead itself. The lid of the port in the door is oddly top-hung on a pair of finely made hinges, while all the rest throughout the model, including the other one in the bulkhead, are hung on ordinary hooks. On any particular model, the hinge straps of inboard bulkhead doors and port lids generally have the same design as those of the broadside ports.

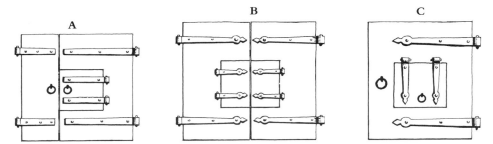

Fig 34 *Gun ports in bulkhead doors.*
A *Sixth Rate Lizard, 1697. Two pairs of doors in both the forecastle and quarterdeck bulkheads.*
B *Third Rate Boyne, 1692. Two pairs of doors in the forecastle bulkhead.*
C *Third Rate, 1692. Two single doors in both the forecastle and quarterdeck bulkheads.*

Port ropes

Port ropes for raising and retaining lids in the open position are rarely fitted on models. A finely detailed and rigged model of a Fourth Rate known as the *Medway*, 1742, at the National Maritime Museum, is one of the few noted. The lower deck port lids are fitted with double rope lifts which are led through the side above the ports in the usual way, while those on the upper and quarterdecks in way of the aft accommodation are single, and taken up outboard to the top of the side where they are made up on the stanchions below the fife rail. One of the best examples of port ropes is seen on a large scale midships section of a mid-eighteenth-century Third Rate at the Pitt-Rivers Museum. The lifts of the lower deck lids are double and led through the side where they unite to a single tackle. Small wooden toggles are worked in the lifts outboard, which limit the raising of the lid to slightly above the horizontal position.

Port rigols

From about 1675, port rigols are fairly frequently seen on models. Although practical in that they prevented rainwater from entering the ports, rigols were also decorative. In their usual forms, rigols are either a simple arch or a double ogee. The arch is generally a segment of a circle with varying degrees of curvature, but some are flattened in the middle with ends curving sharply down each side of the ports. A common practice on First and Second Rates was to fit arched rigols to the middle deck ports and the ogee type to the ports of the lower tier, or sometimes the other way round. Rigols are not normally fitted below channels or where a projecting wale is close to the upper edge of a port, but there are exceptions to this general rule. Rigols are usually very slender—little more than a scale 3in or 4in in width and thickness—and delicately moulded. They would be tedious and difficult to make, particularly the ogee type which appear to be mostly made from a single piece of wood, but it is possible that some are jointed at the apex.

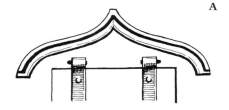
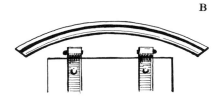

Fig 35 *Gun port rigols. Both these types of rigol are seen on models from the 1670s onwards.*

Lights

The glazing material used for stern and internal bulkhead lights, and also lanterns, can be broadly defined as being mica in the seventeenth century and glass in the later period. It would appear that the transition in shipbuilding happened around

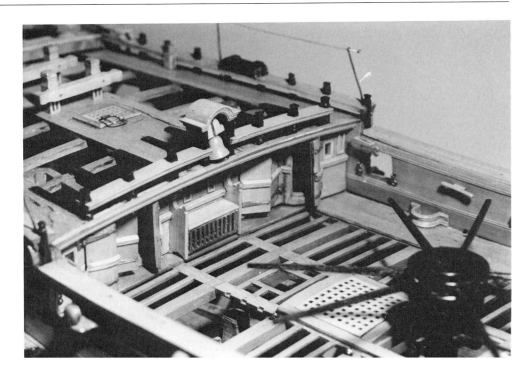

Plate 15 *Upper deck of a Fourth Rate of about 1710, framed with two tiers of short carlings each side. The housings can be seen in the carling where a few ledges are missing (Model No 19).* Author.

1690, for contracts before then generally specify 'muscovy glass' or sometimes 'mustovia glass', while those of a later date call for 'stone ground glass'.

Until approximately 1690, the mica is engraved either on the inside or outside to simulate the narrow strips of lead that held the many small panes together. Various designs are illustrated in Fig 36. On the First Rate *Prince*, 1670, and a few other early models, small dots of gold paint indicate the separate panes. Lights fitted with frames and glazing bars first appear around 1690, and while they may still be glazed with mica on models, it shows the change of use from the earlier 'leaded lights' to larger panes of glass. The frames are made by several different

Fig 36 *Designs for 'leaded lights' (all stern lights)*
A *Third Rate, 1692 (Model No 11).*
B Coronation, *Second Rate, 1685 (Model No 9)*
C *Second Rate of about 1675 (Model at the National Maritime Museum).*
D *Fourth Rate of about 1690 (Model in the Kriegstein Collection).*

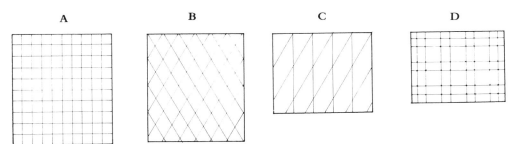

methods. Some are assembled from short lengths of thin strip wood jointed together, but more common types are fretted out of thin sheet wood, metal or, on a few of the later models, ivory. These are very finely made on most good quality models, but the frames fretted out of sheet wood have not stood the test of time, as in many cases the glazing bars—usually the horizontal ones—have either wholly or partially fallen away due to the extremely short grain of the wood. By far the most delicate, and also the most frequent, are lights framed from lengths of slender round or square metal wire soldered together. Sometimes two different types of framed lights are fitted on the same model. For example, the Third Rate *Bredah*, 1692, at Trinity House has fretted metal frames on the quarter galleries and upper tier of stern lights, while those on the screen bulkhead of the open gallery are made from wire. One of the advantages of metal frames is that they can be readily bent to shape to conform with the curved panes of glass often seen on quarter gallery lights. The metal used for making lights appears to be copper or brass on some models, but many of them are a grey to blackish colour which suggests the use of pewter, or even perhaps silver.

Gratings

Just as other features of models were simplified, so was the manufacture of gratings. Until well into the eighteenth century, with very few exceptions, the gratings were simulated by piercing squared holes in solid wood. Some of the earliest examples are a little crude, with perforations well over size, but the majority are remarkably precise and the best gratings are so well made it takes more than a passing glance to detect whether they are in fact pierced or built in the proper way. This type of grating is commonly marked out both fore and aft and athwartship with a fine sharp knife, and it is probable that the holes were first drilled out and then the corners squared with a tiny chisel by using the knife cuts as a guide. The average size of the holes in the gratings of a $\frac{1}{4}$in scale model appears to be about $\frac{1}{16}$in square, or a little more, and the same distance apart. The thickness of wood varies from about $\frac{1}{16}$in to as much as $\frac{1}{8}$in in some cases. The grain of the wood can sometimes be detected as running fore and aft, or occasionally athwartships, but there are many gratings that are completely featureless and have no apparent grain direction at all. These are suspected as being made from *end* grain wood, which is perhaps surprising but not illogical. As an experiment, I have made gratings from wood with conventional and end grain, and while both methods are extremely tedious, it is far easier to pierce the holes in end grain, and the wood is less liable to split. Where long tiers of gratings are shown, the pierced type is often made in a continuous length. On the *Royal Oak*, for example, the ventilation grating of the quarterdeck is made from a single piece of wood some 9in long and 1$\frac{1}{2}$in broad. The round up, or athwartship camber of most gratings is slight, and was probably achieved by steaming. On one seventeenth-century model, however, where the camber is more pronounced, tool marks on the underside of the gratings suggest that they were shaped out of solid wood before piercing the holes.

Pierced gratings are seen on some models until at least as late as the 1730s, but

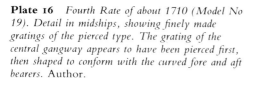

Plate 16 *Fourth Rate of about 1710 (Model No 19). Detail in midships, showing finely made gratings of the pierced type. The grating of the central gangway appears to have been pierced first, then shaped to conform with the curved fore and aft bearers. Author.*

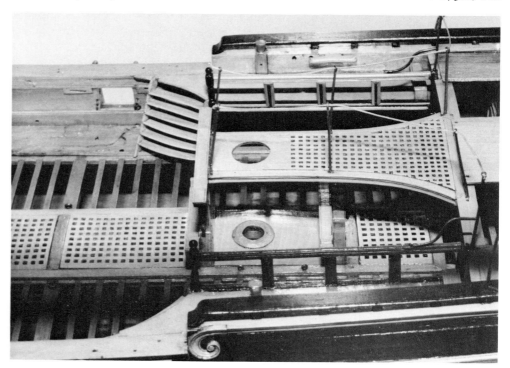

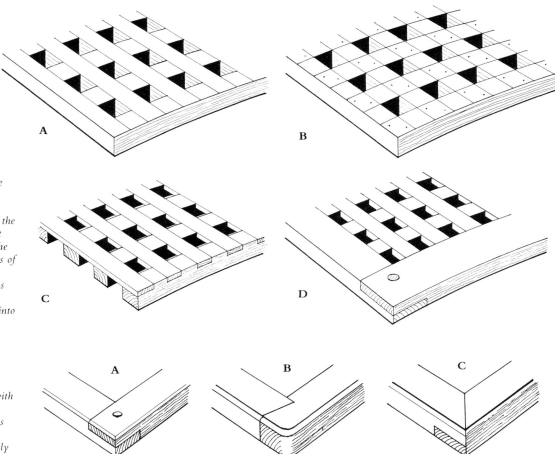

Fig 37 *Gratings.*
A *Solid grating marked out to simulate the fore and aft battens.*
B *Solid grating of the Boyne, 1692, marked with double fastenings at the intersections of the 'battens' with the 'ledges'. The grating is set out both ways with fine knife cuts, giving the illusion that it is made from many tiny cubes of wood.*
C *A built grating with thin fore and aft battens let into the thicker athwartship ledges.*
D *Built grating of the St Michael, 1669, set into a frame with half-lapped corners.*

Fig 38 *Coaming joints. The coamings at the sides of hatches and ventilation gratings are commonly fitted to their respective head ledges with a simple mitre, but various other joints are seen.*
A *Half-lapped joint on the upper deck coamings of the Second Rate St Michael, 1669.*
B *Recessed angled joints similar to this are fairly common on upper deck coamings of eighteenth-century models. Also used for fitting athwartship ledges between individual gratings, and at the fore and aft sides of capstan partners.*
C *Mitred half-lapped joint. Late eighteenth-century Fourth Rate (Model No 24). Used for all coamings on the upper, forecastle and quarterdecks.*

from early in the eighteenth century built ones begin to appear and become common on most of the better quality models by around 1720. These 'proper' gratings are generally superbly made with very thin fore and aft battens let into the heavier athwartship ledges, unlike the cross halved method popular with modelmakers today, which is not only incorrect practice but actually entails more work. Very few built gratings are seen on seventeenth-century models, a notable one being the Second Rate *St Michael*, 1669. A fixed grating on the upper deck near the main mast and another on the quarterdeck are the pierced type, while three more in the waist and one on the forecastle deck which lift out are built, and set into a frame with half-lapped and treenailed corners.

Capstans

The miniature versions fitted on models are by far the most reliable source of information on early capstans, not only for their dimensions, but for their form, disposition and number of whelps and bars. Only the upper part of the jeer capstan in the waist can normally be seen, but hidden away below the decks they are mostly fitted in detail, and in many cases equipped with bars and pawls. Significant developments took place, but change was very slow, and main capstans on two- and three-deckers remained much the same over a period of some 60 years.

The early type of capstan with four bars taken through the head at different levels was obsolescent by the 1670s, and is last seen on the three-deckers such as the *St Michael*, 1669, the *Prince*, 1670, and another First Rate at the National Maritime Museum, which is dated at about 1675. At some uncertain date prior to around 1680, the newly invented drumhead appears on main and jeer capstans

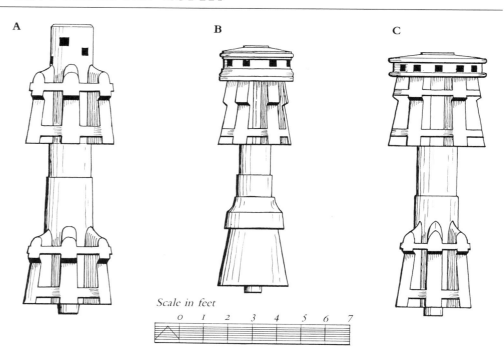

Scale in feet

Fig 39 *Fore jeer capstans.*

A *St Michael, 1669. Five whelps on both lower and upper capstans, with the head pierced for three, or perhaps four, through bars. Made from two pieces of wood, with a joint in the middle of the barrel.*

B *Fourth Rate of about 1691 (Model No 10). The lower part of the capstan suggests that it was intended to be a warping or veering drum, but a more simple explanation is that it may have been left unfinished. Five whelps on the upper capstan, with the drumhead pierced for ten bars. Made from a single piece of wood.*

C *A typical early eighteenth-century jeer capstan as fitted on Third and Fourth Rates. Five whelps on the lower capstan and six on the upper, with the drumhead pierced for twelve bars.*

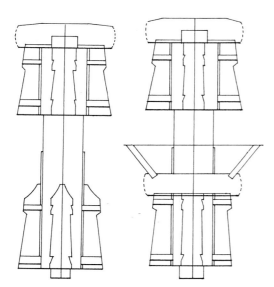

Fig 40 *Fore jeer capstans. (Traced from the original drawings in the Draught Room at the National Maritime Museum.)*

Although these drawings are of uncertain date, they are of interest for apparently showing the transition from the earlier type of capstan to an improved one with the addition of a 'trundlehead' on the lower part. Trundleheads are mentioned in the 1719 Establishment in connection with 'iron pawls', and it is possible that the drawings date from around that time. The capstans illustrated here are for Fourth Rates of 60 guns. The one on the right shows representations of angled pawls hanging from above, the lower ends of which would probably engage in a serrated iron rack set into a groove worked round the periphery of the trundlehead to prevent the capstan from running back under load. The horizontal line above the pawls appears to indicate the underside of the deck beams.

which allowed the use of more bars all at the same height.

Main capstans. Main capstans on models of ships with two decks are single, and placed on the lowest gun deck abaft the main mast, with the barrel—usually tapered—taken down and stepped on a fore and aft beam between two pillars at the level of the orlop deck. An unusual exception to this occurs on the Fourth Rate *Mordaunt*, 1681, which has a main capstan on the upper deck. Double drumhead main capstans with the head on the upper deck generally appear in the 1740s, and the lower barrel disappears. A very early example of this type of main capstan appears on the Fourth Rate *Lion*, 1738 (Model No 21).

Main capstans on three-deckers from the time of the *St Michael*, 1669, to the Second Rate of about 1740 (Model No 22) are also single ones on the lowest gun deck abaft the main mast. No example of a double main capstan has been noted on models of three-deckers, but the change presumably happened at around the same time as on the smaller ships. On any particular model, main capstans are similar to the head of the jeer capstan only a little larger in diameter. Thus the *St Michael*, 1669, has a main capstan of the early type with four through bars, while that on the *Coronation*, 1685, is fitted with a drumhead.

Jeer capstans. Models of two-deckers fitted with the early type of jeer capstan with through bars are very rare, and it is unfortunate that on one of them the capstan is lost (see Model No 2). One of the best examples of the early jeer capstan is seen on the Third Rate of about 1655 (Model No 1) which has a tapered barrel stepped on the lower gun deck, but no whelps fitted on the lower part. The earliest model to show a drumhead jeer capstan is probably the Fifth Rate (Model No 5) which conceivably dates from as early as the 1660s. The capstan is a double one, but only worked with bars on the upper drumhead, and this became the standard type of jeer capstan on two-deckers for approximately 50 years. A very typical example is illustrated in Fig 39C. Although this type is occasionally seen as late as the 1740s, drumheads, or 'trundleheads', generally appear on the lower part from around 1720. Over a period of some 20 years, these early trundleheads are plain and not pierced with sockets for bars. This is evidently not because of a simplification on the part of the modelmaker, for in each case, the drumhead of the main capstan on the same deck is pierced for bars and sometimes fitted with them. An early reference to trundleheads on jeer capstans is found in the 1719 Establishment in connection with pawls:

Number of iron pawls, four to each where they can be fitted, two of which to fall upon the trundleheads, and to answer the pawls on the deck.

Although hanging pawls are not seen on models, this would suggest that, at first, the trundleheads may have been fitted only to support the necessary serrated rack for the pawls to 'fall upon' (see Fig 40). By the 1740s, however, they were fitted for bars, and thus both main and jeer capstans become double drumheads and worked with bars on the lower and upper gun decks. An early model showing this new arrangement is the Third Rate *Yarmouth*, 1748 (Model No 23).

The arrangement of jeer capstans on First and Second Rate three-deckers is confused and not enough examples have been noted to arrive at a general conclusion. There are generally two: a fore jeer capstan with a head on the upper deck in the forward part of the waist, and a main jeer in midships with the head on the middle deck. The fore jeer capstan is single, double or triple, and the main jeer (which is not always fitted) is either single or double. On the Second Rate of about 1740 (Model No 22) the fore jeer capstan is a single drumhead and the main jeer a double drumhead. An interesting example of a triple fore jeer capstan (which is specified in the 1719 Establishment) is fitted on a Second Rate of about 1703 at the National Maritime Museum. The barrel is taken down and fitted with whelps at the level of the lower and middle decks and is worked only by the bars on the upper drumhead.

The height of drumhead capstans is fairly consistent at around 4ft 6in to the cap and 3ft 6in to the centre of the bars. On the early type, there is a difference of about 1ft 3in to 1ft 6in between the upper and lower bars, and the mean height from the deck appears to be a little more than on drumhead capstans at around 4ft 0in. The men were probably mustered to the bars according to their height!

The diameter of seventeenth-century drumheads varies little between the different Rates. For instance, the diameter of the drumhead on the jeer capstan of the *Hampton Court*, 1678 (Model No 6), is the same as that on the Sixth Rate *Lizard*, 1697, at 3ft 0in. In the eighteenth century the difference between the Rates is more pronounced, and on models of the larger ships the diameter of the drumhead can be the same as the overall height, or even more. On any one model, the diameter of the main capstan is a little greater than the jeer capstan. The number of whelps fitted is generally five on early capstans for all Rates. By the end of the seventeenth century, six become common on main and upper jeer capstans of the larger ships, with five on smaller ships, and on the lower jeer capstans. The number of bars on any one capstan is usually twice the number of whelps, but there are exceptions where twelve bars are fitted on five whelp capstans, and sometimes vice-versa.

In the manufacture of capstans, we can see once again the early modelmaker's preference for making items from solid wood rather than building them up with separate parts. Those of the seventeenth, and many of the eighteenth century were turned to profile from a single piece of wood, then the areas between the whelps cut out, leaving the cross chocks in situ. Sometimes it can be seen on the whelps that fine lines were scribed on the capstan while still in the lathe to indicate the position of the chocks. These are beautifully made from a hard and fine grained wood, with no trace at all of a turning tool, or even a chisel mark. Some of the eighteenth-century capstans appear to be made the same way, but with separate chocks fitted to the whelps with a recessed angled joint.

The drumheads of seventeenth- and early eighteenth-century capstans are often decorated with broad shallow flutes radiating out from the central cap. Sometimes, as on the Fourth Rate of 1703 (Model No 16), the drumheads are not truly circular, but fashioned with 'flats' corresponding to the number of bars. Most well made capstans have a fine moulding worked round the drumhead above and below the sockets for the bars.

The partners of double capstans are typically two pieces of wood about a scale 6in to 9in thick which rest in rabbets worked along the edges of the coamings (see

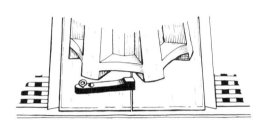

Fig 41 *Detail of the jeer capstan on a Fourth Rate of 60 guns of about 1745, showing a deck pawl (model at the National Maritime Museum). When fitted on early models, there is usually a single pawl at the fore side of the capstan which would be swung round to stop the capstan in either direction of rotation. In the eighteenth century, a pair close together at the fore side of the capstan is often fitted, but one each side is not uncommon, as illustrated here. This one is of particular interest for showing what is evidently a removable retaining pin to prevent the pawl being accidentally employed. When required, the pin would be lifted out and the pawl swung round to engage with one of the whelps.*

Fig 41). They are generally loosely fitted to enable the capstan to be lifted out. The partners are usually rounded up athwartship, and conform with the camber of the adjacent gratings.

Staircases and ladders

Among the more prominent of the inboard features on the open decks are staircases and ladders, together with their associated gangways. There are many variations in these structures, and it is not intended to go into any great detail concerning their development other than to make some general observations. The illustrations given here, and others under the headings of the respective models, will provide some idea of the changing fashions during the period 1670–1750.

Stairs or ladders are not often shown on the earliest models before about 1670, although the side gangways are sometimes fitted. Even the detailed and well made *St Michael*, 1669, is not fitted with either stairs or gangways to any of the open decks, but hidden away behind a pair of doors in the quarterdeck bulkhead is a flight of 'bell stairs' leading down to the middle deck. Bell stairs — which are normally fitted only between decks on the centre line — have perfectly symmetrical curved strings, and are not to be confused with any of those at the side gangways. They are typically fitted on early eighteenth-century Third and Fourth Rates, usually leading down from a companion on the forward part of the quarterdeck. The bell stairs on the Fourth Rate *Lion*, 1738, are fitted with risers, but in most cases they have open treads (see Model No 21).

Until around the mid-eighteenth century, stairs were seldom fitted to the forecastle deck except on seventeenth-century First and Second Rates. The Fourth Rate of 1682 (Model No 8) is notable for the earlier period in that small winding staircases and short gangways are fitted each side to the forecastle in the manner that was normally reserved only for ships with three decks. The Third Rate *Royal*

Fig 42 *This quarterdeck staircase, from the First Rate* Prince, *1670, is typical of those fitted on seventeenth-century First and Second Rates, but not all have such elaborate balustrading. Similar stairs, but smaller, are fitted at the forecastle and poop deck gangways. It is only about 1¼in high to the upper tread.*

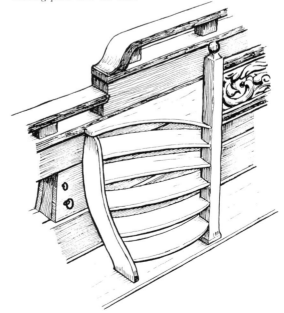

Fig 43 *Quarterdeck gangway and ladder from the Third Rate* Boyne, *1692. This is one of the earliest examples of the type which provides access to the waist from the gangway and also from the entering place over the side.*

Fig 44 *Poop deck stairs from the Boyne. Most models of large ships from the seventeenth century are fitted with gangways to the poop, but there are a few exceptions, such as this example.*

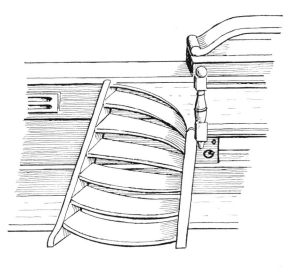

Fig 45 *Quarterdeck ladder from a Third Rate of 70 guns of about 1705.*

Guns

Oak, of uncertain date but probably early eighteenth century, is unusually fitted with a pair of open treaded ladders directly against the break of the forecastle in the arrangement that became commonplace only after about 1750.

On all Rates until the last decade of the seventeenth century, the side gangways from the quarterdeck, and therefore the stairs, terminate well short of the usual entering place over the side. On models of two-deckers and smaller ships, there are sometimes separate ladders placed directly against the bulwarks abreast the external boarding steps. A good example of this is shown on the Fourth Rate of about 1691 (Model No 10). These extra ladders may have been portable ones, which might explain why they are not more generally fitted on models. On Third Rates from about 1690 and smaller ships from 1700, the quarterdeck gangways extend farther forward, and the distinctive type of twisted dual-purpose stairs appear, providing access to the waist both from the gangways and the entering place over the side. There are many variations in this type of stairs, but all have an ingenious design and are cunningly made. They are basically very steep, but the going is made much easier by the gradually changing shape of the treads. The dual-purpose stairs never appeared on First and Second Rates, and unlike the smaller ships, there is no access to the waist from over the side until later years. An interesting point arises here, for on models of three-deckers dating from before the mid-eighteenth century, the external boarding steps always terminate at the entry ports on the middle deck. The inference is that all ranks, including the seamen, boarded the ship via the entry ports. In the second half of the eighteenth century, however, models of three-deckers are universally fitted with boarding steps which continue on past the entry ports up to the top of the side, where there is a gangway and a ladder down to the upper deck in the waist.

Seventeenth-century models are generally fitted with winding stairs or ladders to the poop deck. These are connected to the deck with short gangways in most cases, particularly on First and Second Rates, but there are a number of exceptions on models of smaller ships where the stairs are directly against the poop bulkhead. The primary purpose of gangways was to enable the stairs to be placed between the gun ports, and it is surprising that they were not fitted on the *Boyne*, for instance, where the stairs seriously obstruct the ports. Stairs or ladders to the poop deck on models of the first half of the eighteenth century are variable, and on many there is no means of access at all, even on the most detailed examples. First and Second Rates are often fitted with winding stairs and short gangways each side similar to those of the earlier period. When fitted on Third Rates and below, there is usually a plain straight ladder each side but with no gangways.

An unusual exception to this is seen on the remarkable model of the *Royal Oak*, where there are very long gangways extending over two of the quarterdeck ports, the purpose of which is not readily apparent. A Fourth Rate of 1703 (Model No 16) has a single semi-circular step fitted each side in the angle of the poop bulkhead with the bulwarks. It was a fairly common practice from around 1740 to place a ladder each side beneath the break of the deck, with access to the poop through small square scuttles.

Although models equipped with guns are relatively uncommon, they are seen in all periods from the 1660s onwards. One of the earliest is the Second Rate *St Michael*, 1669. The guns on this model are exceptional for the seventeenth century in that the rather roughly made carriages are fitted with two pairs of small 'trucks', or wheels. Until around the turn of the eighteenth century, trucks are rarely fitted on gun carriages, even on models of the very best quality such as the Third Rate of 1678 known as the *Hampton Court* (Model No 6). Considering the work entailed in making the detailed capstans and finely made fittings such as the whipstaff on the model, all hidden away below the fully planked upper deck, this is odd to say the least. The barrels are beautifully turned, and the carriages—although of a

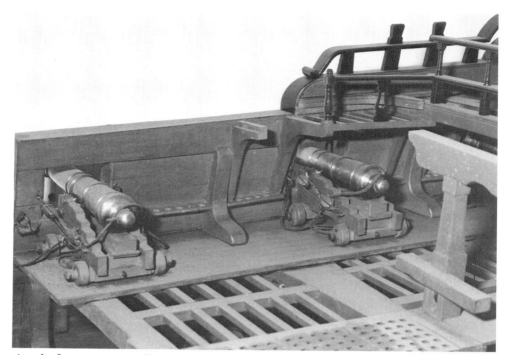

Plate 17 *The upper deck of the same model as Plate 19, showing a pair of 18 Pounders. The guns are fitted with tampions, which are attached to the muzzles with short lanyards. Author.*

Plate 18 *A fine and well detailed example of a mortar on a ½in scale model of a mid-eighteenth-century bomb vessel. This model is also in the Pitt-Rivers Museum, Oxford. Author.*

Plate 19 *A ½in scale model of a 24 Pounder on the lower deck of a mid-eighteenth-century Third Rate. The gun is in its stowed position, with the muzzle lashed to two eye bolts in the beam clamps. The weight of gun, and its number, is painted in white on the right-hand side of the carriage, which is red. The barrel is polished brass. Note the method of attaching the breeching tackle to the cascabel. The model is in the Pitt-Rivers Museum, Oxford. Author.*

simple form — are well made, and the additional task of making and fitting trucks to at least the visible carriages on the open decks would have been slight in comparison. If it were not so unusual, it might be believed that the guns were not intended to be fitted with trucks. A logical explanation may be that trucks were not fitted so that the carriages could be glued to the deck plank to keep them in position, although that was not found to be necessary in later years. Another curiosity is seen on a First Rate of around 1670–1680, in a private collection, where the modeller went to the trouble of making and fitting carriages to all of the 110 broadside ports, but never got round to fitting any barrels to them! There were at least seventeenth-century guns known with only one pair of trucks, which are clearly seen on a longitudinal section of a First Rate drawn by Edmund Dummer in about 1680. The guns are shown with a pair of trucks at the front end of the carriages, and short stubby feet at the back ends. Examples of these are fitted on the quarter- and forecastle decks of the Third Rate *Bredah*, 1692, at Trinity House, while the guns on the upper deck have two pairs of trucks.

The barrels of seventeenth-century guns are usually painted black or sometimes a greenish colour, and appear to be mostly turned from wood, but it is possible that some may be brass. On most seventeenth-century guns, the barrels are not bored out, but there are exceptions such as those on the *St Michael*. The early gun carriages on models are made from a single piece of wood, which is either left solid with a half-round groove to receive the barrel, or hollowed out.

From early in the eighteenth century, very finely made and fully detailed guns appear, with polished brass barrels and properly built up carriages complete with the various ring and eye bolts. Particularly good examples are seen on the Third Rate of about 1705 at the Pitt-Rivers Museum. Tackles are fitted to the guns on a Third Rate of about 1745, at the National Maritime Museum, but this detail is rarely shown on models. Whether or not a model is fitted with guns, ring and eye bolts at the sides of the ports for the tackles are nearly always fitted, as are ring bolts in the deck for the training tackles. A point to note regarding the training tackle ring bolts is that they are always fastened through a beam, which may not necessarily be directly opposite a port, particularly in the waist, where the beams are of widely variable spacing due to the hatches and mast and capstan partners.

The barrels of eighteenth-century guns appear to be mostly bored out, but they are often stopped up with a plug, presumably to represent a tampion. The muzzles of gun barrels are sometimes painted red back to the first reinforcing ring.

Lanterns

Stern lanterns are an interesting group of fittings, not only for their attractive and elegant forms, but for fine craftsmanship in making them. Considering their small size — little more than an inch in height, and often smaller — the best examples are meticulous. Although there are a great many different designs in the bases and finials of lanterns, there are only three basic shapes. Spherical or ovoid ones are commonplace until the early years of the eighteenth century when the hexagonal, or sometimes pentagonal, tapered type of lantern generally appears. In a transitional period from about 1680 to 1700 or a little later, lanterns with straight and parallel sides were also fashionable, which are again mostly hexagonal but pentagonal ones are not uncommon.

The spherical lanterns are seldom perfectly round as on the Second Rate *Coronation*, 1685, but rather of a shape formed by six, or sometimes five, curved and flat-sided segments. They are nearly always gilt, but it seems that all the spherical type lanterns are constructed from metal, with soldered joints, and glazed with mica. The advantage of mica in these cases is that the material is extremely flexible and readily withstands the heat of a soldering iron. Being malleable, it is probable that pewter was widely used. Some corrosion on the finials of the lanterns on the Sixth Rate *Lizard*, 1697 (Model No 12) suggests that they were made from lead. How these lanterns were assembled, with the mica inside the framework, is at first difficult to understand, particularly as they are mostly painted red inside. But a close examination shows that at least some of them were constructed with an inner and outer framework with the mica sandwiched in between. The truly round and many paned centre lantern on the *Coronation* is also made from metal and glazed with mica, but whether it has an inner frame is uncertain. Mica readily bends in one direction, but certainly not two, and there is probably one narrow segment corresponding to each of the twelve panes round the circumference of the lantern.

From early in the eighteenth century, if not before in the case of the parallel-sided ones, lanterns are mostly made from wood left with a natural finish and glazed with very thin glass. Although some of the early lanterns are glazed on all sides, and show an all-round light, the majority are blocked in on the forward side with only the three segments facing aft being glazed, thus showing only a stern light. A number of eighteenth-century lanterns superficially appear to show

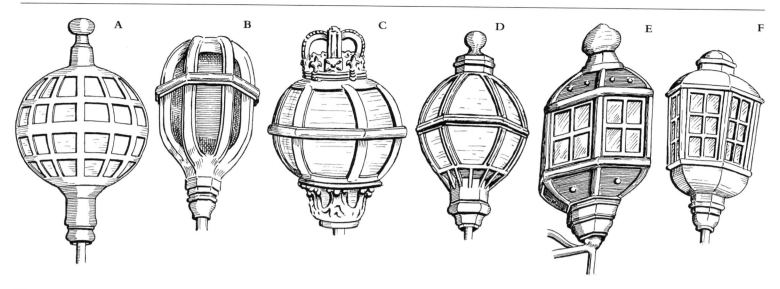

Fig 46 *Stern lanterns.*

A *Second Rate* Coronation, *1685 (Model No 9).*

B *A very unusual lantern from a Fourth Rate of about 1695. It is unglazed and appears to be made from a single hollowed out piece of wood with added horizontal bars. Gilded and painted red inside (model at the National Maritime Museum).*

C *Fourth Rate of about 1692. Gilded with a red interior (model in the Kriegstein collection).*

D *Third Rate Boyne, 1692. Gilded with a red interior (Model No 11).*

E *First or Second Rate of about 1702. White frames and glazing bars; blue upper and lower panels, with the remainder gilt. Red inside (Model No 13).*

F *Fourth Rate Medway, 1742. Natural wood with frames and glazing bars made from brass. Painted red inside (model at the National Maritime Museum).*

an all-round light, but these are deceiving in that the forward three sides are fitted with dummy glazing bars and sometimes glass which is backed by black painted panels. Lanterns of this period are also invariably painted red inside. The lanterns are typically mounted on a single vertical metal bracket with an angled strut each side, and are sometimes braced at the upper end with thin metal wire stays to the tafferal. Particularly attractive brackets are made from thin strip metal which is twisted, creating a spiral effect.

An interesting little detail is seen on the *Royal Oak* which does not have any stern lanterns, but a small one is fitted aft of the main top. Inside this tiny lantern there are two cylindrical objects which appear to represent chimneys for oil lamp wicks, or possibly large candles.

It is apparent that many models were never fitted with lanterns; on others the brackets, or evidence of their fastenings, remain, while all three lanterns are missing. Sometimes only the centre lantern is shown on a model, such as the *Hampton Court*, 1678 (Model No 6) and others, but this should not be taken as evidence that ships were fitted only with a single lantern, as in most of these cases it is because the ones at the sides are lost.

Lanterns look very nice on models, but the centre ones frequently, and frustratingly, completely conceal what can be important details in the tafferal decoration. For instance, if it had not been possible to lift off the centre lantern of the Third Rate *Yarmouth*, 1748 (Model No 4), the Coat of Arms of that town would not have been recognised, without which the model would probably never have been identified.

Rudders

When rudders are fitted on the earliest models (which is not always) they are mostly simply hung on the stern post, and no attempt was made to represent the braces correctly with their respective gudgeons and pintles. A common practice was to fit bent pieces of wire at the upper and lower ends of the rudder which engage in two eye bolts in the stern post. An improvement on this was to fit all the rudder braces, but with pintles only on the upper and lower ones which again pivot on eye bolts in the post. From around 1680, some meticulous work is evident on the better quality models, and the braces—mostly made from brass—are all fitted with pintles and gudgeons in the proper manner. The ends of braces are generally left square, and sometimes turned back round the aft edge of the rudder, but quite often they are finished in the same fancy design as those on the port lid straps. The rudders are usually very close to the stern post, and to allow the swing from side to side, the fore edge is 'bearded' or bevelled back on each side, and the stern post is left square.

Plate 20 *The rudder of the Third Rate Yarmouth, 1748. The braces, which are made from brass, are let in flush with the rudder and fastened with almost invisible brass rivets. Although at the fairly small scale of 1/60, the work is finely done.* NMM (Author).

Models of the late seventeenth century are of considerable interest for showing the transition of the rudder head from being entirely outboard of the counter to being enclosed within it. This appears to have begun about 1690 and was complete by 1700. A curious belief was once held concerning rudder heads, which has been more or less repeated on and off ever since.[5] This was that when only the tiller was taken through the counter, a helm port of considerable width was necessary which made it difficult to prevent the entry of sea water, and that the rudder head was 'taken well up' into the counter by around 1700, which enabled the helm port to be better closed by a rudder cloth. There are three main points here that do not bear examination. Firstly, when only the tiller was taken through the counter, the helm port need be only very small. The helm port was almost directly above the pivoting point of the rudder, and it does not take the working of a rudder on a model to realise that there was virtually no lateral or sideways movement of the tiller at that point, and therefore the helm port could be easily waterproofed by a flexible cloth. Secondly, the rudder head was not taken *up* into the counter, but rather shortened and cut off a little above the mortice for the tiller. It was a measure enforced on the builder by the increasing rake aft of the counter, which enclosed what was left of the rudder head. Thirdly, when the large square rudder head *was* enclosed by the counter, the helm port was necessarily a huge one, and due to the twisting movement of the rudder, there must have been extreme difficulty in closing it with a rudder cloth.

At some uncertain date, the rudder head was extended up through the upper deck on two-deckers or the middle deck on First and Second Rates and pierced with a mortice for an emergency tiller. This is not seen on early eighteenth-century models, and it probably did not happen until around the middle of the century. On a Fourth Rate of the 1719 Establishment at the Science Museum, there appears to be a small part of the deck in the open stern gallery of the upper deck which lifts out. This is directly above the rudder head, and it was presumably to allow the rudder to be lifted up and then dropped down on the gudgeons.

On seventeenth-century models, where the rudder head is entirely outboard of the counter, the aft end of the tiller is often cast down and passes through the helm port in the raking counter at right angles, but this is not seen when the rudder head is enclosed, and the tiller is generally straight throughout its length.

Fire hearths

Very many eighteenth-century models, and a few of the earlier period, are fitted with galley stoves, or 'fire hearths' as they were more generally called. Except for one example on a single-decker, only those on models of ships with two decks can be mentioned. Fire hearths on two-deckers are always on the upper deck immediately forward of the forecastle bulkhead, and are fairly visible although some are partially enclosed by partitions. On First and Second Rates they would be in the same position, but on the middle deck. It is probable that fire hearths are fitted on the more detailed models of three-deckers, which would no doubt be little different from those on smaller ships except a little larger, but no example has been noted.

The earliest fire hearth I know of is fitted on the *Hampton Court*, 1678 (Model No 6). Unlike all the later ones, it has a single copper with the open fire facing aft which is very close to the forecastle bulkhead. The next (chronologically) is the interesting fire hearth on the Sixth Rate *Lizard*, 1697 (Model No 12) which is fitted on the starboard side below the forecastle deck (see Fig 47). This was probably the normal position on a single-decker to avoid the inconvenience of the anchor cables, which would come inboard on the same deck. Where the chimney would be on this fire hearth, and how it would affect the fore shrouds directly above, I have no idea. A Fourth Rate of 1698 at the National Maritime Museum (illustrated in Chapter IV) is fitted with a fire hearth beautifully painted in red and white to represent brickwork. The fire hearth is about 6ft 0in square in plan,

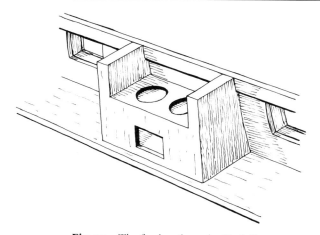

Fig 47 *The fire hearth on the Sixth Rate Lizard, 1697. It is on the starboard side between the first and second gun ports.*

and about 3ft 6in high to the aft side of it, which is taken up by two large coppers. At the forward side is an open fire fitted with fire bars, and the chimney is taken up to the deck head in the same width as the lower part, ie 6ft 0in, or perhaps a little more. This is the standard form of fire hearth seen on all models of the first half of the eighteenth century, but they vary greatly in detail. Fire doors to an enclosed separate fire-box beneath the coppers are shown, and sometimes there is a small door on the side of the upper part of the chimney. Although the chimney part is broad, the internal flue would probably be only about 1ft 6in square, and it seems that the doors in the chimney were for a bread oven, somewhat similar to those in the chimney breasts of old cottages. The most detailed fire hearths are panelled with wood, with the corners reinforced by metal angle plates which are sometimes decorated with fancy ends similar to port lid straps. Strangely enough, the early brick fire hearths were evidently clad with timber and bound with iron. The only reference to early brick fire hearths I have come across is in a group of contracts for late seventeenth-century Sixth Rates, but this probably applied equally as well to larger ships, and those of a later period.[6] The relevant section reads:

> To build on each inside within the bulkhead, one small firehearth for a double kettle, lining the side in the wake thereof with double white plates, and to cant the same with good oak quarters, and fixing it with good oak plank in every respect fitt for the bricklayers works, and to bind the same with iron to keep the brickworks from shaking loose.

It appears that the timber structure was built first, then filled in with the brickwork. 'White plates' are also specified in contracts for roofs of quarter galleries, but what they are I do not know, unless they were thin tinned sheets of iron, or possibly an alloy of some sort.

Brick fire hearths were generally replaced by iron ones from soon after the mid-eighteenth century, although they were known long before, and one was fitted on the Fourth Rate *Charles Galley*, 1676.[7] Very fine fire hearths of this type are seen fitted on models, and highly detailed too. They are fitted with opening doors to the fire-boxes and ovens, an ash pan below the open forward fire, taps from the coppers, guard rails at the sides, and a pair of ring bolts low down on each side to lash the whole contraption down to the deck. An excellent example is fitted on a model of the Third Rate *Lion*, 1777, at Dorset County Museum, Dorchester, which is made from thin plates of natural brass with the joints soldered together. Most of the 'iron' fire hearths are painted black, but it is probable that they were generally constructed from brass. In general layout, these later fire hearths are much the same as the brick ones, except that the iron chimney is of small section and the oven is placed between the enclosed fire-box under the coppers and the open fire at the forward side.

Footnotes

1 Public Record Office, Adm 106/3070, contract for the Sixth Rate *Penzance*, 1695.
2 *Ibid*, Adm 106/3071, contract for the Third Rate *Yarmouth*, 1695.
3 *Ibid*, Adm 106/3071, contract for four frigates dated 1673.
4 See Note by R C Anderson, 'A possible Commonwealth model', *The Mariner's Mirror*, Vol 27, p 168–9.
5. G S Laird Clowes, *Sailing Ships, their History and Development, Part 1. Historical Notes*, 1932.
6. Public Record Office, Adm 106/3070.
7. Article by A W Johns, *The Mariner's Mirror*, Vol XI, p 185.

IV
Scales and
Dimensions

To obtain the dimensions of the ship that a model represents, it is necessary to determine the scale at which it was built, and very often this can be difficult. During the period in which models were built, the standard was 1/48, or $\frac{1}{4}$ in to 1ft, the usual scale at which draughts were drawn, and the majority of models are evidently precisely built to this scale, and directly from the draught. As well as this common scale of 1/48, a great variety of others were used, which can be placed in three main categories. In the first group are scales based on 'common' fractions of an inch, such as $\frac{1}{8}$ in, $\frac{3}{16}$ in, $\frac{5}{16}$ in and $\frac{3}{8}$ in. The second group consists of scales derived from 'decimal' divisions of an inch, such as $\frac{1}{10}$ in and $\frac{1}{5}$ in, the last being the most common after $\frac{1}{4}$ in, and used extensively from about 1700. In the third group are some models that are built on apparently odd scales that cannot be related to any normal fraction of an inch, and can be expressed only as a ratio.

It is these abnormal scales that are hard to understand, but there are several possible reasons as to how they came about. There appear to be two distinct principles involved when the scales of models depart from the normal 1/48. The first is that many models, mainly eighteenth-century, were obviously built from reduced or sometimes enlarged copies of a normal $\frac{1}{4}$ in draught, to whatever scale was required. The other principle is a little complex, but briefly it is that a model would have been built directly from the lines of a standard draught, and to represent a smaller or larger ship, it was achieved by varying the scale. The evidence of this is confined to seventeenth-century and early eighteenth-century models. To understand a little of the principle, it is revealing to take a look at some scales used by early shipwrights which helps to explain why some models are built on seemingly unusual ratios. The use of variable scales was well known in early times, and was an elegant and ingenious alternative to preparing separate draughts for ships of different dimensions. The best illustration of how the method works can be found in the multiple scales which appear on the beautiful draughts in a book known as *Fragments of Ancient English Shipwrightry* ascribed to the shipwright Matthew Baker which dates from the late sixteenth century.[1] One of the draughts (page 21) has six scales on it for the purpose of building ships with widely differing dimensions from a single set of lines. Five of the scales are $3\frac{3}{4}$ in long overall, the same as the moulded breadth of the midship bend on the draught, and are divided and marked in feet for breadths of 20, 24, 30, 40 and 44ft. The purpose of the sixth scale is unclear, as it is not marked in feet, but over the same length of $3\frac{3}{4}$ in it has slightly under 17 divisions, which would give a breadth of about 16ft 9in. Except for two very small discrepancies, the scales work out at $\frac{11}{128}$ in, $\frac{3}{32}$ in, $\frac{1}{8}$ in, $\frac{5}{32}$ in, $\frac{3}{16}$ in, and $\frac{7}{32}$ in, which are illustrated in Fig 48 as they appear on the draught. To be strictly accurate, the scale of $\frac{11}{128}$ in actually gives a breadth of 43.64ft instead of exactly 44ft, and $\frac{7}{32}$ in gives a breadth of 17.14ft instead of 16ft 9in, but considering that they were drawn by a draughtsman in the late sixteenth century, they are remarkably precise. The significance of these scales is that five of them can be found from equally spaced divisions of a series of converging lines, or a 'diminishing scale', with the sixth at one quarter of a division.

The diagram in Fig 48 shows a possible method by which Baker found his scales, but it can be constructed in various other ways, such as in a triangle. No doubt he would have required the scales for ships of any other breadth, and the diagonal line on the diagram shows how this can be found.

45

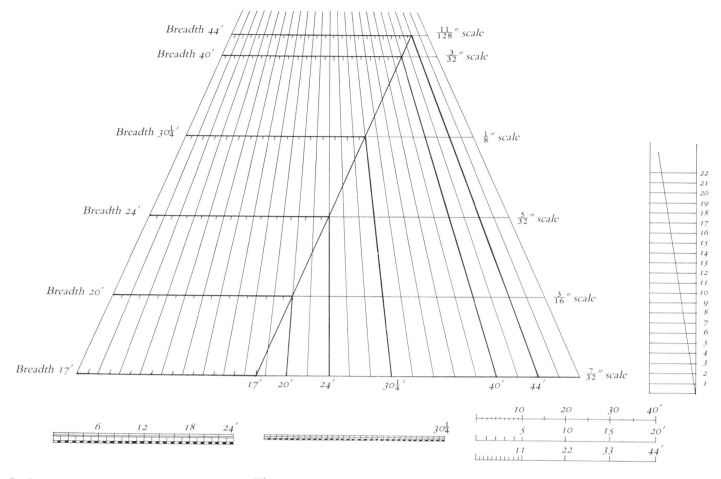

Fig 48 *Late sixteenth-century scales from a draught ascribed to Master Shipwright Matthew Baker. The six scales shown below and to the right of the diagram are as they appear on the draught, apparently for the purpose of building ships of varying breadths, but the same proportions, from one set of lines. The diagram illustrates a possible method used by Baker to obtain his scales. If a scale is required for any other breadth, it can be found by following up the appropriate line from the bottom of the diagram, and striking a horizontal line at the intersection with the diagonal. Every other converging line in the diagram is omitted for clarity.*

The same principle is explained in a work on shipbuilding written in about 1625, in which the anonymous author describes a draught as of 'mean proportions between the greatest and least, the rather because by an increasing or diminishing of the scale we may keep the same mould and build any other ship of more or less burthen at pleasure'.[2]

By the second half of the seventeenth century, it appears that shipwrights were still using variable scales, but to a far less extent than in earlier years. An example is found on a draught of a Sixth Rate dating from around 1670, which has one scale of ¼in giving approximate dimensions of 83ft 0in on the keel, and with a breadth of 26ft 0in.[3] Another scale of $\frac{3}{16}$in on the same draught produces a keel length of 69ft 0in and a breadth of 21ft 0in. These dimensions are at about the upper and lower limits for a Sixth Rate at that time, and to build a ship of any intermediate dimensions the appropriate scale would be calculated, perhaps by the same method illustrated in Fig 48.

Also in 1670, we have the valuable works of Anthony Deane. In his *Doctrine of Naval Architecture*, Deane describes a scale as:

> a piece of board, brass or paper, whereon you make with your compasses several equal parts, the greater or lesser as your plate or design will afford, the larger the better regarding the design in hand, and considering a ship, a body of many feet, which will take up a great room, I choose to suppose a quarter of an inch to one foot, or as my plate will admit of, more or less.

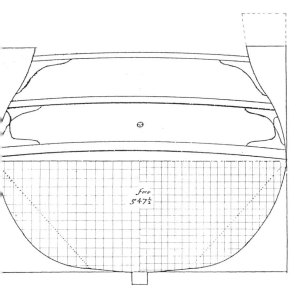

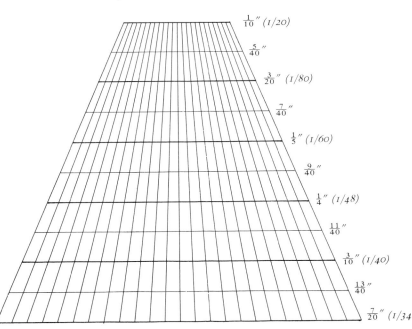

Only one example of a scale by Deane exists, which is found on a draught for a Third Rate which is illustrated in the *Doctrine*, and to fit his 'plate' he chose a fairly small one. The scale has thirty-two divisions in a length of $4\frac{1}{2}$ in, which works out at a ratio of 1/85.3, or exactly $\frac{9}{64}$ in to 1ft. Although this appears unusual, it can be found on a diminishing scale based on common fractions (see Fig 50).

The midship bend illustrated in Fig 49 is one of a series of body sections believed to be of the *Rupert*, a Third Rate built by Deane in 1666, from which he has calculated the underwater volume in feet.[4] A number of oddities can be seen on the drawing which are at first difficult to understand, such as the way the knees are drawn, the three decks, and the puzzling relationship of the upper deck beam with the top of the side. But what Deane has apparently done here is to convert the body sections of a Third Rate to a much larger ship with three decks, simply by changing to a smaller scale. The way the knees are drawn suggests that the body sections were intended to represent the inner sides of the hull timbers. The breadth of the midship bend is 8in, or 32ft 0in at Deane's preferred scale of $\frac{1}{4}$ in. If within the timbers, the breadth outside plank would become about 34ft 6in, which is the same as that originally intended for the *Rupert*, although she was completed with a breadth of 36ft 3in.[5] The bend itself is clearly that of a two-decker, which is evident by the height to breadth proportions, but at a $\frac{1}{4}$ in scale the height between decks is only about 5ft 3in and the underwater volume is only about 334ft compared with the $547\frac{1}{2}$ft given on the drawing. By trial and error, it can be found that to obtain $547\frac{1}{2}$ft Deane must have used a scale of 1/61.5, which gives a height between decks of about 7ft 0in as it should be, and a breadth of 41ft 0in. Again, if within the timbers, the breadth outside plank would be about 44ft 0in, very near to that of the three First Rates built by Deane in the early 1670s. All that remains to be done to complete the drawing to represent the midship section of a three-decker is to extend up the top of the side 4 or 5ft. If this can be done on a draught, a model (or a ship) of a First Rate can of course be built from a $\frac{1}{4}$ in draught of a Third Rate, which almost certainly explains why the model of a First Rate of about 1670 is at a scale of about 1/55 (see Model No 4). Another example of a seventeenth-century model built to a scale of around 1/55 is a Second Rate of about 1680. According to Culver,[6] the model has a breadth of 9.4in which again suggests that it was built from a $\frac{1}{4}$ in draught of a Third Rate with a breadth of about 37ft 6in. At 1/55, the breadth becomes 43ft 0in, that of a normal Second Rate of 90 guns.

It was the body plan that was all important in rescaling draughts, with the

Fig 49 *Anthony Deane's midship section of a Third Rate, showing how he converted it to a larger ship with three decks by changing the scale. The grid of squares does not appear on the original drawing, and has been added to illustrate the scale of 1/48 on the left and the scale of 1/61.5 on the right, which Deane must have used to obtain the underwater volume of 547½ft.*

Fig 50 *Diminishing scale based on common fractions of one inch. An infinite variety of scales can be found by equally dividing a series of converging lines.*

Fig 51 *Diminishing scale based on decimal fractions of one inch.*

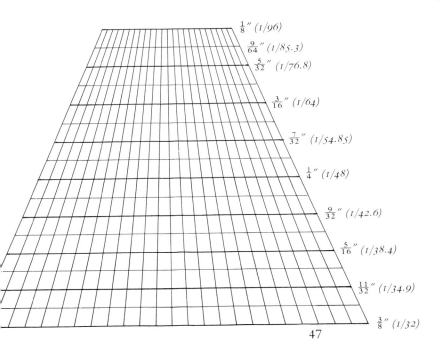

change in scale calculated from the breadth, and any alteration in the length/breadth proportions would be achieved by a very small adjustment to the timber and room.

Evidence which suggests that models were built from rescaled draughts in the eighteenth century is found in a Queen Anne Third Rate of 70 guns in the possession of Mr Montagu. According to the dimensions given on the label, the model measures $32\frac{1}{4}$in on the gun deck, with a breadth of $8\frac{3}{4}$in. To provide suitable dimensions for a Third Rate at that time, an odd scale of 1/56 is required, which gives full-sized dimensions of 150ft 6in on the gun deck and a breadth of 40ft 10in. It is possible that the model was constructed from a reduced copy of a standard draught, or one actually drawn to a scale of 1/56, but a more logical explanation is that the hull itself was built for convenience from a $\frac{1}{4}$in scale draught of a smaller ship. In other words, if the model is measured at a $\frac{1}{4}$in scale, it has almost the exact dimensions of a typical Fourth Rate on the 1706 Establishment, ie 129ft 0in on the gun deck and a breadth of 35ft 0in.

Sometimes the change in scale would not be very great. The model illustrated in Plate 21 is dated 1698 on the cradles, and initialled FH which can be taken as being those of Shipwright Fisher Harding. At a scale of 1/48, the model has a gun deck of 150ft 0in and a breadth of 39ft 6in, near enough the dimensions of the *Bedford*, a Third Rate of 70 guns built by Harding in 1698. But with its very short poop deck and number and arrangement of ports, the model clearly represents a Fourth Rate of 60 guns. The hull of the model may have been built from the draught of the *Bedford*, but completed as a ship of 60 guns, in which case the dimensions would need to be calculated from a scale of 1/46. This gives a length on the gun deck of 143ft 9in and a breadth of 37ft 9in which is the same as the *Montagu*, 60 guns, 1698, another ship built by Fisher Harding.

Although it is impossible to verify, there are probably models which were built from draughts drawn to imperfectly divided scales. An example of this can be found on the draughts drawn by William Keltridge in 1684. Two of the draughts are drawn to scales of $\frac{1}{8}$in and $\frac{3}{8}$in which are accurate, but several more, obviously *intended* to be at $\frac{1}{4}$in, vary between 1/49 and 1/50. But these are not really inaccurate, as if a draught is drawn to a certain scale and dimensions are taken off that draught by the same scale, no error arises. It is only when a model is measured with a perfectly divided modern scale rule that the discrepancy would appear, although we are not aware of it. This is an unknown quantity, but it would explain a number of models which have dimensions that are apparently too large or too small for the ship it represents when measured on even scales. This is probably the reason why the Second Rate *Coronation*, 1685, is built at a scale of 1/51 (see Model No 9). Another example of a model which may have been built from an inaccurate scale is a Fourth Rate dating from the early 1690s at the National Maritime Museum. At a $\frac{1}{4}$in scale, the breadth is at least 1ft 6in too great for any of the many Fourth Rates built at that time. But it has suitable proportions, and if it were measured at 1/46, the model would have a breadth of 34ft 6in and a gun deck of 125ft 6in, almost the exact dimensions of several Fourth Rates built in the early 1690s.

Diminishing scales were probably widely used by shipwrights and modelmakers, not only to convert one scale to another but to obtain them, and they may have had them marked out on a wide board as long as a large draught. The apparently odd ratios at which some models are built can be explained as originating from a diminishing scale. The diagram in Fig 50 is based on common fractions, and illustrates how any intermediate scale between $\frac{1}{8}$in and $\frac{3}{8}$in can be found. Deane's scale of $\frac{9}{64}$in appears at the top of the diagram, and the $\frac{9}{32}$in at which a First Rate of about 1715 was built, which was determined by its draught of water marks.[7] The scale in Fig 51 is based on decimal fractions of an inch, and shows the unusual scale of $\frac{7}{20}$in which was used to build a large-scale model of the *Victory*,[8] 1737. Very accurate divisions can be obtained when diminishing scales are perfectly

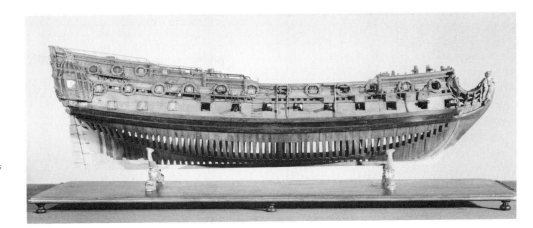

Plate 21 *This model of 1692 has the dimensions of a Third Rate of 70 guns when measured at the normal scale of 1/48, but it appears to represent a slightly smaller ship of 60 guns, and built to a scale of about 1/46.* NMM.

constructed, but if the horizontal lines are slightly misplaced, errors arise, and this may be the reason for the inaccurate scales mentioned previously.

The many smaller-scale models of the eighteenth century were probably built from quite simple reduced copies of standard ¼in scale draughts. To build the hull of a model, it would only be necessary to make a reduction of the body plan, and perhaps the profile of the stem, with all other dimensions taken off with adjustable proportional compasses, which were known from the early seventeenth century. Parallelograms and pantographs were also well known from about the same time. Some of these instruments were very large, with arms of 3ft or more in length, and it is possible that body plans were reduced by this method. An interesting illustration of a parallelogram is seen at the Science Museum, London, which bears the inscription, 'An Instrument to Augment or Diminish any Draught of Fortifications, Ships, Lands, Buildings & Co in any Proportions'.

A more accurate way to make a reduction is by the use of squared paper. To make a reduction from 1/48 to 1/60, for example, a grid of ¼in squares would have been drawn on the original body plan, from which the lines could be readily transferred to paper with squares of ⅕in. An undated device of a glass plate engraved with squares is on display at the Science Museum, which originated from the Admiralty. In use, the plate would have been placed on the drawing from which the reduction was to be made, instead of spoiling it by drawing in the grid of squares.

Dimensions of ships and models

Assuming the scale is known, the dimensions obtained from a model are of considerable value. This is not only for the principal ones of gun deck, breadth and keel, to compare with those of a particular ship, but for the scantlings of wales, etc, the important 'timber and room', and for illustrating the various fashions of the fore and aft rakes. Also of great interest are measurements of details such as fish davits and capstans which are difficult to find from any other source. For instance, the only dimension given in seventeenth-century contract-specifications and the later Establishment lists for capstans is the diameter of the barrel, and it is only from models that the height and diameter of the drumhead can normally be found. The dimensions and terms used, which are given under the headings of the respective models, require explanation, and the following is based on evidence found in contracts, early works on naval architecture, and on draughts. Where mention is made of how a dimension has been taken from models, this refers to those that have been measured by myself.

Length on the gun deck. From the late seventeenth century, when this dimension first appears on draughts and in contracts, the length was generally given as 'on the gun deck from the rabbet of the stem to the rabbet of the post'. In later years it was clarified as 'on the gun deck from the aft side of the rabbet of the stem to the fore side of the rabbet of the stern post'. In other words, this was the outside of the timbers, but it is probable that the actual 'as built' length given in the ship lists is to the outside of plank, as was the breadth, and this is the dimension which has been given for the models.

Breadth. Until around the mid-seventeenth century, the breadth was normally given as 'within the plank'. This later became known as the 'moulded breadth', which was measured to the outside of the timbers. From about 1650 onwards, the breadth is usually specified as 'outside to outside of the plank', which is the dimension given in the ship lists. The term 'breadth extream' is often found, but this is still outside the plank, and not over all the projecting wales as might be thought. An excellent definition of the breadth is found in the 1719 Establishment list:

> The Extream Breadth is to be taken from the outside to the outside of the Plank or thick stuff either above or below the Wales, where the Ship shall be broadest, always deducting the Doubling or Sheathing from the said Breadth.

Models do not generally have any plank fitted below the wales, and the dimension has been obtained by deducting the thickness of the wales from the overall breadth and adding a suitable thickness for the plank.

Length on the keel. During the second half of the seventeenth century, three distinct methods of measuring the keel were in use—the 'tread', the 'touch' and the theoretical 'calculated' length. The tread, which is always the longest length, was measured along the bottom of the keel to the angle where the fore edge of the cut-water began to rise. The touch length was taken from the aft end of the keel to the point where the rabbet of the stem began to curve up from the keel. Sutherland defined this as 'the rising of the keel or part where its upper part ceases to be straight, called by shipwrights the Touch'.[9] On most models, the touch corresponds with the aft end of the keel/stem scarph, but there are many exceptions such as the *Hampton Court* (Model No 6), where the keel length given on the draught agrees precisely with the forward end of the scarph. The calculated length was measured from the aft end of the keel to a perpendicular dropped from the fore side of the stem at the level of the upper edge of the lower mainwale, or 'harpin'. Three-fifths of the breadth was then subtracted to give the calculated length of keel, which Sutherland called 'Shipwrights Hall Rule'. Whether the touch or calculated keel was shortest depended on the fore and aft rakes, but it is fairly safe to say that prior to the 1670s, the touch length was the shortest. After this time, the touch length varied, from being about the same as the calculated to very much longer, due to the general adoption of short fore rakes of the stem. There were evidently a number of variations in measuring the calculated keel, which are explained in the accompanying extract from the 1719 Establishment. At the same time, a new and more complicated method was proposed, which is impractical to apply to models. In all periods from about 1650, tonnage was found by multiplying the length of keel by the breadth, the product by the half breadth, and dividing the sum by 94. Until the 1670s, the formula for tonnage was worked out from the touch keel. During the 1670s and '80s, all three widely differing keel lengths were used indiscriminately to obtain tonnage, but from then on, the calculated keel was used exclusively, and became known as 'length on the keel for tonnage'. The keel lengths given in Pepys' *Register of Ships* of 1685, and other lists of the late seventeenth century, are a confused mixture of the tread, touch and calculated. Without knowing which is which, it is impossible to compare the keel length of a model with a particular ship, but a lot can be done, and very often two of the lengths can be found for the same ship, and sometimes all three. In many cases, the tonnage listed for a ship is derived from a keel length other than that which is given, particularly in Pepys' list. This is of great value, as by working the formula for tonnage backwards, one of the other keel lengths can be found. One example is the *Coronation*, 1685, which is given in Pepys' list as a keel of 140ft 0in but with a tonnage of 1427 which is derived from a keel length of 134ft 0in. The keel lengths of the model of the *Coronation* have not been obtained, but the fore rake of the stem is fairly short, and no doubt the 140ft 0in would agree to the touch, with the 134ft 0in being the calculated.

The twenty Third Rates built between 1678 and 1680 are an interesting group as far as keel lengths are concerned. The main dimensions of all these were virtually identical, at 150ft 0in on the gun deck and 40ft 0in in breadth, but keels varied from 120ft 0in to 140ft 0in, and ten of them are listed in Pepys' list with a tonnage that does not agree with the given keel length. The longest lengths are clearly to the tread, and the shortest the calculated, with those in between at about 130ft 0in being the touch. For instance, the *Northumberland*, 1679, is listed in Pepys' with a keel length of 137ft 0in which must be the tread, and a tonnage of 1050 which derives from a length of 121ft 6in and this has to be the calculated keel. Another list of 1685 known as Gloria Britannica gives a keel of 130ft 0in for the *Northumberland*, which is evidently the length to the touch. Keel lengths given in the various lists for the same ship very often widely differ due to the different methods of measuring. The Fourth Rate *Charles Galley*, 1676, is a good example, which had a keel of 124ft 0in according to Dimension Book B, with Pepys' list giving 114ft 0in. From the scale on an early draught of the *Charles*, it can be found that it is the tread that measures 124ft 0in, and Pepys' 114ft 0in works out at the calculated. The touch length from the draught is about 118ft 0in. Although it is of interest to take the calculated keel and tonnage from a model, it has little practical value for identification purposes. In all periods, it is the measurement to the touch and tread that is of real use, and then only when it can be verified as such in the lists, but there are many uncertainties. The touch keel length is never given in eighteenth-century lists, but it is still of value to take from a model if it is suspected as being of a particular ship, and a draught exists to make a comparison.

To Determine the Burthen in Tuns

From the 1719 Establishment. NMM Adm 170 (429)

> First, instead of Measuring from the Back of the Main Post to the Perpendicular or Square from the Keel at the fore part of the Stem at the top thereof, or from a square or Perpendicular from the Keel at the Fore part of the Stem at the Upper Edge of the Lower Harpin, as hath been usuall, both which extreames are liable to many uncertainties, and may be Considerably Varied by increasing or lessoning the Main or False post without the Rabbet abaft, or by raising or lowering the Harpin forward, the Raking the upper part of the Stem more or less, or adding or diminishing to the Scantlings of the Same before the Rabbet of the Stem; none of which are essential for determining the Tunnage. Therefore instead thereof, Erect a Square or Perpendicular from a Line Ranging Straight with the Lower part of the Rabbet of the Keel to the after part of the Plank (or Rabbet) at the Upper Edge of the Wing Transome; and also another Square or Perpendicular from the Forepart of the Plank (or Rabbet) of the Stem, at 5/6 Parts of the height of the Wing Transome. Then measure the Length between these Perpendicular Lines, and add thereto 1/24 of the Extream Breadth for the Scantling of the Stem before, and the Post abaft the Plank (without regarding whether there be a False Post or no) from which sum Subtract 6/25 of the Height of the Wing Transome (for the rake abaft) and 3/5 of the Main Breadth (for the Rake forward), the Residue is to be accounted the Length of keel for Tunnage, which multiplied by the Extream Breadth, and the product by the Half Breadth, and that sum divided by 94 gives the Burthen in Tuns. This for square sterned ships.

Fore and aft rakes. In the seventeenth century, the rake aft of the stern post was a horizontal measurement taken from the end of the keel to a perpendicular dropped from the back of the post at the level of the 'main' or 'wing' transom. The fore rake of the stem was also a horizontal measurement, taken from the touch of the

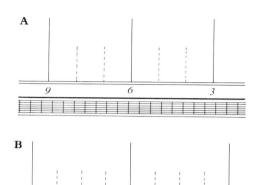

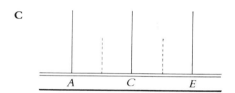

Fig 52 *To build a Navy Board framed hull from an Admiralty draught, the 'timber and room', and the siding of the timber required for the frames, can be found by the numbers or letters indicated at the station lines. These are three typical examples.*

A *Distance between station lines, 7ft 6in. Three timber and rooms of 2ft 6in. Siding of the timbers, 1ft 3in.*

B *Distance between station lines, 9ft 0in. Four timber and rooms of 2ft 3in. Siding of the timbers, 1ft 1½in.*

C *Distance between station lines, 5ft 6in. Two timber and rooms of 2ft 9in. Siding of the timbers 1ft 4½in.*

Footnotes

1. Pepysian Library, Magdalene College, Cambridge, Ms 2820.
2. *A Treatise on Shipbuilding and a Treatise on Rigging, c* 1625. Society for Nautical Research. Occ Pub No 6, edited by W Salisbury and R C Anderson, p 14.
3. NMM Draught Room, Box 5, Neg No 6815.
4. Pepysian Library, Ms 2501.
5. Brian Lavery, *Deane's Doctrine of Naval Architecture*, Conway, 1981, p 11.
6. Henry B Culver, *Contemporary Scale Models of the 17th Century*, New York, 1926 (Model in the New York Yacht Club).
7. *Catalogue of ship models*, National Maritime Museum, p 49.
8. *Ibid*, p 82.
9. William Sutherland, *Shipbuilding Unveiled*, 1711.
10. Public Records Office, Adm 106/3070.

keel to a perpendicular dropped from the fore side of the stem, either at the stem head or at the level of the upper edge of the lower mainwale, or harpin. The former method was probably in use until about 1670, from which time contracts generally specify the fore rake as 'at the harpin'. In the earliest contracts, a specific dimension is given for a total of the two rakes, but from about 1670, individual dimensions are specified for both the stem and the post. By 1690, although the rake of the post was still given as a dimension, the rake of the stem was specified as a proportion of the breadth. A good example of this is the model of the *Boyne*, 1692, which has a fore rake of a little under three-fifths of the breadth. The contract for the *Norfolk*, 1693, a sister ship of the *Boyne*, specifies 'Rake forward at the harpin 3/5ths part of the main breadth, the which it is not to exceed'.[10] In the Establishments of the eighteenth century, the stem is not mentioned, except for a very small fore rake above the level of the gun deck, but the stern post was specified to rake aft 2½in in a foot, or about 12 degrees.

Timber and room. Throughout the seventeenth century, and in the early eighteenth, the 'timber and room' was a division of the length of a ship equal to the fore and aft width, or 'siding', of one floor plus one futtock, where 'timber' was the floor and 'room' was the space between the floors in which the futtocks tightly fitted. In the 1690s the term is sometimes found in contracts as 'room and space of the timber and room', but from then on it was always known as 'room and space'. Each timber and room was allocated a number in the aft body and a letter in the fore body, but except for on a few early draughts, only those at the station lines are so indicated. The station lines shown on Admiralty draughts are normally spaced at three, or sometimes four, timber and rooms until the 1750s, when two became usual (see Fig 52). In the seventeenth century, the sidings of one floor and one futtock completely filled up the timber and room, but a very small tolerance was allowed of between ¼in and 1in, presumably for fitting. A typical contract would specify the timber and room as 'noe more than 2ft 3in', with the siding of the floor given as 13¼in and the futtock as 13½in, amounting to 2ft 2¾in. Sometimes only the timber and room and the siding of the floors is given, but with the futtocks specified to 'fill the rooms'. It was an important dimension in shipbuilding, and vital in building a Navy Board hull accurately to length. On most models, the siding of the timbers is remarkably consistent, but there are many examples of adjustments having been made by introducing slightly thicker or thinner timbers at intervals, to agree with the spacing of the timber and rooms and station lines of the draught it was built from. Because of this necessary accuracy, and because there were distinct changes in the dimension of the timber and room at different periods, it can on occasion be an aid to establishing the approximate date of a model (see Chapter V, on identification). For accuracy, the dimension of the timber and room of models has been obtained as an average of a measurement taken over ten frames.

Depth in hold. The depth was normally measured in midships from the top of the ceiling, or internal plank, to the upper edge of the lower deck beams.

Height between decks. This was taken from the upper side of the plank on one deck, to the upper side of the plank on the deck above.

Gun ports. Where dimensions are given for the gun ports of a model, this has been taken for convenience as a measurement of the lids. The true size of the actual opening of the ports through the hull timbers is a little less than that given due to the rabbet.

V
Identification of Ship Models

One of the more perplexing aspects in the study of Navy Board models is that there should be any need for them to be identified at all. Apart from a very few which are known from documentary evidence to be of a particular ship, and a handful of others where the name is displayed on the stern, or sometimes at the break of the poop, they are completely anonymous. It is because of this lack of provenance that the interpretation of models as to what they represent can only be suggested on the evidence that they themselves provide. But perhaps this is not surprising considering their age and the fact that models passed through many hands have become separated from their original display cabinets, and it is probable that many of them never had contemporary descriptions. All models have of course modern labels, but it has to be said that not a few of them are susceptible to an alternative opinion, particularly with respect to their date, and also sometimes the Rate. The subject is complex, difficult, and more often than not, frustrating, but at the same time it is a fascinating and absorbing one, and when a model can be suggested as being representative of a ship known to have been built, it can be extremely rewarding and well worth all the effort. This can rarely be done today, for most models capable of being identified already have been, but there are still a few that can be named, and others where at least a tentative suggestion can be made. Before anything in that way can be attempted, the Rate and date of the ship needs to be established, and also when the model was made, which is not always the same as when the ship was built. Interlinked with all facets of identification is the scale at which models were built, and the dimensions.

Full credit must be given to the late Dr R C Anderson and others who in the early years of this century laid down the fundamental techniques of identification. This was to measure a model, and by assuming a scale, the full-sized dimensions could be recovered and compared with those recorded for a particular ship. This basic principle is as valid today as it was then, except that there has always been far too great an emphasis on precise scales, and that to be identified, a model should necessarily have dimensions very close to those of the ship. This school of thought has at times been carried to extremes. Those models that have already been identified by name certainly meet the above requirements, but they were partly identified *because* of this which would not always be the case. Dimensions are important, otherwise the whole principle of identification by measurement would collapse, but a lot of allowance has to be made for several possible reasons.

Firstly, dimensions are of no value unless the scale is known, and, as discussed in the previous chapter, this can cause the greatest difficulty. The problem is that there is no standard dimension from which the scale can be obtained except for those few models where draught of water marks are indicated on the stem and stern post. In many cases, the scale can only be approximately calculated by working backwards from the probable dimensions of the ship represented by a model, in which case the dimensions are meaningless for identification purposes except for providing the length/breadth proportions. The great majority of models, however, are built to 1/48, or other even scales such as 1/60, which can generally be taken as accurate and the dimensions reliable. But it can never be assumed that even these are *always* precise over a length of 3ft or more, and by measuring a model with an accurately divided modern scale rule, errors of several full-size feet can easily occur, although it would not be realised.

Secondly, we have to consider the differences between design dimensions and those of the ship as completed. With certain reservations, it is logical to believe that a model would be built accurately from a draught, which does not mean that a ship built from that same draught would turn out the same. It is convenient to compare the dimensions of a model with those in the ship lists, but we always have to bear in mind that they give 'as built' dimensions, which—particularly in the seventeenth century—may be considerably larger than the design dimensions: up to 6ft or more in length and 2ft in breadth was not uncommon.

Thirdly, we have to question the accuracy to which models were built from

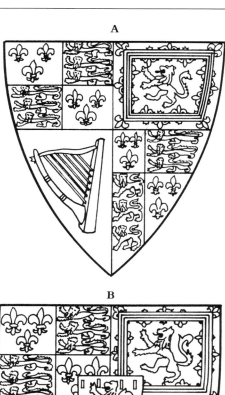

A

B

C

the draught. It can probably be taken that the breadth and depth are accurate for the hull would have to be shaped from patterns of the body sections, but the very method by which the hull framing was built could easily lead to errors in length. To build an accurate hull, a certain number of floors and futtocks have to go in a certain length, and to prepare timber to such a thickness that when over a hundred pieces are put together it will agree precisely with a predetermined length is very difficult indeed. It can often be seen on models that adjustments were made to the siding of the hull timbers, and sometimes thin packing pieces are inserted between the floors and futtocks which was obviously done so that the framing would agree with the spacing of the station lines. On many others, however, the siding of the floors and futtocks is so precisely the same, it leads one to suspect that the timber was prepared as closely as possible in thickness, and if that led to the hull being a little too short or long then it was ignored. In the length of a large model built to 1/48, an error of say 1in would be easy to make and it would be visually undetectable, but it would make a difference of 4ft on the scale, although it is again an unknown quantity. This would explain numerous models which are apparently too long or too short in proportion to their breadth.

All this will probably appear to be an exaggeration of the difficulties encountered in the dimensions of models, but it can in fact happen and has to be allowed for. What it amounts to is that if there are clear indications that a model is of a certain ship, that should take priority, and if the dimensions do not agree, within reason, it can be put down to any one of the above factors.

As an example, a Sixth Rate at the National Maritime Museum can be cited which has a length on the gun deck of 89ft 0in and a breadth of 23ft 0in at a scale of 1/48. On the cradles is the date 1706 and the initials BR which are almost certainly those of Benjamin Rosewell of Chatham Dockyard. Only one Sixth Rate was built at Chatham around that time — the *Nightingale*, 1702, which had as built dimensions of 93ft 0in on the gun deck and a breadth of 24ft 6in. The model cannot be identified as the *Nightingale* on this evidence alone, but the point is that it *might* be, and it should not be thought otherwise just because it is 1in too short and $\frac{3}{8}$in too narrow. The proportions are suitable, and in all probability the model was built from a draught drawn to a slightly inaccurate scale.

The date of a model can be found in various ways, the most obvious being when it is actually on the model itself, or more often, on the cradles. Unfortunately this is comparatively rare, and only found on a few models dating from the seventeenth and early eighteenth century.

Until the end of Queen Anne's reign in 1714 the Royal Arms were displayed on many models, mostly as a carving somewhere on the stern, but a few examples of Royal Standards exist, and one or two are seen on figureheads. During this period, the Arms changed several times and can date a model, sometimes within fairly narrow limits. Charles II and James II both used the Royal Arms of the Stuarts which cannot be distinguished from each other. The first change is seen in 1689 at the accession to the throne of William III. The Arms are still those of the Stuarts, but with the addition of William's paternal Arms of Nassau in pretence. This was contained in a small shield placed in the centre of the Stuart Arms which can nearly always be seen on models, although other details of the Arms are often poorly defined. Queen Anne used the ordinary Stuart Arms until 1707, when they were changed at the Act of Union with Scotland. Another alteration to the Arms took place in 1714 at the beginning of the long Georgian period during which they did not change again until 1801.

Monograms of kings and queens — often beautifully carved and of attractive designs — are commonplace throughout the period. Again these are only of value for dating purposes before 1714, as it never occurred to the carver to indicate whether the monogram GR was that of George I or II, for example, which would have been useful for dating models to before or after 1727.

All this evidence of date has to be taken as being the period during which the

D

E

Fig 53 *The Royal Arms. (Traced from originals in* The Romance of Heraldry, *C Wilfred Scott-Giles, 1929)*

A *Charles II (1660–1685), James II (1685–1688), Anne (1702–1707).*
B *William III (1688–1702).*
C *Anne (1707–1714).*
D *George I, II and III (1714–1801).*
E *George III (1801–1816).*

model was made, or at least completed, which is not necessarily that of the ship it represents. A good illustration of this is a Third Rate at the Science Museum, which is known to be the *Captain*, 70 guns, 1708. But prominently displayed on the quarter galleries is the monogram GR which shows that the model was not finished until at least after 1714 when George I succeeded to the throne. There are numerous examples of this sort of thing, and there is a logical explanation for it. As it is clear that models were sometimes built over a number of years, it follows that if one was begun, for instance, during the reign of William III and completed in the reign of Queen Anne, it would show evidence of the later period although it would be of an earlier ship. Such a one is the galley-frigate at the Pitt-Rivers Museum, which not only has the date of 1702 on the cradles and the monogram of Queen Anne on the stern, but also the Royal Arms of William III, and in all probability it is a model of an even earlier ship (see Model No 15).

As a guide to the approximate date of a model, the 'timber and room' or 'room and space' of the hull framing can be of considerable value. There were distinct and well defined periods during which a certain dimension for the timber and room of a particular Rate of ship was in use, and it is clear that on each of these models, the number and spacing of the floors and futtocks exactly corresponds to the spacing of the station lines on the draught it was built from. For instance, the Sixth Rate *Lizard*, 1697 (Model No 12) has the station lines and individual timber and rooms of 1ft 10in marked on the side of the keel, which is the same as that specified for late seventeenth-century Sixth Rates. Another example is the Third Rate *Yarmouth*, 1748 (Model No 23) where the timber and room of 2ft 5in agrees with the draught of that ship, and also with that which was laid down in the Establishment of 1745. The dimension of the timber and room is small, but it can be obtained from models very accurately to the nearest full-sized inch when the scale is reliable as an average of a measurement taken over a number of frames. Ten is convenient. On the model of the Third Rate *Royal Oak* (Model No 25), for example, this measures 5.4in which divided by 10 becomes 0.54in for each individual timber and room or 2ft 2in at a scale of 1/48. What this means is that the hull of the model was built from a draught with station lines spaced at multiples of 2ft 2in, no more and no less. Although the *Royal Oak* is believed to be the ship as rebuilt in 1741, there are many features about the hull which suggest that it was made at a much earlier date, and the unusually small timber and room supports this. The timber and room in use at any particular time can be found mostly from contract-specifications for the seventeenth century, and draughts and Establishment lists in the eighteenth century. For Third Rates, 2ft 2in or 2ft 3in was usual in the 1690s and the first few years of the eighteenth century. From then until 1719 the timber and room was generally around 2ft 4in to 2ft 6in. The 1719 Establishment specifies 2ft 7in which was evidently rigidly enforced. From a random selection of about twelve draughts for Third Rates dating from 1719 to around 1740, including two for the *Royal Oak*, all have station lines spaced at three timber and rooms of at, or very near, 2ft 7in. For a short period after about 1740, several draughts show a timber and room of 2ft 5in as it was specified in the 1745 Establishment. By the 1750s, there was a comparatively large increase to 2ft 8in or 2ft 9in which remained the standard timber and room for Third Rates for many years. There was a definite reason for this last increase, as for the first time it allowed the principal double frames to extend up to the top of the side without being obstructed by the ports. An interesting example of the transition can be seen on two draughts for 74s prepared in 1756 to the designs by Sir Thomas Slade for the *Hero* and *Hercules*. The *Hero* has station lines spaced at three timber and rooms of 2ft 5in which in no way correspond with the ports, but the *Hercules* has station lines spaced at two timber and rooms of 2ft 8½in which exactly agrees with the arrangement of ports.

Returning to the *Royal Oak*, the evidence of the timber and room suggests that it could not have been built from the draught of the 1741 ship, but rather from one dating from the early eighteenth century, although this is not certain.

Another illustration of what can be done is seen on a Fourth Rate at the National Maritime Museum which is dated approximately to 1725, and on the 1719 Establishment. The dimensions are given as 137ft 0in on the gun deck and a breadth of 36ft 0in at a scale of 1/64. At this scale, the timber and room is 2ft 3in. But if it were a Fourth Rate on the 1719 Establishment, the timber and room *should* be 2ft 7in, the same as a Third Rate, and going strictly by the dimensions, the model is 3ft 0in too long on the gun deck. The scale of 1/64 is not common and if the model were measured at 1/60 it has a gun deck of 128ft 6in and a breadth of 33ft 9in, which is very close to the dimensions of ships on the earlier Establishment of 1706. At the new scale of 1/60, the timber and room becomes 2ft 1in which agrees favourably with the 2ft 0in to 2ft 3in usual for the Fourth Rates of that period.

It should be stressed that the theory is tentative, based on the limited data I have been able to gather, and is not infallible. But if it were developed further, and the timber and room recovered from many more draughts and models, no doubt a more reliable and complete pattern would emerge.

Establishing the Rate of a model is generally straightforward, although some difficulty can be encountered with certain classes. Ships of one, two and three decks are of course instantly recognisable, but it is not always certain whether a three-decker is a First or Second Rate, for example, and Third and Fourth Rates can sometimes be confused. As dimensions are often inconclusive, the number and arrangement of gun ports is the main guide to finding the Rate. This is very complicated because some ships are pierced with the same number of ports as guns they were Rated for, while others had either more or less. A fairly reliable guide for seventeenth-century three-deckers is that First Rates were pierced with 14 ports on one or more of the main tiers, while Second Rates had no more than 13. In the later period, the ports on the main tiers were often similar for First and Second Rates, but the latter class can usually be distinguished by fewer ports on the quarterdeck. The number of ports on Third Rate 70s ranged from 62 to 68 with the majority being pierced with 66, the remainder made up by guns on the forecastle and sometimes the poop which fired over the rails and did not require ports. Several Third Rates of 70 guns are described in catalogues as ships of 66 guns because they have that number of ports, and the usual four on the forecastle deck have not been allowed for. Fourth Rates of 60 guns can sometimes be mistaken for larger ships. Not counting any on the forecastle and poop, 60s were actually pierced with 60 ports in the late seventeenth century, 62 in the early 1700s, and as many as 64 towards the mid-eighteenth century. In most cases, these can be distinguished from Third Rates by having no more than five ports a side on the quarterdeck, and by their much shorter poop.

Van de Velde portraits and drawings are an invaluable guide to the arrangements of ports for the seventeenth century, as are contract-specifications which generally give the number of ports on each deck, although unfortunately there are none for First and Second Rates. For the eighteenth century, draughts are the principal source. The identified models are also important for showing the port arrangement of a particular Rate and date.

The name of the ship, like the date, is most obvious when it is actually on the model, but apart from block models only a handful are known. In most cases the name can be taken as being reliable, such as the *Britannia*, 1682, the *Boyne*, 1692, the *Royal George*, 1756, and a few others. Several more are at least suspect, and difficult to relate with a ship known to have been built. The *Barfleur*, for instance, is not easy to explain, nor is the *Sheerness* (see Model Nos 22 and 2). Another mystery model is a small Fourth Rate at the National Maritime Museum which has the name *Bristol* and the date of 1666 carved on the stern. At a scale of 1/48, the length of keel and breadth are similar to the dimensions of the Fourth Rate *Bristol* built in 1653, and it is possible that the model represents an unrecorded

Fig 54 *Monograms of Kings and Queens.*
A *Charles II (1660–1685). Second Rate* St
Michael, *1669. Central panel between the
stern lights.*
B *James II (1685–1688). Second Rate*
Coronation, *1685. Between the quarter
gallery lights.*
C *William III and Mary II (1689–1694).
Fourth Rate of about 1691. Two panels below
the stern lights.*
D *William and Mary. Third Rate* Boyne, *1692.
Between the quarter gallery lights.*
E *William III (1694–1702). Third Rate*
Bredah, *1692. Central panel between the stern
lights.*
F *Anne (1702–1714). Fourth Rate, 1701. On
the upper counter.*
G *George II (1727–1760). Fourth Rate* Lion,
1738. On the roof of the quarter galleries.
H *George II, Third Rate of about 1740. On the
tafferal.*
I *George III (1760–1820). Frigate,* Triton,
1796. On the tafferal.

rebuild of that ship in 1666, although there are a number of features about it which
are very early for that date.

A certain indication of the name is when the Heraldic Arms of a town are
incorporated in the decoration. Very many ships had names of towns, and it is
surprising that this is not found more often on models. Only three come to mind
(the Fourth Rate *St Albans*, 1687, at Trinity House, and the Third Rates *Ipswich*,
1730, and *Yarmouth*, 1748, both at the National Maritime Museum) but there may
be others perhaps still unrecognised. A number of models have distinctive decorative
features which suggest the name, although it can never be absolutely certain. For
instance, if the *Royal Oak* had not had the name on the counter it might have
been recognised from the oak leaves decorating the figurehead, friezes and tafferal
carvings. As an example, the Fourth Rate (Model No 19) can be cited, which has
a distinctive pattern of diamonds on the upper counter and stools of the quarter
galleries. Assuming the scale of 1/48 is accurate, the model appears to be one of a
small class of Fourth Rates built in the early eighteenth century. Only a few were
built, and one of them was the *Diamond*, 1708, and the model has almost exactly
the same dimensions as that ship.

The carved quarter pieces on the stern of the Second Rate *St Michael*, 1669,
appear to indicate the name of the ship. A tall and imposing male figure holding
a long stave stands on a plinth supported by a crouching evil-looking creature
with long pointed ears and cloven hooves. This undoubtedly depicts St Michael
himself, with the vanquished archangel Lucifer as the Devil at his feet. Early
illustrations of this show St Michael without wings, as on the model, which differs
in this respect from the modern version of the myth seen in the bronze by Sir
Jacob Epstein at Coventry Cathedral.

For the seventeenth century, models can be compared with the great number
of ship portraits by the Van de Veldes and other artists, but with caution. These
depict ships as they were at a particular time, often many years after the launching
date, and as they were constantly being rebuilt, altered, had variable port
arrangements and new carved work due to rot and damage in action, portraits can
be completely misleading. Because of this, it is quite possible that an unidentified
three-decker of about 1675 at the National Maritime Museum is another model
of the *St Michael*, perhaps as she was after being made a First Rate in 1672. The
models are very similar except that the identified one has a flush stern while the
other has an open stern gallery. Ports are inconclusive, as the following table
shows, in comparison with those from a known portrait of the ship by Van de
Velde the Elder.

	Lower deck	Middle deck	Upper deck	Quarter deck	Total
Identified model	26	26	26	8	86
Portrait	26	26	26	12	90
Unidentified model	28	26	28	12	94

At an exact scale of 1/48, the unidentified model is 3ft 0in longer on the gun deck
and 1ft 0in broader than the one known to be the *St Michael*, but this is of no
great significance. The clue is found in the figurehead. On the two models, and
three drawings of the ship by the Van de Veldes, the figurehead is shown as a
large bird drawing a seated figure in a chariot. All are different from each other,
but what is important is that all illustrate the same theme, and apparently no other
ship of the time appears to have had such a distinctive figurehead. The model is
quite likely to be another one of the *St Michael*, and any anomalies can be put
down to it being made at a different period, which would reflect changes in the
ship's appearance. The models were almost certainly not made by the same
craftsman, and this would explain many differences in the detail work.

Initials and dates on models can usually be linked with known shipwrights, and are valuable for identification purposes, but again with caution. Initials can be misleading in that while some can be taken as being those of Master Shipwrights, others may be of ordinary shipwrights or Assistants. Models were probably often built by ordinary shipwrights, and an example can be seen in the Third Rate *Captain*, 1708, which was made by William Hammond although the ship itself was built by Master Shipwright Podd. What this means is that initials on models are not necessarily those of Master Shipwrights, and as ordinary shipwrights and Assistants were often promoted to Master at the same yard, this can be confusing. It is all speculation, of course, but as an example a Fourth Rate in the Rogers collection at Annapolis has the initials JB and the date 1703 on the cradles. This could be taken for John Burchett of Rotherhithe, who was Master Shipwright there from around 1700. The earliest Fourth Rate built by Burchett was the *St Albans*, 1706, but the model almost certainly has no connection with that ship, for it has all the characteristics of the William III period. In all probability, Burchett was working at Rotherhithe in the late seventeenth century and it is quite possible that he made a model of one of two Fourth Rates built there in the 1690s — the *Dartmouth*, 1693, built by Shish, and the *Winchester*, 1698, built by Wells, the date 1703 being when the model was completed. The task of identification is considerably eased when a model has unusual proportions or represents a type of ship of which very few, or only one, was built. One of these is the galley-frigate at the Pitt-Rivers Museum, which is possibly the *Charles Galley*, 1676.

For the eighteenth century draughts are important, particularly when they show details of the carved decoration, but unfortunately this is not often. A few models which are known to be of a certain ship show that they were built very accurately from the draught. The Third Rate *Ipswich*, 1730, at the National Maritime Museum, for example, has a very distinctive stern with tall Corinthian columns each side, and is a late two-decker with two open stern galleries. This corresponds very closely with the draught of the ship, and the model could have been identified from that alone, apart from the Arms of Ipswich on the stern. The Third Rate *Yarmouth*, 1748, also has the Arms of that town on the stern, but with its unusual proportions, arrangement of gun ports and many other details, the model could be recognised as having been built from the draught of that ship, albeit one at a reduced scale, although the carved work is not shown.

The impression has probably been given that most models can be identified by name but this is far from being the case, and the great majority remain unknown. But what are they? The question is not easy to answer, but it is improbable that a modelmaker would build one of an imaginary ship. Nor is it likely that a model is unidentifiable because it was a design for a ship that was not built, altered while building or cancelled, which is sometimes suggested, as it is probable that these incredibly detailed models are not actual designs at all, at least not the eighteenth-century ones.

Although these will perhaps remain anonymous, much could be done by taking off the hull lines from models and comparing them with draughts. Until around the mid-eighteenth century, Master Shipwrights prepared their own designs for individual ships, and the lines would vary to a certain extent from one builder to another for ships of the same Rate. A very large number of draughts exist from about 1700, and by comparing the lines it might be possible to say that a certain model was made from a certain draught, and these are often indicated with the name of the ship. In the case of a model built to a scale of 1/48, the actual measurements in inches could be compared directly with a draught without worrying about scales and full-sized dimensions. Apart from the main dimensions, the rakes of the stern post, stem and cut-water, the timber and room, the heights to the wales, and many other measurements would also be useful.

It is scarcely possible that this could be done, but anything that would throw more light on models is desirable, and it would no doubt allow more to be identified than there are at the present time.

Stern of the Second Rate St Michael, 1669. The superbly detailed and carved Royal Arms is probably the finest example seen on seventeenth-century models. The model is the earliest which is known to be of a certain ship. NMM (Author).

Broadside detail in midships of the lovely Second Rate Coronation, *1685, showing the entry port. Note the gilded gargoyles decorating the scuppers from the upper deck. Kriegstein Collection (Author).*

Bow of the Coronation, *showing the splendid Lion figurehead and the typical carved brackets, or 'terms', on the head timbers. Kriegstein Collection (Author).*

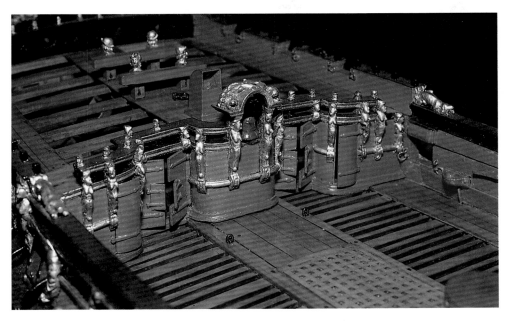

Stern of the Third Rate Boyne, 1692. The relief carving on the upper counter and between the lights is one of the earliest examples of a short-lived fashion which died out around 1702. NMM (Author).

Forecastle bulkhead of the Boyne. The framing of the upper deck is unusual for having no outer tier of carlings. NMM (Author).

Broadside detail in midships of a very fine Third Rate known as the Hampton Court, 1678, showing the main channel. The plank between the wales is made from figured walnut. The Earl of Pembroke (Author).

Stern of an unidentified Fourth Rate from the William and Mary period, about 1690. A finely carved bust of a horse is concealed behind the centre stern lantern. Kriegstein Collection.

The Fourth Rate Lion, 1738. Gilded decoration is uncommon on models dating from the mid-eighteenth century. The combination of black, gold, and red paint contrasting with the natural wood creates a luxuriant colour scheme. Note the unusual white 'boot-topping' below the main wales, and the oriental character of the paint work on the port lids and roundhouses. Other points of interest are the very exposed seats of ease forward of the bollard timbers and at the sides of the roundhouses, and the delicate twist-turned balusters above the beak-bulkhead. Kriegstein Collection.

Bow of the Third Rate of about 1702. Kriegstein Collection.

Bow of the Queen Anne Fourth Rate. Kriegstein Collection.

The very detailed and finely built stern of the First Rate Royal William, 1749. Four models of the Royal William exist, three at the National Maritime Museum and one at the United States Naval Academy Museum, Annapolis. NMM (Author).

Stern of a Third Rate, of about 1702. The beautiful decorative work on this stern is basically of quite simple construction, and consists of only three horizontal pieces which are moulded on the edges and carved in relief, except for the tafferal which is cut clear through and backed by panels. The vertical joint with the quarter galleries can be seen, which appear to be fashioned and carved entirely from single hollowed out pieces of wood. A bust of Queen Anne is shown on the centre of the tafferal, and her motto, SEMPER EADEM, is in the frieze below the lights. Kriegstein Collection.

The stern of a Fourth Rate known as the Medway, 1742. NMM (Author).

Bow of the Third Rate Yarmouth, 1748. NMM (Author).

View of the upper deck in the waist of the Yarmouth. Although at the fairly small scale of 1/60, the detail shown is remarkable but typical of the period. Note the lead of the tackle from the fish davit to the capstan via the large block siezed to the deck near the bitts. The two red marks on the inner edge of the gunwale appear to indicate the position of the midship bend, or 'dead flat', but the draught of the Yarmouth shows it just aft of the same gun port. NMM (Author).

Stern of the Yarmouth. *The Heraldic Arms of Yarmouth are concealed behind the centre lantern. The simple but elegant arch of the stern is very typical of ships built in the 1740s. NMM (Author).*

The stern of a Fourth Rate, probably late eighteenth-century. It is possible that the model may represent the Leopard, *1790. This model is very well made, but the quality of the carvings does not compare with the best work produced earlier in the century. Pitt-Rivers Museum (Author).*

VI
Hull Supports, Baseboards and Display Cabinets

It appears that only a relatively small proportion of models are still resting on contemporary supports, most of them being of modern or fairly modern origin. Assuming that all models did have contemporary supports at one time—and it is difficult to believe that they did not—how and why they disappeared is a mystery. Take the *Boyne*, for instance, which would almost certainly have been on decorative carved cradles originally. There is at least an explanation for the Third Rate of about 1705 at the Pitt-Rivers Museum (Model No 18), which rests directly on its keel. It was made by William Lee as a commission from Dr George Clarke, and it is hard to imagine that Lee would have delivered the model or that Clarke would have accepted it without any means of support. The model was placed in its present case in the nineteenth century, and due to the height of the main mast, it would not have fitted in if it were on cradles, and they were probably discarded at that time and subsequently lost.

By comparing photographs of the same model, it can frequently be found that they are on varying types of supports at different times. Others are confusing for being on supports which actually belong to another model, sometimes of a widely different date, and therefore anomalous. For example, a model of the Second Rate *Princess Amelia*, 1773, in the Rogers collection is illustrated in the Catalogue as on small carved cradles.[1] The same cradles are also seen with several other models, and it is not easy to detect which one they originally belonged to, but it is probably a late seventeenth-century Fourth Rate. Another model in the same collection, of a Third Rate 80 dating from the early 1690s, originally had cradles carved with the initials WL which are probably those of the aforementioned William Lee. But the model is illustrated in the Catalogue as resting on simple wooden supports, while its cradles are apparently associated with a Fourth Rate of around the early eighteenth century. It is probable that in these cases the cradles were 'borrowed' from another model simply for the purpose of taking photographs, but it is misleading none the less. Despite all this, many models of course *are* still on their original cradles or other form of support, and some very fine examples exist, particularly from the seventeenth century.

Seventeenth-century models are universally supported on a pair of carved wooden cradles, either with or without baseboards. These are mostly with a gilded finish but painted ones are seen, and some are decorated with both gilding and paint. Others are left with a natural varnished wood finish. The unusually shaped cradles of the Fourth Rate, 1701 (Model No 16) are curiously painted to represent a burr wood. The early cradles are commonly carved with dolphins or fabulous sea creatures, and are sometimes initialled and dated. The illustrations provide some idea of the various and distinctive designs. A Second Rate of about 1680 at the Merseyside County Museum, Liverpool, is highly unusual for the period in being on a slipway, with the hull supported by closely spaced raking shores each side at the turn of the bilge.

Various types of plain wood cradles are fairly common in the first half of the eighteenth century. Some are made from natural polished brass with elegantly scrolled feet, such as on the Third Rate *Royal Oak* (Model No 25). Two Fourth Rates of about 1715 at the National Maritime Museum are distinctive for being mounted on an edgeways board. The boards are about 3in broad and 1in thick the full length of the keel, and terminate in fancily shaped ends. They are finely veneered in oak with figured walnut borders and edges and inlaid with decorative black and white lines. They were no doubt both made by the same man. The models must have been mounted on the stands at an early stage in building before the internal work was begun, and fastened through the keel in some way.

The most common form of support of eighteenth-century models is by two, or sometimes three, turned pillars under the keel. The pillars are of very many different designs, some slender and delicate in the classical style, while others are quite plain. They are mostly turned from wood, either natural or stained black, but brass ones are not uncommon. Most models on this type of stand are further

Fig 55 *The cradles of a Stuart Royal yacht of about 1680. They are left with a natural wood finish. Model in a private collection.*

supported by a single slender brass strut each side in midships, which are sometimes of a spiral form.

Baseboards are of little interest — they are mostly just a board of plain wood — except for original ones dating from the William III and Queen Anne period. These are absolutely typical of the fine cabinet making at that time, and without considering the date of the model, the baseboards could actually be placed to approximately between 1690 and 1715. It was only during this period that mouldings of cross-grained walnut were applied to the edges of table tops, etc, and this is often seen on the baseboards of models. At this time, the tops were veneered with walnut in leaves of the finest quality, with broad cross-banded borders and inlaid with stringings. Some are laid with marquetry in a geometric pattern of different coloured woods. The baseboard of a Queen Anne Third Rate has a large star in the centre in a complicated design of diamonds similar to those often seen on compass roses.

Fig 56 *The cradles of a Fourth Rate from the William III period. These are gilded. Model in the Kriegstein Collection.*

The baseboard of a Second Rate of about 1702 at the National Maritime Museum is of interest, for on the smooth pine of the underside is the gun deck plan of a large ship drawn in ink to a scale of 1/48. The model is at the smaller scale of 1/60, and to provide a suitable size for the baseboard, much of the starboard side and stern of the plan was sawn away, but from the half breadth it can be found that the main breadth outside plank would have been approximately 48ft 0in, compared with 47ft 6in for the model. The plan was obviously for a First or Second Rate three-decker, but no suggestion can be made as to what ship it was for, its date, or whether it was the same one represented by the model. If this was the sort of fate destined for draughts after they had served their purpose, it is not surprising that they are scarce from about that time, particularly deck plans. But it certainly agrees with the remark made by Samuel Pepys in the late seventeenth century that draughts were '...done in the usual manner upon boards'.

Models still contained in their contemporary display cabinets are extremely rare and only a handful are known, but it is clear that most of them would have been originally. For instance, the collection formed by Samuel Pepys in the seventeenth century was housed in 'handsome glass cases',[2] and a contemporary writer described the models in the collection of the Duke of York (later King James II) as 'remarkable objects enclosed in glass cases'.[3] Many models are known to have originated from the Royal Households, for example the *Boyne*, 1692, and others now at the National Maritime Museum, which were once owned by King William IV. Others came from the great stately houses of England, where they had probably been since they were first built. These too would most certainly have been in

Plate 22 *This Fifth Rate of the King Charles II period is probably the earliest model still in its contemporary display cabinet. The cabinet is a very fine example, and still has its original glass. The model is in the Kriegstein collection.* (Author).

contemporary cabinets, but how and why they have apparently disappeared is uncertain. It cannot be believed that while models have survived, their cabinets have not, and there is at least one possible explanation. According to the splendid cabinets that do exist, they would have been highly desirable as pieces of furniture in their own right, and as models clearly passed through many hands over the years, it is easy enough to imagine that when they were disposed of, their cabinets were retained and used for other purposes. There are probably many ship model cabinets scattered around that are now fitted with shelves and containing collections of other precious objects.

The early contemporary cabinets are quite unlike those of today. They are free-standing on various types of support, have solid backs, and a pair of doors at the front which are generally glazed with small panes of glass. Among the finest examples are those of the famous Sergison collection at the United States Naval Academy Museum which date from the William III and Queen Anne period. According to photographs of the cases, they are superb quality and fine examples of English cabinet making at that time, and probably of as great an intrinsic value as the models they contain.

Footnotes

1. *Henry Huddleston Rogers Collection of Ship Models*, Naval Institute Press, 1971.
2. *Further Correspondence of Samuel Pepys*, edited by J R Tanner, 1929.
3. Extract from the 'Travels of Cosmo the 3rd, Grand Duke of Tuscany, through England, 1699', *The Mariner's Mirror*, Vol 4, p 157.

The Models

One of the more difficult tasks in preparing this book was to reduce the large number of models that exist to a small selection for the purpose of publication. In part, this was determined by the availability of models for study and measuring. The primary requirement, however, was to illustrate a representative cross-section of different types of ship from the period 1650–1750. One model, although dated at present at about 1740, is probably of a much later ship, and this has been included for its interest and fine craftsmanship.

For each model, the description is headed with the identification by which it is currently known. Some of these attributions have been queried, not so much for models whose name has been well established for many years, but for those where the date, and sometimes the Rate, is suspected as being other than that given on their labels. This is not by any means intended as a deliberate contradiction, but rather as an alternative, personal opinion based on the reasons given — which of course are susceptible to being disproved.

Where models have been measured by myself, this is indicated by an asterisk against the dimensions. The models have been measured as accurately as possible, but an allowance of plus or minus 6in on the scale should be allowed for the length on the gun deck and 12in for the touch keel length due to the difficulty in establishing exactly where the 'touch' is on some models, particularly those early ones with a long fore rake of the stem.

The full-sized dimensions have been calculated from the given scale. In the case of a few models where the scale may be in doubt, this is explained in the text. For models identified by name, the main dimensions of the ship herself are also given for comparison, and in general, from which ship list they have been obtained. Where sufficient measurements have been taken, the tonnage for both the 'touch' and 'calculated' keel lengths is given for seventeenth-century models, which has been worked out from the formula described in Chapter IV. In the case of a named seventeenth-century model whose main dimensions are very close to those of the ship, one or other of the tonnages also agrees very closely, and this can sometimes be valuable in determining which keel length is given in the ship lists. Apart from this, the tonnage is given for interest only, and should not be used for identification purposes.

For details of the ships' contemporary rigging, readers are referred to specialist books on the subject, such as the definitive *The Masting and Rigging of English Ships of War, 1625–1860* by James Lees.

Ship List References

Samuel Pepys' *Register of Ships*. This list covers new ships built between 1660 and 1686, and also those which were still in existence at the Restoration in 1660. Published in 'A Descriptive Catalogue of the Naval Manuscripts in the Pepysian Library', *Navy Records Society*, Vol 26.

Dimension Book B. This list covers the period up to about 1740, and is the only major one from which the length on the gun deck for seventeenth-century ships can be found, although there are many omissions. Original in the Public Record Office, Kew, and a photographic copy in the Draught Room at the National Maritime Museum.

'A list of the Navy, 1685', published in *Navy Records Society* Vol ? *The Life of Steven Martin*.

R C Anderson, *Lists of Men-of-War, 1649–1702*, Society for Nautical Research Occasional Publication No 5.

Colledge, J J, *Ships of the Royal Navy; An Historical Index*, Vol I, 1969.

Extensive lists for the period 1600–1836 in Brian Lavery, *Ship of the Line*, Vol I, 1983.

A list of ships compiled by Anthony Deane in 1670. Published in Brian Lavery (Editor), *Deane's Doctrine of Naval Architecture*, 1981.

A list entitled 'Gloria Britannica or the Boast of the British Seas, AD1685'. Published in Charles Derrick, *Memoirs of the Rise and Progress of the Royal Navy*, 1806. This list can also be found in E H H Archibald, *The Wooden Fighting Ship in the Royal Navy*, 1968.

1. Ship of 50-58 guns c1655

Location: **National Maritime Museum**
Scale: 1/48

Dimensions ★ (at a scale of 1/48)		*Height below decks*	
Gun deck	147ft 9in	Upper deck	7ft 0in
Breadth	34ft 9in	Quarterdeck	7ft 0in
Keel (touch)	119ft 3in, 766 tons	Forecastle	6ft 0in
Timber and room	2ft 5in	Poop	7ft 0in
Depth in hold	14ft 6in, top of floors to upper side of lower deck beams		
		Gun ports	
Rake of the stem	24ft 0in at the harpin	Lower deck	26
Rake of the stern post	7ft 0in at the transom (19°)	Upper deck	26
		Quarterdeck	6
Height to lower edge of mainwales		Total	58
At the stern	20ft 9in		
In midships	13ft 6in		
At the stem	17ft 3in		

This model is unidentified and the date is not exactly known, but it is generally believed to be one of the earliest examples of the Navy Board type, and may very well be the oldest in existence. The long and narrow proportions, and the dimensions of the model at a scale of 1/48, closely agree with the Third Rate frigates built in the period 1650–1655. Fourteen were built, all with as-built dimensions of between 116ft 0in and 120ft 0in on the keel, breadths of 32ft 0in to 36ft 0in, and depths in hold of around 14ft 0in. Although the model has often been associated with the *Speaker* or the *Fairfax*, both launched in 1650, or the *Antelope* of 1651, there are no particular features to suggest that it represents a known ship except for the dimensions, which in this case does not help a great deal.

The date of the model is uncertain, as all the above-mentioned ships were built during the Commonwealth period of Oliver Cromwell, and would not be decorated with the Stuart Royal Arms prominently displayed at the stern. There are three possible explanations for this. First, the Arms are those of Charles I, and the model was made before his execution in 1649; second, the model was made after the Restoration in 1660, and the Arms therefore were those of Charles II; third, the model dates from the Commonwealth period, but the stern decoration was altered at the Restoration and the Stuart Arms added, as happened on the ships themselves. There is no evidence that the stern decoration has been tampered with. Although this would not be expected after over three hundred years if it were well done in the first place, it is improbable. On the whole, the structure and general appearance of the model is very early compared with those that certainly date from after the Restoration, and a possible explanation is that it was made in the 1640s as a preliminary design for an

Plate 23 *Quarterdeck and poop. The raised level of the quarterdeck can be seen directly abaft the companion, with the break in the beam clamps noticeable just below the hance at the top of the side. NMM (Author).*

intended Royalist ship, but the design was then used for a ship which was actually built for the Parliamentary fleet a few years later, conceivably the *Fairfax, Speaker* or *Antelope*.

Despite its great age, the model is remarkably intact, with only the cat heads and supporters and a few bits of carving missing. The model was in the collection formed by Dr R C Anderson and was presented by him to the Museum in 1935.

Hull framing

The hull construction is little different from any of the later models except that it is not quite so well made and has a somewhat rough finish. The long rakes of the stem and stern post are typical of ships built before about 1660. The timber and room of the hull framing, at 2ft 5in, was usual for a fairly large ship of the time. With the

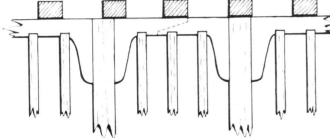

Fig 57 *Detail of the upper deck beams and double lodging knees. The knees are made in pairs from a single piece of wood, but if this was full-sized practice, there would have been a scarph in the fore and aft arms as indicated by the pecked line.*

absence of top side planking, it can be seen that the top timbers are reduced in their siding upwards of the scarph with the futtocks.

Outboard details

The mainwales are 12in broad, 9in thick and widely spaced at 2ft 6in between the two strakes. The lower deck ports are quite small at 2ft 3in broad and 2ft 0in deep. The lower edge of the ports is formed by the futtock heads, but with a separately fitted upper cill. On the upper deck, the ports are circular in the waist, with those under the quarterdeck and forecastle being rectangular. No mizzen channels are fitted.

Plate 24 *Aft part of the upper deck in the waist. Note the straight bulkhead and the plain heads of the bitts. NMM (Author).*

Plate 25 *Forward part of the upper deck in the waist, showing the jeer capstan and the belfry. NMM (Author).*

Inboard details

The upper deck beams are partially let down on the clamps, and fitted with two lodging knees at each end instead of the usual one hanging knee and one lodging knee. On the forecastle, quarter- and poop decks, the beams are let down flush with the clamps and fitted with hanging knees only, but these have mostly fallen away and left the athwartship arms of the knees still attached to the beams. Aft of the mizzen mast, the quarterdeck is at a raised level of about 1ft 6in, presumably to provide extra headroom in the Captain's cabin. Four small scuttles are pierced in the riser of the deck for the use of the helmsman on the whipstaff on the deck below — two looking through the open front of the covered companion forward of the mizzen mast position, and one each side. The inboard bulkheads are

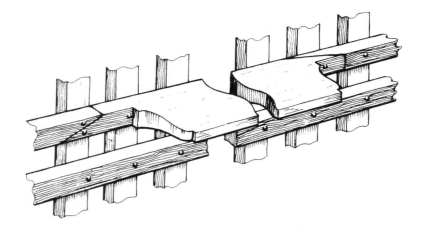

Fig 58 *Main channel on the port side. Unlike on later models, the channel is actually a broadened part of the chainwale itself, with an extension each end which is scarphed to the wale proper. No deadeyes or chain plates are fitted.*

Plate 26 *Forecastle deck. There is a total absence of top side or deck plank on this model. NMM (Author).*

Plate 27 *Hull framing at the stern*. NMM (Author).

Plate 28 *Hull framing at the bow*. NMM (Author).

straight and flat, with none of the bays and protruding cabins that became usual after the Restoration. The jeer capstan in the waist is very similar to that on the model of the *St Michael*, except that there are no whelps fitted on the lower end of the barrel for use on the lower deck. The belfry at the break of the forecastle deck is of interest, and is possibly the earliest evidence of the fitting in that position.

Decoration

Except for the carvings and moulded rails, which are gilt, the whole of the model is painted a dark bluish-grey colour. The carved work appears to be simply executed, but it is probably quite detailed beneath the thick coating of gesso. The unusual design of the port wreaths is particularly attractive.

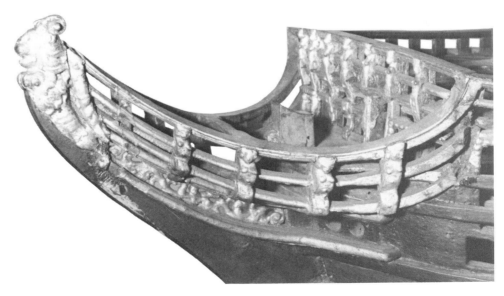

Plate 29 *View of the head showing the long shallow head rails and the high position of the cheeks and hawse holes. The lion figurehead is very different from those of later years*. NMM (Author).

2. Fifth Rate of 36-40 guns c1660

Location: **National Maritime Museum**
Scale: 1/48

Dimensions★ (at a scale of 1/48)		Gun ports	
		Lower deck	22
Gun deck	115ft 6in	Upper deck	14
Breadth	27ft 0in	Quarterdeck	4
Keel (touch)	93ft 6in, 362 tons		—
Keel (calculated)	98ft 9in, 383 tons	Total	40
Rake of the stem	22ft 6in at the harpin		
	25ft 6in at the stem head		
Rake of the stern post	2ft 6in at the main transom		

Early models of the smaller Rates are extremely uncommon, and this intriguing little example is possibly the oldest existing one known. The name *Sheerness* is carved in a panel on the upper counter and looks as though it is original, but the model is certainly of an earlier date than the only comparable ship of that name, which was a Fifth Rate of 32 guns launched at Sheerness in 1691, with a length on the gun deck of 105ft 9in and a breadth of 27ft 6in. The latest date can be traced to some time in the 1670s by the main capstan, which is the old type that preceded the drumhead. This is a puzzling model in many respects, and it is difficult to arrive at any positive conclusions. The Royal Arms at the stern and the circular port wreaths indicate a date after the Restoration of Charles II in 1660. On the other hand, the long and narrow proportions, very long rake of the stem and several other possible reasons suggest that the model may be an early Commonwealth Fourth Rate. At the Restoration, the ships of the Navy that were already in existence had the offending Commonwealth decoration removed from the stern, and replaced by the Arms of the Stuarts. The only remnant of the Arms on the model is the Unicorn supporter, which is attached directly to the stern timbers without any backing piece. But it is clear from the remains of glue on the timbers that there was originally a complete panel in this area, which appears to have been removed and

Plate 30 *Port broadside. The long and lean lines of this ship, with little sheer, are evident from this view. NMM.*

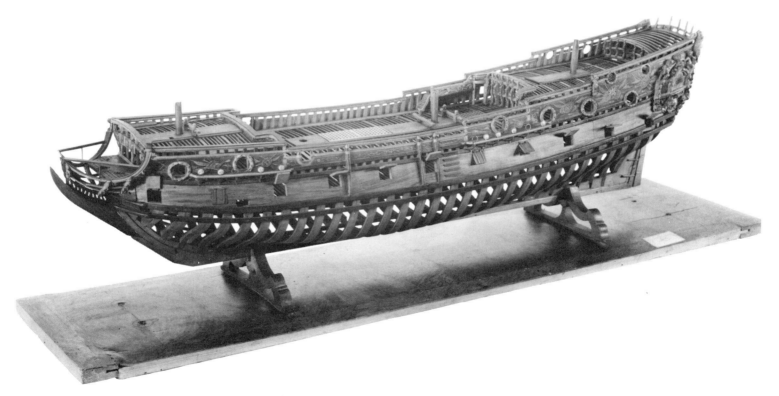

Fig 59 *Profile of the rake of stem and stern post. The very long fore rake of the stem, at 25ft 6in, is almost equal to the breadth. The combination of a long fore rake and a short rake of the stern post seems to be unusual.*

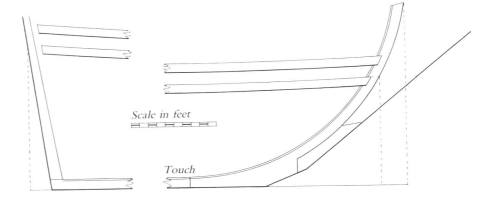

Scale in feet

Touch

replaced by the Stuart Arms. Another clue that suggests a pre-Restoration date for the model can be seen in the carvings above the quarter badges. These are curious things which may not have any meaning, but it is worth mentioning, as the like of it has not been seen on any other model. On both sides, there are trumpet-blowing figures suspending the Royal crown directly above ugly and grotesque heads. This is not the way to flatter the King, as it appears to be a symbol of derision against the Monarchy. The question arises as to whether this sort of thing would be displayed on a model built after the Restoration or before, perhaps as early as around the time Charles I was executed in 1649, and we can imagine a Parliament man with a sense of humour putting these strange carvings on a model.

Another oddity is that along the full length of the hull a number of the frames are wired together, and from marks on the timbers it can be seen that many more were once wired, which was later removed. The wire, which is quite thick, is looped round the frames below the mainwales and taken inboard across the lower deck, where the ends are twisted tightly together. Assuming that this was not done at the time the model

Plate 31 *Hull framing at the stern. The solid block forward of the stern post is scarphed to the shallow deadwood. Note that the short grain of the wood has allowed the toes of some of the timbers to fall away at the deadwood, and has exposed the joint, which otherwise may have been considered a simple slot. Author.*

Plate 32 *Hull framing at the bow. The upper part of the knee of the head appears to be a repair. Some of the wire can be seen below the wales. Author.*

Plate 33 *The stern is very low and broad, with little tumblehome at the sides, compared with later models. It is interesting to note that the man who made this model knew very well that the mica he used for the glazing did not take kindly to glue, as he has pierced it where it contacts the timbers to improve the adhesion. The religious-looking figure to starboard is carved from bone or ivory. Author.*

was built, which is unlikely, it would have entailed the removal of almost all the inboard structure above the lower deck. When, and for what purpose, this was done is a complete mystery, as the hull appears to be quite sound. It may be recent, but the decks do not seem to have been disturbed. One possibility is that the model underwent an alteration to the inboard structure at some early period, but this still does not explain why it was necessary to wire the frames together.

Identification

No reasonable explanation can be offered for this model and the puzzling name *Sheerness*. All the evidence seems to suggest that it is possibly a small Fourth Rate of an unknown date prior to 1660, and after about 1650 when the forecastle deck was introduced on these small ships, but there

is nothing conclusive about it. The model cannot be identified with any of the many Fourth Rates built in the 1640s and '50s, and it is unsatisfactory to look at dimensions, as by a slight change of scale it could be made to fit a number of them. But of them all, at a scale of 1/48 the model has almost the exact dimensions of the *Adventure*, 1646, which had a gun deck of 116ft 2in, a breadth of 27ft 9in and a 'touch' keel of 94ft 0in. The *Adventure* was known for her ideal proportions, and the model may very well have been built from that design. It is a great pity that the figurehead and tafferal are missing, as these would have given an almost certain indication of whether the model dates from before or after the Restoration. The figurehead, probably a lion, would not be crowned before 1660, and the tafferal would most likely have been finished with a simple moulded rail instead of carvings.

Hull construction

The hull is one of the very few that are built on a completely different principle to the distinctive Navy Board type, and is very early evidence of the use of double frames with all the timbers butted together. The frames are composed of floors, first and second futtocks, and a single top timber. Between the main frames are further top timbers, which extend upwards from the lower edge of the upper mainwale. In most cases, these lie alongside the heads of the second futtocks, but in others, they have

Plate 34 *The quarter gallery, or 'badge', showing the curious carving of a crown above an ugly head. The eyes of the beast and the other figures are picked out with tiny dabs of paint. One of the odd 'lintels' can be seen set into the plank above the gun port. Author.*

70

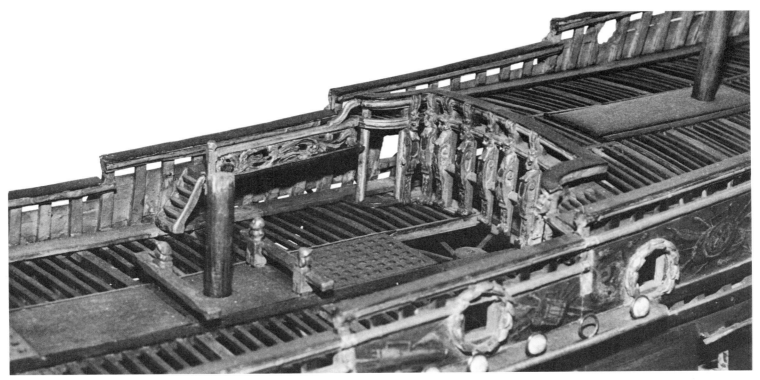

no connection at all, and just seem to be suspended by the wales and top side plank. The double frames are fastened together with treenails at the ends of the timbers. The series of small vertical timbers fitted between the transoms are not common on models, but it was probably a normal practice in shipbuilding, when the transoms were widely spaced, as in the seventeenth century. These very short timbers are particularly well fitted into shallow scores in the transoms. In the hold, a single fore and aft footwale is laid each side at the floor heads, and a very slender keelson is fitted.

Ouboard details and fittings

The gun port configuration, with none on the upper deck in the waist, is typical of mid eighteenth-century Fifth Rates. An odd feature is that there are small pieces of wood let into the plank above the lower deck ports, somewhat similar to a lintel over a doorway. Some of the deadeyes are missing, but their straps and chain plates are still in place. The deadeyes are made of bone or ivory, and are few in number, with five on the fore channel and six on the main. The channels are not braced by the usual arched spurs, and no mizzen channels are fitted. This is probably not an omission by the modelmaker, but rather that the shrouds would be taken up by tackles inboard of the bulwarks. The upper part of the knee of the head is of a different wood than the rest of the structure, which is probably an old repair. Seldom seen on early models are the berthing rails fitted to the main head rails. They are made of wood, and are supported in the centre by single metal stanchions. The topside plank between the wales appears to be walnut.

Inboard details and fittings

The jeer capstan in the waist is missing, but the main capstan is in place on the lower deck just abaft the mizzen mast position. It has an octagonal head which is pierced and fitted with four through bars at different levels. Also on the lower deck, there is a single pair of riding bitts immediately abaft the foremast position.

All decks are framed with widely spaced beams and a single tier of carlings each side, except for the upper deck below the forecastle where there is a single carling on the centre line. An unusual feature of the quarterdeck is that the ledges rest in rabbets worked along the edges of the carlings, instead of being housed. Further details of the upper and forecastle decks are illustrated in the section on deck framing (Chapter III, Plate 13).

The internal bulkheads are of simple

Plate 35 *After part of the waist and the quarterdeck bulkhead. The head of the main capstan can just be seen through the open hatch.* Author.

open framed construction, with no panels or doors. Access through the bulkheads is provided by a single opening on the port side only, except for at the poop where the entry is central. No belfry is fitted, a feature that is believed to have been generally introduced soon after the Restoration in 1660. The cat head, which is only in place on the starboard side, is very short at about 2–3ft, and its tail is turned aft and fastened to the inner side of the bulkwarks.

Decoration

The quarter badges are finely carved, and appear to be made from single pieces of wood which are pierced and rabbeted to receive the mica glazing. A Union Flag, painted in colours, is incorporated in the lower part of the badge. The friezes at the top of the side are painted with trophies of arms in soft dull colours, and the model is probably the earliest known with this type of decoration. One of the trophies includes another Union Flag which is oddly rotated about 45 degrees from its correct angle. The port wreaths are carved with a simple laurel leaf design.

3. St Michael, Second Rate of 90-98 guns 1669

Location: **National Maritime Museum**
Scale: 1/48

Dimensions*	Model	Ship
Gun deck	155ft 0in	155ft 2in
Breadth	40ft 9in	40ft 8½in
Depth	—	17ft 5in
Keel (touch)	126ft 0in, 1113 tons	125ft 0in, 1101 tons
Keel (calculated)	127ft 0in, 1121 tons	
Timber and room	2ft 5in	
Rake of the stem	25ft 6in at the harpin	
Rake of the stern post	6ft 3in at the main transom (16°)	

Height to lower edge of mainwales	
Aft	24ft 6in
Midships	16ft 0in
Forward	19ft 9in

Gun ports		Broad	Deep
Lower deck	26	3ft 6in	2ft 9in
Middle deck	26★	3ft 0in	2ft 9in
Upper deck	26	2ft 9in	2ft 6in
Quarterdeck	8		
Total	86		

★ Includes one luff port each side, forward of the cat supporter. Dimensions of the *St Michael* have been taken from Pepys' *Register of Ships*, except for the length of gun deck, which has been taken from Dimension Book B. The *St Michael* was built in 1669 by Sir John Tippets at Portsmouth.

This lovely and important model is the earliest one known which is positively identified, and it has long been established as representing the *St Michael*. The identification was made by reference to several Van de Velde drawings of the ship,[1] and by the dimensions, which agree very closely to those listed at a scale of 1/48, the breadth being that before she was broadened by girdling in 1674. Although the depth in hold was not obtained, it is interesting to compare the draught of water. Pepys lists this as 19ft 8in for the *St Michael*, which agrees with the lower edge of the upper mainwale on the model, while the portrait of the ship shows it at the upper edge of the lower wale, a difference of about 2ft. One of Van de Velde's drawings is a pencil and wash portrait of the port broadside, and there is a close resemblance. The gun ports agree, except that there are four ports each side on the quarterdeck of the model and six indicated on the portrait. The other drawings, in pencil, consist of two views of the figurehead, one of the quarter gallery and some of the decorative details. In the case of the figureheads, the drawings are somewhat vague and differ in some respects from each other and with that on the model, but all show the same basic theme of a large eagle-like bird drawing a figure seated in a four-wheeled chariot. The quarter gallery of the model is also very similar to the drawing, except that the aftmost upper deck port is fitted with a circular wreath instead of a square one.

Hull construction

The hull framing is of standard construction, except that as on a few other early models, the floor heads are cut off horizontally instead of square. A longitudinal section of a First Rate drawn by Edmund Dummer in about 1680 clearly shows horizontal floor heads, and it may have been a quite common practice in shipbuilding. The timber and room, at 2ft 5in, is normal for a Second Rate of the time. A very unusual choice of wood was made for the hull framing, as it appears to be walnut, or even perhaps mahogany. Internally, there are two heavy footwales each side—one at the heels of the futtocks and another just below the floor heads. The keelson is fitted, on which stand square stop-chamfered pillars

under every other gun deck beam. No mast steps are fitted, and the masts rest directly on the keelson. Long fore and aft knees are fitted at the wing transom. There is no internal plank fitted at the sides on the lower and middle decks, which reveals the scarphs between the futtocks and top timbers, and the manner in which the ports are framed. The futtock heads in general terminate at about the level of the chainwales, but with considerable variation. Some reach up to the middle deck port cills, while others are very much shorter. The lower deck ports are pierced through the solid timber at the scarph of the futtocks with the top timbers, and no cills are fitted. This was a simple matter, but framing the middle and upper deck ports evidently entailed a lot of work, as much packing and cutting into the timbers was needed due to the difference in spacing of the ports and timbers, and all the cills are fitted with finely made angled joints. Quite a lot of debris was lying in the hold—bits of mica, deck ledges and other odd small pieces of wood—which appears to have fallen in while the model was being made.

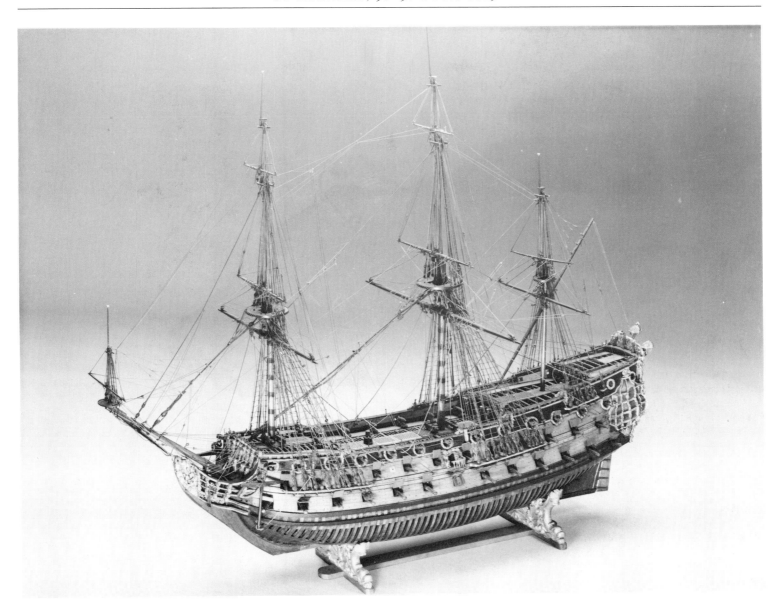

Outboard fittings and details

The mainwales are 1ft 6in broad, and 10in thick, with the two strakes spaced 2ft 0in apart. The chainwales are 12in broad, 6in thick and 12in apart. All these strakes are fastened with closely spaced treenails. There are no upper wales on this three-decker, just one large moulded rail. This was the 'great rail', which defined the lower limit of the 'black work' at the top of the side. The fore and main channels are 3ft 0in broad, with the inner edge the same thickness as the breadth of the chainwales, tapering to about half that at the outer edge. The channels are braced from above by the usual large spurs—five on the fore, six on

the main and three small ones on the mizzen channel. An entry port is fitted on the port side only. The dead block for the fore tack in between the head rails is an early illustration of this fitting, and is confirmed by the Van de Velde drawings.

Inboard fittings and details

The lower and middle decks are framed in the conventional manner, with two tiers of short carlings each side and narrow strips of plank for the guns to stand on. On the upper deck, the long and short carlings are shown. The 'long carlings' forming the sides of the hatches extend the whole length of the waist, and are let down on the beams

Plate 36 *Broadside of the* St Michael. *One of the earliest of identified models, it is in a wonderful state of preservation.* NMM.

so that the upper side is flush, and separate coamings are fitted, unlike most of the seventeenth-century models which are combined in one timber. The gratings are the pierced type, except for several in the waist on the upper deck which are quite different. It is possible that they are not original, but whether they are or not, the craftsman went to great lengths in making them. A frame was made first with halved joints at the corners fastened with large treenails, and a properly built grating was then inset within the frame. On reflection, they are probably contemporary, as the colour and patination

A curious omission on this very detailed model are the side gangways and stairs leading up to the quarterdeck and forecastle from the waist. On the poop deck is a large raised ventilation hatch with coamings about 1ft 6in high. No gratings are fitted, but the hatch has three intermediate beams athwartship, which are finely jointed to the coamings with dovetails.

Fig 60 *The belfry at the break of the forecastle, from aft. It gives some idea of the sheer scale of the carved work on ships of this period.*

Fig 61 *Detail of the quarterdeck bulkhead. The central pair of doors lead directly to a covered flight of bell stairs down to the middle deck.*

Decoration

This model, and the First Rate *Prince*, 1670, at the Science Museum, can be considered as the finest existing examples to illustrate

of the wood is similar to the rest of the structure, and it is hard to believe that anyone would go to these lengths to replace missing gratings.

The lower end of the barrel of the fore jeer capstan is fitted in the aftmost of three separate positions on the middle deck. The foremost of these appears to be the correct one as it has a raised circular step, the others being just holes bored through the deck plank. It is possible that the capstan was misplaced at some time, and that the aftmost position was actually for a normal main jeer capstan with the head on the middle deck, which has perhaps been lost, or maybe

Plate 37 *This is a beautiful example of the tall and slender stern of a Restoration three-decker. The Achievement of Arms of the Stuarts, in this case those of King Charles II, are particularly finely carved and detailed. The portrait busts in the compartments each side of the tier of lights on the middle deck are an early illustration of a fashion, which became common during the Reign of William and Mary. NMM.*

never fitted. On the lower deck abaft the main mast is the single main capstan. It is very similar to the jeer capstan but much larger, and has a barrel of around 3ft in diameter. Four through bars are fitted. Each of the capstans is beautifully fashioned from single pieces of wood, the double jeer capstan being joined just below the partners. Except for on the quarterdeck and the luff ports on the middle deck, guns are fitted to all the ports. The barrels are nicely turned from wood and are fitted on very simple carriages. Only those on the upper deck are fitted with small trucks. The guns are held in position by long pins driven through the barrels into the port cills. The drawing of the belfry at the forecastle bulkhead gives some idea of this highly elaborate structure, and the sheer size of the carvings. The two central figures represent carvings of about 10ft tall. In contrast, the quarterdeck bulkhead is comparatively plain compared with other seventeenth-century three-deckers. The large central pair of doors is not the main entry into the coach, as may be thought, but leads to an enclosed flight of bell stairs leading down to the middle deck.

the magnificence of carved and gilt decoration in the Restoration period of King Charles II. It is very difficult to describe adequately this beautiful work, but the illustrations give an idea of the quality and fashion in ornament at the time. The figurehead is a singular one, and obviously depicts a story from classical mythology. The seated figure in the chariot drawn by a double-headed eagle has been described by some authorities as Jupiter or Zeus, presumably because of the association with an eagle.[2] The figure does not look at all similar to the usual representation of Zeus, but is rather that of a handsome youth. A more likely explanation is that it portrays the mortal Ganymede, son of the King of Troy. According to legend, Zeus was entranced by the beauty of the young man and caused him to be carried off by an eagle to live among the gods on Mount Olympus. Another version of the myth is that Zeus himself took on the personification of an eagle to take off Ganymede. The chariot is shown on a representation of a small cloud, and a winged cherub above is holding reins from the eagle's beak. Unlike the *Prince*,

75

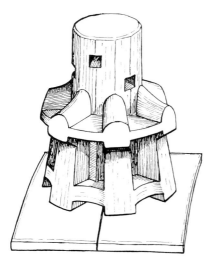

Fig 65 *The jeer capstan on the upper deck in the waist. It appears to be pierced only for three through bars but other examples of this type have four. The partners are split in two halves athwartship, and rest in the rabbets of the fore and aft coamings at the side of the hatches.*

Plate 38 *Detail of the head. There is a further gun port on the middle deck forward of the cat supporter, which is obscured by the anchor. NMM.*

the beak bulkhead is two decks deep, and contains chase ports on both the middle and upper decks. On the bulkhead are two tiers of carved 'terms' — four on the lower and eight on the upper, which are separated by a moulded rail. They are very similar in style to the carvings on the head timbers and internal bulkheads. In the usual fashion of the seventeenth century, the terms are

all depicted with female breasts, although their heads may be either male or female.

Dominating the upper part of the stern is the Royal Arms of the Stuarts. This is the complete Achievement of Arms, and the carving of it is quite exceptional. The tafferal is decorated with a cherub in the centre holding a pair of cornucopias. At each side, more cherubs are sitting astride seahorses, which are supported by a broken arch pediment. In the centre panel between the two tiers of stern lights is the crowned monogram of Charles II. The lower counter is painted with bold designs of Trophies of Arms, which are divided by small figures with female breasts and cloven hooves and with large grotesque mask heads. The rudder head is decorated with the head of a lion. The quarter pieces are tall male figures dressed in Roman-style tunics and holding long staves. They stand on plinths supported by crouching evil-looking charac-ters with cloven hooves and pointed ears. The portrait busts on each side of the lower tier of stern lights are an early indication of a fashion which became common during the William and Mary period.

Colour scheme

Red: Gun carriages; inside of port lids.

Black: Mainwales; frieze at the top of the side; inside of the head rails; plank sheer and fife rails; compartments of the stern, quarter galleries and bulkheads; gun barrels; spirketting on the upper deck.

Gilt: All carved work; moulded rails of the head, stern, broadside and bulkheads; cheeks of the head; stern lanterns; channels and spurs.

Fig 64 *Lower finishing of the quarter gallery. Winged heads of cherubs are by far the most common type of finishing seen on models prior to the beginning of the eighteenth century.*

Fig 62 *The entry port to the middle deck. It is shown on the port side only. The balusters are made alternately from bone and wood.*

Fig 63 *Three of the carved 'brackets on the head timbers. They are typical of those on ships of the second half of the seventeenth century. The dead block for the fore tack, if original, is an early illustration of this fitting.*

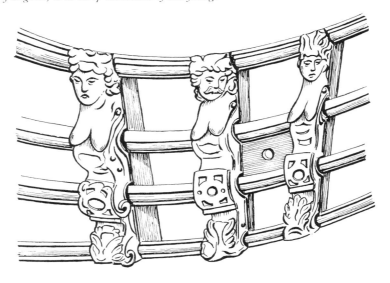

Footnotes

1. NMM No 537, 544 and 545. All these are reproduced in Frank Fox, *Great Ships* (Conway, 1980).
2. L G Carr-Laughton, *Old Ships' Figure-heads and sterns* (London, 1925).

4. First Rate c1670

Location: **National Maritime Museum**
Scale: **1/54 (approx)**

Dimensions* (at a scale of 1/55)			
Gun deck	164ft 6in		
Breadth (moulded)	42ft 9in (43ft 4in)		
Breadth (outside plank)	43ft 9in		
Keel (touch)	131ft 9in (131ft 5in), 1341 tons		
Keel (calculated)	134ft 9in,	1372 tons	
Rake of stem			
(at the stem head)	31ft 9in (32ft 6in)		
(at the harpin)	29ft 6in		
Rake of post			
(at the main transom)	6ft 6in (6ft 7½in)		
Length of post	26ft 4in (26ft 4in)		
Timber and room	2ft 6in (2ft 6in)		
Height to wales (lower edge)			
At the stern	23ft 6in (24ft 0in)		
In midships	15ft 3in (15ft 4in)		
At the stem	18ft 9in (18ft 4in)		

Height below decks			
Upper deck	6ft 10in		
Forecastle	5ft 2in		
Quarterdeck	6ft 11in		

Gun ports		Broad	Deep
Lower deck	28	2ft 10in	2ft 7in
Middle deck	26	2ft 3in	2ft 3in
Upper deck	28	2ft 3in	2ft 3in
Quarterdeck	12		
Total	94		

* The dimensions in brackets are those for a First Rate, taken from *Deane's Doctrine of Naval Architecture*, to compare with those of the model.

Compared with other seventeenth-century three-decker models, such as the well-known *St Michael* (1669) and the *Prince* (1670), this example is fairly simple in construction, with little detail, not quite so well built and in an unfinished state, but it is an important model and of considerable interest. It has often been suggested that the model has a connection with the Master Shipwright Anthony Deane, and that it may be a design for his first three-decker — the *Royal James*, launched in 1671.

Dimensions

In 1670, Deane produced his great work on ship design, *Deane's Doctrine of Naval Architecture*,[1] which includes a sheer draught and rigging plan of a First Rate that is very similar to this model, with the same number and disposition of ports and the same highly unusual triple mainwales. The figurehead and quarter galleries are virtually the same on both model and draught, and the only real differences are that the model has circular port wreaths instead of square, has

an entry port on the starboard side, and a slightly different arrangement of the head rails. Apart from this superficial resemblance to Deane's First Rate, it is the dimensions, and the probable reason why the model was built to an unusual scale, that are of most interest. It should be emphasised that the scale is not perfectly known, but the model clearly represents a First Rate, and to produce the dimensions of a ship of that class it is evidently at, or close to, 1/55. At this scale, the dimensions of the model are very close to those of the *Royal James* (1671) which had a breadth of 45ft 0in and keel lengths of either 132ft 6in or 136ft 0in, depending on what list it has been taken from, which is probably the 'touch' and 'calculated' respectively. But as the model may be a preliminary design, it is perhaps more relevant to compare the dimensions with those given by Deane in his *Doctrine*, and there is a remarkable similarity. The work contains an extensive list of the dimensions and scantlings for all Rates, and calculations, based on the moulded breadth to obtain the rake of the stern post, etc, but does not actually give the breadths except for a Third Rate. Deane thought that the fore rake at the stem head

was to be three-quarters of the breadth: '...sufficient for a ship of war of any rank whatsoever'. As the fore rake of the stem is given at 32ft 6in, this would have been derived from a moulded breadth of 43ft 4in. The only other dimension that is not directly given is the rake aft of the stern post, which was calculated for a Third Rate at $\frac{11}{12}$ of $\frac{1}{6}$ of the moulded breadth. This would be in proportion to that for a First Rate, and works out at 6ft 7½in compared with the 6ft 6in of the model. On the model is a false post abaft the main stern post which extends down to the bottom of the keel, where it is 1ft 6in broad fore and aft. This has not been included in the length of the keel and rake of the post, which have been taken from the actual end of the keel.

Scale

As to the scale, there are two possible reasons for it, the first being that the model was actually built from a draught drawn to a scale of 1/55, but this seems improbable. The alternative is a little complex, but perfectly feasible. In Chapter IV we have seen how Anthony Deane used a midship bend of a ship with a breadth of 32ft 0in at a scale of 1/48, and by simply changing to a smaller scale of 1/61.5, converted it to a three-decker with a breadth of 41ft 0in. The principle of applying different scales to standard draughts for building ships of varying dimensions was well known to early shipwrights, and there is no reason why a model should not be built the same way. The scales were worked out to give the required increase or decrease of the moulded breadth, and if it were necessary to alter the proportions, it was done by increasing or decreasing the timber and room. The dimensions of this model suggest that the hull was built from a draught of a Third Rate drawn to a scale of 1/48 with a moulded breadth of 37ft 3in. In other words, if the model is measured at this normal scale it has a breadth of 37ft 3in, and by converting the scale to 1/55, the breadth becomes 42ft 9in. The body plan

Plate 39 *Starboard broadside. The gun port wreaths are very small and give the impression that the ports are circular. It would have been impossible to fit lids as the wreaths cut across the corners of the ports.* NMM.

sections of a Third Rate would not need to be changed as they would serve equally as well for a First Rate, and all that is necessary is to extend the top of the side up about 5ft 0in. As there may be a connection with Deane, it seems appropriate to compare the model with his draught of a Third Rate. Part of this draught is illustrated in Fig 66, which shows how it can be converted to a First Rate. Deane's draught is drawn to the small scale of 1/85.7, and probably a reduced copy of the draught for his *Resolution* (1667), specially drawn to illustrate his *Doctrine*. The original draught was almost certainly 1/48, the scale that Deane favoured, and to make the comparison it has to be assumed that the upper draught in Fig 66 is at that scale. It can be seen that there are the same number of station lines, timber and rooms, and therefore timbers in both draughts, instead of more for the larger ship as might be expected. But this was certainly the way Deane worked, as it is clear from the *Doctrine* that there would be exactly the same number of timber and rooms in the first three Rates, and that the difference in length was achieved by varying the dimension of the timber and room. From the *Doctrine* we find that for a First Rate this was 2ft 6in, for a Second Rate 2ft 5in and for a Third Rate 2ft 4in.

By dividing these timber and rooms into the lengths of keel given for the three Rates, in each case it works out at 52, ignoring fractions. This is significant, as Deane's draught also has 52, and it seems to be more than mere coincidence that the model has 52 as well. There is only one slight problem in comparing the two draughts. Everything is in proportion except the length/breadth ratio, as First Rates were a little shorter in proportion to the breadth than were the Third Rates. By taking off the timber and room from the draught at the 1/48 scale it is found to be 2ft 4in, as it should be, but at 1/55 scale it becomes 2ft 8in, which is 2in too great, and therefore the keel is too long. The modeller would know this, and all he had to do to construct the hull was reduce the timber and room to a scaled 2ft 6in to give the correct keel length; there would be no need to shorten the sheer draught to do this. As a matter of interest, the keel/breadth ratio of Deane's draught is 3.25/1, and that of the model is 3.08/1, compared with 2.95/1 for the *Royal James*. On the body plan of the modified draught, the foremost station lines have been extended almost straight up instead of the usual 'tumble out'. This agrees with the model, as the tumblehome continues all the way to the beak bulkhead, with the upper

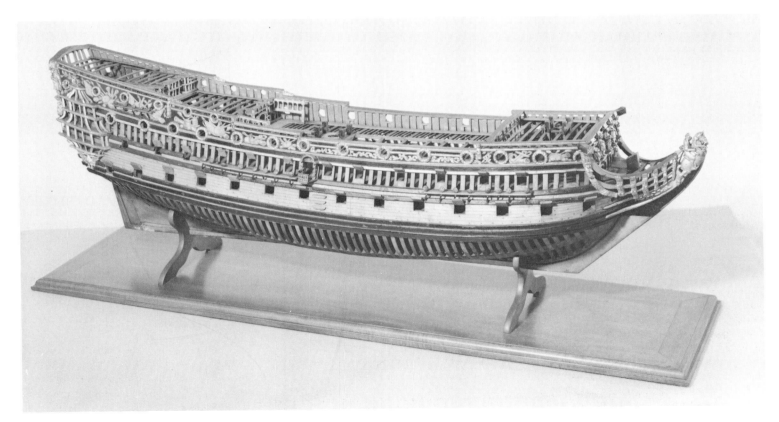

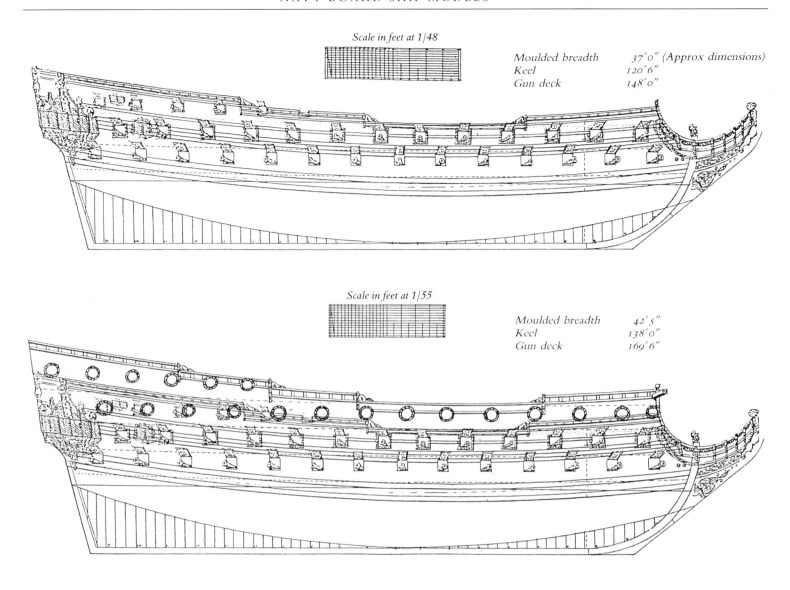

Scale in feet at 1/48

Moulded breadth	37'0" (Approx dimensions)
Keel	120'6"
Gun deck	148'0"

Scale in feet at 1/55

Moulded breadth	42'5"
Keel	138'0"
Gun deck	169'6"

Fig 66 *These illustrations of Deane's draught of a Third Rate at a scale of 1/48 show how it can be converted to a First Rate by raising the top of the side, adding a third tier of ports and reading the draught at a smaller scale of 1/55. The top of the side is a little too high, as the heights between decks have not been adjusted to the new scale, and the modified draught is too long. The whole of the head remains at the same level and cannot be raised, as First Rates of this period had chase ports in the beak bulkhead on the middle deck. All that needs to be done is to add another tier to the quarter galleries. The number and disposition of gun ports is exactly the same as on the model and agrees perfectly with the illustration of a First Rate in the Doctrine, except that the foremost port on the middle deck of the model is aft of the cat supporter, instead of forward.*

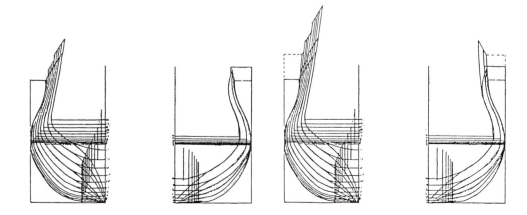

ends of the top timbers almost vertical. The *Royal James* was Deane's first three-decker, and if indeed there is a connection with him, it could well be that he had not prepared a draught for that ship at the time the model was built and, for convenience, modified his draught of a Third Rate.

The reason for the scale of 1/55 has taken some explanation, and does not prove anything, but if it were so, it would provide a fascinating insight into the way ship-wrights manipulated their draughts and scales for whatever purpose they had in mind. It would be of great interest if the body sections were taken off this model for comparison with the body plan of Deane's draught. One final thought: Samuel Pepys mentions a model that Deane made, which he gave to Christ's Hospital, and 'thought'

it was the *Royal James*.[2] Even then Pepys was unsure of the name, but it does prove that Deane did actually build a model of a three-decker, and this model may well be that very one.

Hull construction

In midships, the floor timbers are longer in proportion than on most models, and have a correspondingly long scarph with the futtocks, which terminate about 2ft from the keel. Towards bow and stern, the length of scarph is progressively reduced to about half that in midships. A visual estimate of the floor length in midships is approxi-

mately two-thirds of the breadth, which works out at 28ft 6in compared with 26ft 6in given by Deane for a First Rate. The floors are let down on the keel about 3in, and the timbers at the bow are let into the inner side of the stem, but at the stern the timbers rest directly on the deadwood with no jointing whatsoever. The upper ends of the futtocks terminate at about the level of the middle wales, except for those under the middle deck ports, where they extend upwards to form the port cills. The whole of the stern framing up to the main

Plate 40 *This figurehead is strikingly similar to that on the model of the* Prince, *1670, at the Science Museum. The absence of a belfry and carved heads on the fore top sail and jeer bitts is noticeable.* NMM.

Fig 67 *Detail of the quarterdeck bulkhead. The covered companion way leading down to the middle deck and enclosed by the bulkhead is very similar to that on the St Michael, 1669. One of the large standard knees can be seen against the side, abaft the bulkhead.*

transom is of simplified construction and made from a single piece of wood about 1in thick, which is pierced to represent the separate transoms. In the hold are the usual heavy footwales each side, with one at the floor heads and one at the heels of the futtocks. The keelson is fitted, with a finely fitted hooked scarph in midships.

Outboard fittings and details

The individual strakes of the triple mainwales are 12in broad and 14in thick, giving an overall breadth of 4ft 8in. Several scarphs can be seen on the wales, which are evidently made and not just marked on, and there are probably more which have been obscured by the black paint. The channel wales are the same thickness as the mainwales, but broader at 1ft 3in. No strakes are fitted between any of the wales, and the hull timbers exposed here are painted yellow. The plank between the main- and channel wales is laid on in full-width pieces and fastened with tiny brass nails in a random pattern, but mainly along the edges. This plank is scored to represent the seams between six strakes, and many butts

are marked, but in pencil, as though the modeller intended to scribe them in but in the end did not. As on many models, the spacing of the gun ports does not agree with the spacing of the timbers. There is no difficulty with the lower tier, as the ports are pierced through the solid work at the scarph of the futtocks and top timbers, and these are equally spaced. But unlike the *St Michael* where a lot of work was involved in modifying the top timbers to allow equal spacing of the ports on the middle and upper tiers, these are placed between the timbers, which has resulted in considerable differences in the distance between them. Between some of the ports there are five top timbers, in other places only four, and some of the ports on one side do not correspond in position with their counterparts on the other side. For some obscure reason, the inner sides of the thick port lids are deeply scored with closely spaced diagonal lines, which has produced a pattern of small diamonds. The stern is notable for the large number of gun ports, with four on each of the three main decks. The unfinished nature of the quarter galleries is of interest as it shows the basically simple structure of these features before being concealed by the lights and carvings. An entry port is fitted both to port and to

Fig 68 *Figures such as this are commonly seen on the cat supporters of seventeenth-century models. They are curiously depicted as squatting on tiny legs, with cloven hooves, female breasts and a male head.*

Plate 41 *The unfinished nature of the stern affords a clear view of the basic structure of the quarter galleries and stern timbers. Also evident are the twelve stern ports and the false stern post. The holes in the post suggest that a rudder was once fitted. NMM.*

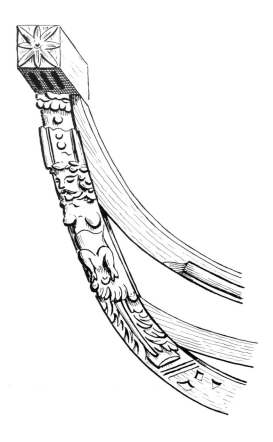

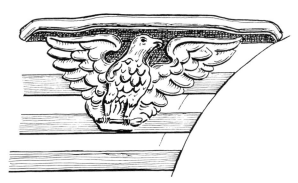

Fig 69 *This large eagle forms the lower finishing to the quarter gallery.*

starboard. They are simply decorated, not at all like the elaborately carved affairs seen on other models of this period. An uncommon feature can be seen at the head, where the main rail dies out against the cat supporter and terminates below the cat head, instead of continuing on up to form the usual timber head.

Inboard fittings and details

Both lower and middle decks are planked with sheet wood in two halves, with the joint on the centre line. The decks are covered with thick paper which is lined in ink to represent the separate planks. A single pair of riding bitts are fitted on the lower deck, which are positioned abreast the fourth port from forward. Several very large standards are fitted each side on the lower and middle decks. The upper deck is framed with a single tier of carlings each side, except for about 15 to 20ft aft, where the beams are closely spaced and no carlings fitted. The carlings are full length in the waist, and let down on the beams to form the hatch coamings. Elsewhere, the carlings are short and fitted between the beams.

Only one capstan is fitted, which is on the middle deck between the fifth and sixth gun ports from forward, and is the type that preceded the drum head. The head is pierced for four through bars at different levels, but unlike others of this period, the capstan is not fitted with whelps, the whole thing being solid and octagonal in section. Shipwrights would think nothing of fashioning a capstan such as this from the butt of a large oak, and it no doubt represents one that was in use at the time. The head is level with the underside of the upper deck beams, and would be approximately 5ft 9in high with a diameter of about 3ft 0in. Two huge standard knees, about 10ft 0in apart, are fitted each side on the upper deck, with the foremost one just abaft the quarterdeck bulkhead. The inboard bulkheads are entirely undecorated and of simple open construction – just the vertical stantions and horizontal rails. No ladders, stairs or gratings are fitted, and there is no indication of a belfry.

Decoration

The equestrian figurehead is probably intended to portray King Charles II, or perhaps his brother James, Duke of York and Lord High Admiral. A fine group of five full length figures decorate the beak bulkhead. The central figure is that of a woman dressed in a long robe, and the others are male, attired in various short tunics, one holding a pike and another about to draw his sword. The large eagles that form the lower finishing of the quarter galleries are in contrast to the winged cherub heads that are commonly seen on seventeenth-century models. The friezes are painted in gold on a black background and depict warlike Trophies of Arms, with flags, guns, drums, shields, axes and spears much in evidence.

Fig 70 *The middle deck capstan. It is about 5ft 9in high, with a diameter of 3ft 0in.*

Colour scheme

Red: Inside of port lids; bulwarks; inner sides of the head timbers; hull timbers inside quarter galleries; companion at the quarterdeck bulkhead.
Black: Main- and channel wales; bitts; cat heads; inner sides of head rails; stem head; knee of the head upwards of the waterline; plank sheers and rails at the top of the side.
Gilt: All carved work; moulded rails; edges of plank sheers; head cheeks; framing of the quarter galleries and internal bulkheads; stern timbers upwards of the main transom.

Footnotes

1. Brian Lavery (Editor), *Deane's Doctrine of Naval Architecture* (Conway, 1981).
2. Navy Records Society, *Samuel Pepys' Naval Minutes* (1925).

5. Fifth Rate of 34 guns, Reign of Charles II

Location: **Kriegstein collection**
Scale: 1/48

Dimensions (at a scale of 1/48)		Gun ports	
Keel (touch)	103ft 0in	Lower deck	22
Gun deck	116ft 0in	Upper deck	12
Breadth	28ft 0in	Total	34

This interesting little model is another of the very few that exist of the smaller Rates from the earlier period. Its date can be broadly defined as between 1660 and 1685, on the evidence of the monogram of Charles II on the tafferal, but it is not easy to be more precise. The drumhead jeer capstan has appeared, which is undoubtedly original and possibly the earliest example known, but when this type was first introduced is uncertain. Although drumhead capstans are generally seen on models of known date soon after 1680, there is no evidence to suggest that they are the first of the new type, and the drumhead may have been in use some time before this. The model certainly appears to be from the earlier period of Charles II, rather than later, and a tentative suggestion for the date is around 1665–1670.

In general appearance, and number and arrangement of ports (with none on the upper deck in the waist), the model is typical of the Fifth Rates built during the Restoration period. Of the seven that were built, the four largest were the *Sweepstakes*, 1666, the *Falcon*, 1666, the *Nonsuch*, 1668, and the *Phoenix*, 1671. These had dimensions as follows, taken from Dimension Book B. Other lists give varying dimensions but the discrepancies are small, except that the breadth of the *Phoenix* is mostly given as 28ft 6in.

Plate 42 *Starboard broadside. The aftmost port on the lower deck is at a lower level than the rest, suggesting that there may be a step down in the deck at the gun room. The drumhead capstan, which can just be seen, has five whelps and is fitted with ten bars. The deadwood aft is built up from four separate pieces, with one long piece on the keel and three short pieces above. No deadwood is fitted forward. Kriegstein collection.*

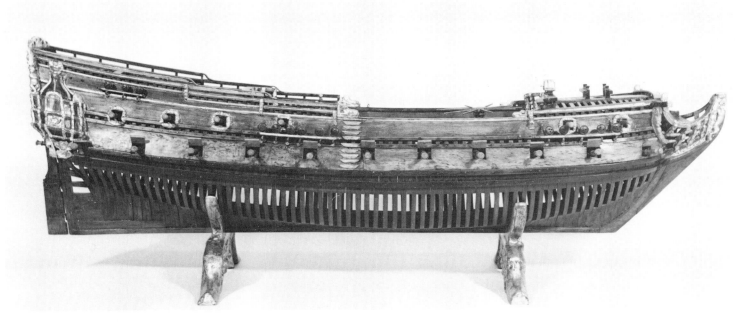

85

Plate 43 *View of the head. The beak platform and head grating are unusually curved up each side, and finish flush with the upper side of the main head rails. Seats of ease, which are seldom shown on the earlier models, can be seen. Although not apparent, the tails of the cat heads are turned aft and fastened to the inner sides of the bulwarks.* Kriegstein collection.

Plate 44 *Details of the main channel on the port side. The channel is very short, with few dead-eyes. If the deadeyes are to scale, they would be about 2ft 0in in diameter, but they are probably oversized.* Author.

	Gun deck	Breadth	Keel
Sweep- stakes	108ft 10in	28ft 6in	87ft 6in
Falcon	–	27ft 6in	89ft 0in
Nonsuch	–	27ft 8in	88ft 3in
Phoenix	–	27ft 0in	90ft 0in
Model	116ft 0in	28ft 0in	103ft 0in

Except for the *Sweepstakes*, the lengths on the gun deck are not known, but it is possible that with the slightly longer keel, the *Phoenix* may have had a gun deck of up to about 112ft 0in. The keel length of the model has been measured to the point where the stem rabbet rises sharply at an angle from the keel instead of at a tangent. It may be that in this unusual case, the true length to the 'touch' is to the beginning of the stem/keel scarph, which is some 6ft 0in farther aft, giving a keel length of about 97ft 0in. The four ships were originally built to carry 30/36 guns, but within a year or two of completion they were made up to Fourth Rates, pierced with a complete tier of ports on the upper deck and armed with 36/42 guns.

A portrait of the *Phoenix* by Van de Velde the Elder depicts the ship as she was

Plate 45 *This stern is very different in both style and nature of the decoration to that on the earlier Fifth Rate.* Kriegstein collection.

Plate 46 *Aft part of the waist, showing the quarterdeck bulkhead, gangway and stairs. The construction of the bulkhead, with no panels, is typical of the period. The heavy carvings on the stantions of the bulkhead are repeated at the bulkheads of the forecastle and poop. Gun barrels are turned from wood and mounted on simple carriages with no trucks.* Author.

in 1675, with eleven ports aside on the lower deck and ten on the upper deck, as the model would have if the upper tier were completed, and three a side on the quarterdeck. Although the model has a striking resemblance to the portrait of the *Phoenix*, no suggestion can be made as to whether it is actually of that ship, or any of the Fifth Rates built, due to its excessive length, particularly on the keel. But there is probably a connection and the model may have been a design for one of the ships, which turned out as built with amended dimensions. Another consideration, suggested by the Coat of Arms at the stern,

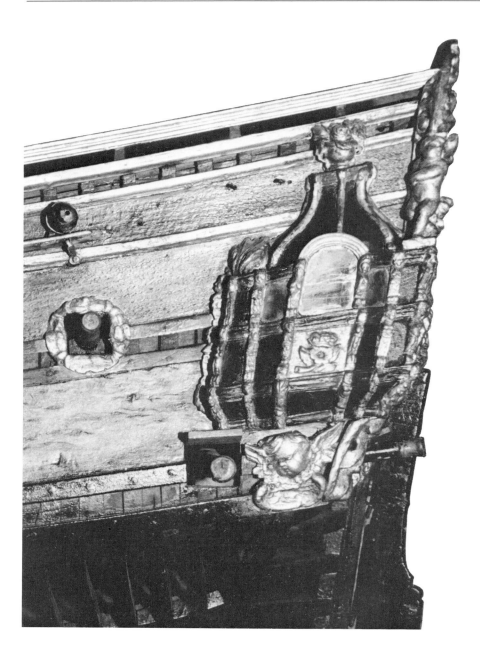

Plate 47 *Quarter gallery. An urn of flowers forms the upper finishing of the gallery, and the crowned rose of England appears in a panel below the window. Note that the inner side of the port wreath is square and flush with the sides of the port, unlike most which are generally circular.* Author.

is that the model may be of an unknown privateer rather than one of the King's ships. The carving is not well defined but does not seem to represent the Arms of the Stuarts, and may be those of a Peer of the Realm such as a Duke or an Earl. The model, which was once owned by Vice Admiral Robert Fairfax (1666–1725), is in a perfect undamaged condition, and still contained in its beautiful and original display cabinet.

Colour scheme

Black: Mainwales; head cheeks; stem head and bollard timbers; plank sheer and fife rails; panels of the quarter galleries and counter; timber heads; deadeyes; bits; gun barrels; breast rails at the breaks of the decks.

Red: Inner sides of port lids; port linings; guns muzzles; gun carriages; stairs to the quarter- and poop decks.

Gilt: All carved work; moulded rails of the head, stern and broadside; edges of the channels; belfry; boarding steps; cradles.

6. Hampton Court, Third Rate of 70 guns 1678

Location: Wilton House, Wiltshire
Scale: 1/48

Dimensions of model★		
Gun deck	150ft 9in	
Breadth	40ft 0in	
Keel (touch)	131ft 0in, 1115 tons	
Keel (calculated)	125ft 0in, 1063 tons	
Timber and room	2ft 5in	
Rake of the stem	17ft 0in at the harpin	
Rake of the stern post	5ft 0in at the main transom (12°)	

Height to lower edge of mainwales	
At the stern	23ft 9in
In midships	15ft 3in
At the stem	18ft 0in

Deck lengths	
Forecastle	29ft 0in
Quarterdeck	64ft 0in
Poop	35ft 0in

Gun ports		Breadth	Depth
Lower deck	26	3ft 9in	3ft 3in
Upper deck	26	2ft 9in	2ft 6in
Quarterdeck	10		
Poop	4		
Forecastle	2		
Total	68		

Draught of water	
Forward	17ft 6in
Aft	18ft 6in

Bower anchor	
Overall length of shank	17ft 0in
Length of stock	18ft 0in
Stock (square in the middle)	1ft 6in
Stock (square at the ends)	9in
Length of arms (crown to bill)	7ft 0in
Breadth of palms	3ft 0in
Length of palms	3ft 6in

Dimensions given on draught	
Length by the keel	131ft 0in
Extreme breadth	40ft 0in
Depth in hould	17ft 3in
Length on ye gun deck	150ft 0in
Draught of water	18ft 0in
Burthen in tuns	1114

Comparison with ship

	Gun deck	Breadth	Keel (touch)	Keel (calc)	Depth	Tons
Hampton Court	150ft 6in	40ft 1in	—	125ft 6in	17ft 3in	1072 (Dimension Book B)
	—	39ft 10in	131ft 0in	—	17ft 0in	1105 (Pepys)
Model	150ft 9in	40ft 0in	131ft 0in	125ft 0in	—	

Port configuration of the three Third Rates built by John Shish

	L/Deck	U/deck	Q/deck	Forecastle	Poop	Total
Hampton Court	26	24	10	—	4	64
Lennox	26	24	10	—	—	60
Stirling Castle	26	26	10	4	4	70
Model	26	26	10	2	4	68

The port configurations above have been taken from a list compiled by Frank Fox from portraits of known ships.[1]

The dimensions for the *Hampton Court* are given from two separate lists, as only Dimension Book B gives the length on the gun deck. This list also gives the calculated length of keel, whereas Pepys' *Register of Ships* gives the keel length to the 'touch'. With the short fore rake of the stem, the 'touch' keel has become longer than the theoretical calculated length.

Of all the seventeenth-century models that exist, this superb example of a Third Rate is uniquely complete – not only for its unusually detailed construction and fine craftsmanship, but for the original rigging, a full array of flags, and above all, a draught of the same ship, which is shown in the back of the contemporary display case. The draught does not indicate the name of the ship, but the model is known as the *Old Hampton Court*, 1678, one of three Third Rates built at Deptford Dockyard by John Shish, the others being the *Lennox*, 1678, and the *Stirling Castle*, 1679. One of the beautifully carved cradles has a small shield with the initials IS, or JS, which are almost certainly those of John Shish, and the date '92. Again we find that a date on a model is not always a reliable guide to the ship it

represents but rather the date the model itself was completed, as it is clearly of an earlier ship. There are several detailed portraits by Van de Velde the Elder of all three of the Third Rates built by Shish. The ships were very similar except that the *Hampton Court* was distinctive in having two projecting open stern galleries, and all had slightly different decoration, with variations in the number and arrangements of the gun ports (see table). Of the three ships, the model bears the least resemblance to the *Hampton Court*, as apart from the stern galleries, the ship had no ports on the forecastle and only twenty-four on the upper deck. The *Lennox* too had twenty-four ports on the upper deck, with none at all on the forecastle and poop. This leaves the *Stirling Castle* which, except for having

Plate 48 *The model is displayed in a large contemporary glazed cabinet, where it has probably remained ever since it was built. A draught of the same ship is in the background. There is no trace of the name of the ship on the draught, or of who the artist was.* Henry Wills. By courtesy of the Earl of Pembroke, Wilton House, near Salisbury.

an extra one each side on the forecastle, had the same ports as the model, and the same foremost ports on the upper deck unusually placed directly below the cat heads.

The dimensions are no help, as the differences between all three ships, the draught and the model are so slight that they can be ignored. In all probability Shish would have built his three Third Rates from the same draught, but completed them with the variations in port arrangement and decoration, and in the case of the *Hampton Court*, with the addition of stern galleries. Perhaps a simple explanation for the model is that Shish built it from the original design draught, which would explain why it does not agree in all respects with any one of the portraits of the three ships as built. The beautifully drawn and extremely rare draught is a work of art in its own right, and embellished with the carved work and other decoration. The similarity between the model and draught is remarkable, not only for the dimensions and general appearance, but for the carvings, designs of the painted friezes, and every conceivable small detail. The draught appears to be of a little later date than the model, and is probably a fair copy of the original, again to illustrate the ship in addition to the model. It can be dated to after the death of Queen Mary in 1694, on the evidence of the monogram WR on the quarter gallery of the draught, whereas in the same place on the model the monogram is an intertwined WM. The existence of a seventeenth-century draught and a model of the same ship provides a unique opportunity to establish which keel length is given in the various ship lists. On both model and draught, the given keel length of 131ft 0in agrees precisely to the 'touch', or the point where the rabbet of the stem begins to rise from the keel (see table). The draught is on two hinged boards, and it is interesting to note in this respect that Samuel Pepys mentions draughts as 'done in the usual manner upon boards'.[2] The model, which is in superb condition, is owned by the Earl of Pembroke, and is displayed in the part of Wilton House that is open to the public.

Hull construction

The construction of the hull framing is of the highest quality, and appears to be made entirely from pear wood. The timber and room of the framing, at 2ft 5in, corresponds exactly with the 7ft 3in between station lines of the draught, which are at intervals of every third timber and room. In midships, the heels of the top timbers extend down below the wales farther than usual, at about 4ft 0in. From midships aft, the line

Fig 71 *Quarterdeck stairs and gangway. On the model, the sheets for the sprit sail and fore course lead through sheaves in the side, and through the two large holes in the upper riser of the stairs,* where they are taken forward and both made up on a single large cleat on the bulwarks. It appears to be an inconvenient arrangement.

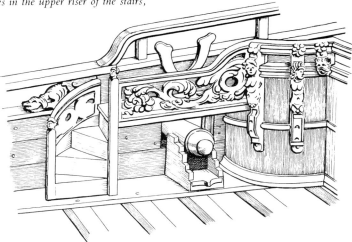

Fig 72 *Poop deck stairs and gangway showing some of the rich carved work. The crouching dogs at the hances are typical of the seventeenth century.* All the gun carriages are of this simple type, with no trucks.

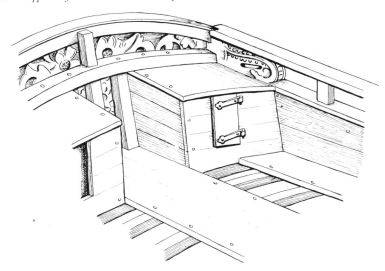

Fig 73 *Aft end of the poop deck. The small cabins are for the ship's trumpeters. These cabins disappeared from Third Rates in the 1690s. The tafferal carvings are cut clear through, with the forward side finished in a simplified design.*

of the heels is parallel with the wales, but forward, the line curves sharply up with the heels disappearing behind the wales at the bow. Between the deadwoods at bow and stern, the heels of the futtocks terminate at about 1ft 6in from the keel. Draught of water marks are indicated in Roman numerals on the starboard side of the stern post, and port side of the stem at 1ft 0in intervals. These are marked between 15ft 0in and 20ft 0in, but a faint waterline scribed on the hull agrees with 18ft 6in aft and 17ft 6in forward. The draught of water given in Pepys' list for the *Hampton Court* is 18ft 6in. The stern post/keel joint is strengthened by small brass reinforcing plates let in on each side. In the hold the keelson is fitted, and a heavy fore and aft strake, about 1ft 6in broad and 9in thick, is laid each side flush with the floor heads. The internal finish of the hull is equally as fine as the outboard, and the craftsman has gone to the trouble of working a small chamfer along the edges of the futtocks between the floor heads and the heels of the top timbers. The orlop deck clamps,

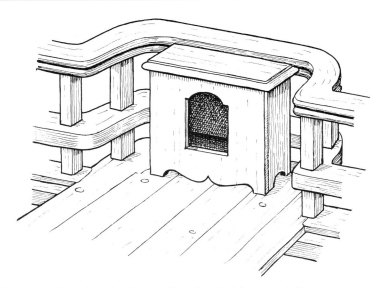

Fig 74   *The compass binnacle is fitted at the forward end of the quarterdeck.*

Plate 49   *The lion figurehead is a splendid example of the 'fierce'-looking beast usual in the seventeenth century, unlike those of later years. Note the small pair of bitts below the bowsprit,* and the extreme forward position of the upper deck port. Author. By courtesy of the Earl of Pembroke, Wilton House, near Salisbury.

Fig 75 *The beautifully carved cradles are finished in natural varnished wood. The upward extensions fit between the hull timbers and lock the cradle in place.*

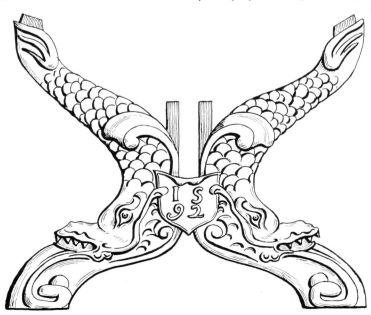

Plate 50 *Quarter view of the stern and quarter gallery showing the fine and extensive carved work. The quarter figure is holding a trident, and probably represents Neptune. The portrait bust below, which is repeated on the starboard side, is that of William III, and portrays the King crowned with a wreath of laurel leaves. Author. By courtesy of the Earl of Pembroke, Wilton House, near Salisbury.*

beams and carlings are fitted, but no plank is laid.

Outboard fittings and details

The mainwales are 10in thick, 1ft 6in broad and 2ft 0in apart. The chainwales are both about 6in thick, with the lower of the pair 1ft 3in broad and the upper 1ft 0in. There is no strake between the chainwales, and the top timbers have been reduced in their siding towards the top of the side. The plank between the main- and chainwales is laid on in one broad piece, and is of a highly figured wood that appears to be walnut. A feature of the broadside not seen on any other model of a two-decker, and rarely in portraits of ships, is that the main course tack is led through an ornamented dead block in the bulwarks, instead of the usual

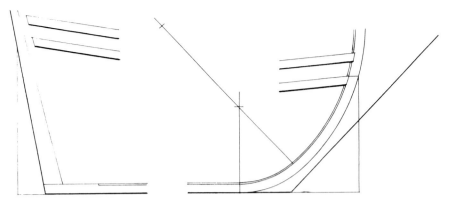

Fig 76 *Profile of the stem and stern post. The fore rake, at 17ft 0in, is very short, and less than half the breadth of the ship. Note the compound curvature of the stem, produced by sweeps of different radius.*

chesstree. This is illustrated on the draught and also, perhaps not surprisingly, it can be seen on two of the portraits of the ships built by Shish, the *Lennox* and the *Hampton Court*. The foremost port on the upper deck is pierced in the angle of the side with the beak bulkhead, completely destroying the cat supporter, the only remnant left being a small carved figure below the cat head, and the eking, which continues on down below the port. Being so close to the bulkhead, the gun is placed at an angle of about 45 degrees. The anchors are beautifully fashioned from a single piece of steel, with the two leaves of the stock secured together with eight brass fastenings. It is surprising to see that the anchors have virtually the same dimensions as those for a much larger Third Rate of a hundred years later. The channels are braced above by serpent-shaped timber spurs. Some meticulous work can be seen in the rudder hangings. The five pairs of braces and straps are made from brass, and let into the rudder and stern post, fastened with tiny brass pins and filed off perfectly flush with the timber. The stern and quarter gallery lights are glazed with mica, which is marked out in fine gold lines to represent very small panes of about 4in × 3in. Delicately moulded rigols are fitted above each of the lower deck ports.

Inboard fittings and details

The upper deck is completely planked, with a single wide piece each side of the centre line fastened to the beams with scattered treenails. Scribed lines on the deck represent planks of about 1ft 6in broad. The drumhead jeer capstan on the upper deck in the waist is fashioned from a single piece of wood, and has a height of 4ft 0in, with a diameter at the drumhead of 3ft 0in. The capstan is fitted with twelve bars and has six whelps. A very early example of a fire hearth is fitted in the usual place on the upper deck, just forward of the forecastle bulkhead. It is in a reversed position to later ones, with the single copper on the forward side and the open fire and chimney aft. The chimney, where it emerges from the forecastle deck, is about 2ft 0in square, tapering to about 1ft 0in at the upper end. Another fitting seldom seen at this period is the fish davit for stowing the anchors. As usual on models, the davit is rigged out on the port side with the inner end held down by a single span shackle on the centre line at the aft end of the forecastle deck. In length, the davit is about three-quarters of the ship's breadth at 29ft 0in, and is 1ft 6in square in the middle, tapering to 1ft 0in at each end. One particular feature on the quarterdeck is perhaps one of the rarest of all fittings seen on models: a beautifully made compass binnacle which is set into a bay in the breast rail at the forward end of the deck. It is not, of course, for the steering compass but for the seventeenth-century equivalent of a 'repeater', for use by the Captain and Master. Of especial interest on this model is the whipstaff steering arrangement. This is functional and complete, with finely made brass fittings at the ends of the tiller and whipstaff, and the 'sweep', or 'quadrant', is fitted below the upper deck beam to support the forward end of the tiller. No lookout is provided for the helmsman, and it is clear on this detailed model that none was intended, and that he would steer 'blind' as on a ship with three decks. A hole about 1ft 6in square is pierced in the quarterdeck directly above the whipstaff, which seems to have served two purposes: first, it provided a means of communication with the helmsman; second, due to its 12ft 0in length, the only way the whipstaff could be fitted was by pushing the upper end up through the hole, then lowering it down through the steering rowle (see Appendix V for details of the whipstaff). Guns are fitted to all ports except the aftmost one each side on the upper deck. With only one port a side on the forecastle, the usual four guns on this deck are made up by two in a permanent position in the chase ports. The gun barrels are turned from wood and painted the distinctive pale green colour of corroded brass.

Decoration

The carved work, as would be expected on a model of this quality, is of superb execution. The Royal Coat of Arms is displayed in the centre of the tafferal and above the quarter galleries, and a complete Achievement of Arms, in minute detail, is at the break of the quarterdeck. At this period the Lion and Unicorn supporters are very often separated from the Arms. In this case the supporters are seen on the quarter galleries, but lower down and each side, at the level of the upper lights. It is interesting to see that on the starboard side, the Lion supporter is on the dexter side for England, and to port, the Unicorn is dexter, in the Scottish manner. A full array of flags is rare indeed on a model of this date. From forward they are: the Union Jack, the Admiralty Flag, the Royal Standard bearing the Arms of William III, the Union Flag, and the Red Ensign. The flags are painted on very thin metal, possibly brass.

Colour scheme

Black: Mainwales, and strake between; knee of the head above waterline; bollard timbers and stem head; lower counter; panels of the quarter galleries and stern; plank sheer and fife rails; all bulkheads; bitts; stantions and rails at the breaks of the decks; string and spirketting in the waist; bulwarks; cat heads.
Red: Inner side of port lids; muzzle, ears, and inside the crown of the Lion figurehead; gun carriages; inner sides of bulkheads; fire hearth.
Gilt: All carved work; moulded rails; edges of plank sheer; head rails and cheeks; lantern.
Pale green: Gun barrels.

Footnotes

1. Frank Fox, *Great Ships* (Conway 1980), p 195.
2. *Samuel Pepys' Naval Minutes*, Edited by J R Tanner, Navy Records Society (1925), Vol 60, p 239.

7. Mordaunt, Fourth Rate of 40-46 guns 1681

Location: **National Maritime Museum**
Scale: 1/48

Dimensions★	Model	Ship	Height to lower edge of mainwales	
			At the wing transom	19ft 0in
Gun deck	122ft 6in	–	Midships	13ft 0in
Breadth	32ft 2in	32ft 4½in	At the stem	13ft 9in
Keel (touch)	105ft 9in, 582 tons			
Keel (calculated)	101ft 8in, 559 tons	101ft 9in, 567 tons	Gun ports	
Timber and room	2ft 2in		Lower deck	22
Draught of water	13ft 6in (forward)		Upper deck	24
	14ft 6 in (aft)	16ft 0in	Quarterdeck	10
			Total	56

Dimensions of the *Mordaunt* from Pepys' *Register of Ships*. The *Mordaunt* was built in 1681 by Captain Castle at Deptford.

This fine model was identified by R C Anderson as the *Mordaunt* on the evidence of the Coat of Arms of Lord Mordaunt displayed at the break of the poop deck, the dimensions, and arrangement of gun ports.[1] No dimension for the length of gun deck has been found for the *Mordaunt*, but as the breadth and length of keel for tonnage agree so closely, there would probably be very little difference with the 122ft 6in of the model. Originally, the *Mordaunt* was a heavily armed privateer, built by Captain Castle at Deptford in 1681 for a syndicate headed by Lord Mordaunt. Soon after, in 1683, the ship was bought into the Navy. Whether the model was built before or after this date is uncertain. The uncrowded Lion figurehead and the Mordaunt Arms suggest that it was before the ship was purchased by the Navy, but on the other hand, the Admiralty badge prominently displayed at the break of the quarterdeck indicates that it may have been after. There are at least two contemporary portraits of the *Mordaunt*, by the Dutch artist Van de Velde the Elder.[2] These are detailed drawings, one showing a clear view of the stern and the other of the starboard broadside. The model bears a remarkable similarity with the portraits, not only in the general appearance and decorative details of the stern, but also with small features such as the unusually high position of the head cheeks. Only one small discrepancy can be seen. In the portrait of the stern, medallions containing St George's Cross appear at the ends of the stern gallery, but on the model these are shown higher, at the level of the lower tier of stern lights. Van de Velde was known to have made use of models for his drawings, and it seems likely that he used this one of the *Mordaunt* for that purpose.

Hull construction

The hull framing is of usual construction

Plate 51 *Upper deck in the waist showing the riding bitts close to the forecastle bulkhead. The hatch coamings, and spirketting and string of the bulwarks have a fine moulding worked along their edges. Note the small gun ports compared with those on the lower deck. The capstans are early examples of the drumhead type.* NMM.

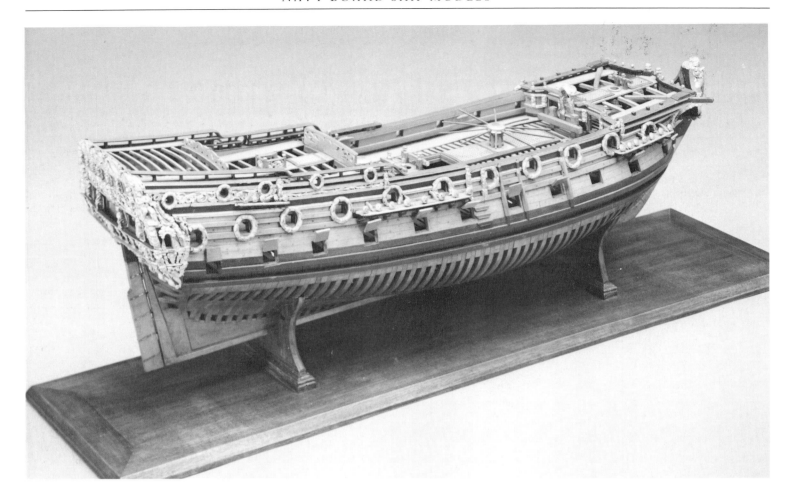

except that the framing does not terminate in the solid block at the stem. The stem is united to the keel with a scarph that is quite unlike those seen on other models of any period. Instead of the usual short scarph, the fore end of the keel is extended forwards and upwards in a long interlocked scarph with the stem, which is secured with brass fastenings. This would be a very strong scarph, and undoubtedly illustrates a method that was in use at the time. Clearly marked on the hull is the draught of waterline, which is 14ft 0in in midships, where it corresponds to the upper edge of the lower mainwale, as it is shown in the broadside portrait. The draught given in Pepys' *Register of Ships* and other lists of 16ft 0in is probably the greatest depth, at the stern, and would be about 15ft 6in in midships compared with the 14ft 0in indicated by the model. In the hold are two substantial fore and aft strakes each side, one flush with the floor heads and one at the heels of the futtocks, about 1ft 0in from the keelson.

Outboard fittings and details

The double mainwales are 11in broad, 9in thick and 1ft 6in apart, with the chainwales of the same scantling, and 1ft 0in apart. The chainwales are fastened with brass pins which have been filed off flush with the wood. The plank between the wales is scored to represent the seams between three strakes. This plank is fastened with a few treenails, with many more simulated by markings with a small punch. The lower deck ports are 2ft 9in broad and 2ft 6in deep. Upper deck ports are very small, at only 1ft 9in square. At the stern the open gallery is at the level of the upper deck, with the breast rail supported by widely spaced carved balusters. Apart from this one, open balusters are never seen on models with a gallery at this low level, as it is in effect the area of the upper counter, and usually berthed up with plank to the breast rail. Perhaps some ingress of water was anticipated, as the gallery deck is unusually laid with gratings. Seldom seen on a Fourth Rate are the four stern ports in the lower

Plate 52   *The starboard broadside.* NMM.

counter, two being the usual number. Another departure from standard can be seen at the head. The beak bulkhead is far forward, and actually built into the bollard timbers, or 'knight heads'. At each side of the bulkhead are three large circular steps leading up to the forecastle deck, with a seat of ease incorporated in the lower one.

Inboard fittings and details

Perhaps the most notable feature of the ship is that the main capstan and riding bitts for the anchor cables are on the upper deck, which is never seen on a usual ship of the Navy. But the hawse holes apparently lead into the lower deck, and cannot be placed any higher as the cables would foul the head timbers. To overcome this problem, long sloping troughs are built into the upper deck, which lead down to the lower level of the hawse holes. An interesting single bitt (Fig 77) is fitted on the upper deck in the forecastle, just aft and to starboard of

Plate 53 *View of the head. The cheeks are in a high position, which has made the head rails very shallow. Normally, there would be a cheek on each* *of the mainwales, or slightly above. The upper end of the keel/stem scarph can be seen.* NMM.

away to provide the width of the port, and cills are fitted.

Decoration

The whole of the decorative work is much the same as on the other models of the period, and this can mostly be seen in the photographs. The Stuart Royal Arms of Charles II is displayed at the stern, which may be another indication that the model was made after the *Mordaunt* was bought into the Navy.

Colour scheme

Black: Mainwales, and one strake above; plank sheer, rails and friezes at the top of the side; beak bulkhead; hatch coamings; lower counter.

Red: Inside of the port lids; bulwarks; bulkheads; bitts; stairs; cat tails; whelps of the capstans.

Gilt: All carved work; cheeks of the head; deadeyes; belfry; mouldings; drumheads of the capstans.

Fig 77 *Athwartship view of the single bitt on the upper deck in the forecastle. The bitt is about 3ft 0in high. (Not to scale.)*

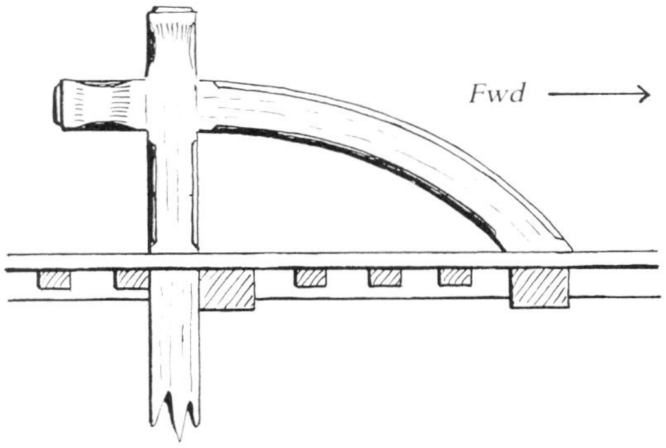

the foremast position, the purpose of which is not entirely clear. It may have something to do with stopping the anchor cables, although in that case one would expect a pair to be fitted. There are no fore jeer bitts fitted in the usual position aft of the mast on the forecastle deck, and it is possible that in this case, the jeers were led down through a scuttle in the deck and belayed to the single bitt below. The model is one of the very few where the cat tails lie at an angle across the forecastle deck. The gratings, if original, are very early examples, made in the proper way with thin fore and aft battens let into the thicker athwartship ledges. Except for the bulwarks in the waist, no inboard plank is fitted and the manner in which the ports are framed can be

Fwd ⟶

seen. Those on the lower deck are pierced through the solid work at the scarph of the futtocks and top timbers and are not fitted with cills. The upper deck ports are pierced between adjacent top timbers which are cut

Footnotes

1. R C Anderson, *The Mariner's Mirror* Vol 2, pp 164/6.
2. NMM Nos 597 and 598.

97

8. Fourth Rate of 50 guns 1682

Location: **National Maritime Museum**
Scale: **1/48**

*Dimensions**			*Gun ports*	
Gun deck	130ft 0in		Lower deck	22
Breadth	33ft 6in		Upper deck	22
Keel (touch)	109ft 3in, 651 tons		Quarterdeck	6
Keel (calculated)	110ft 3in, 658 tons		Total	50
Timber and room	2ft 0in			
Rake of the stem	20ft 6in at the harpin			
Rake of the stern post	4ft 0in at the main transom (11°)			

Height to the lower edge of mainwales	
At the transom	18ft 6in
In midships	12ft 0in
At the stem	15ft 0in

This unidentified model – with the date 1682 painted on the stern – is something of a mystery, and there is no evidence to suggest that it represents a particular ship. There were no Fourth Rates built between 1675 and 1687 apart from the privately commissioned *Mordaunt* and a few smaller rebuilt ships. The draught of water marks on the stem and stern post show that the model was made at an accurate scale of 1/48, and the keel length and breadth are very close to the dimensions of six Fourth Rates built in the 1660s and '70s. Although the model cannot be identified with any of these ships, the hull must have been made from a draught dating from before 1682. Of the six Fourth Rates, the *Kingfisher*, 1675, was notable for her very shallow draught of water which is given in Pepys' list as 13ft 0in, several feet less than for the other five. The length of gun deck has not been found for the *Kingfisher*, but she had a keel length of 110ft 0in and a breadth of 33ft 8in. The waterline is not marked on the model, but it too has a shallow draught of 13ft 0in, measuring it to the usual position at the upper edge of the lower mainwale in midships. It is a minor point, which does not mean that the model is the *Kingfisher*, but it is quite possible that the hull was made from the same draught.

Plate 54 *Port broadside.* NMM.

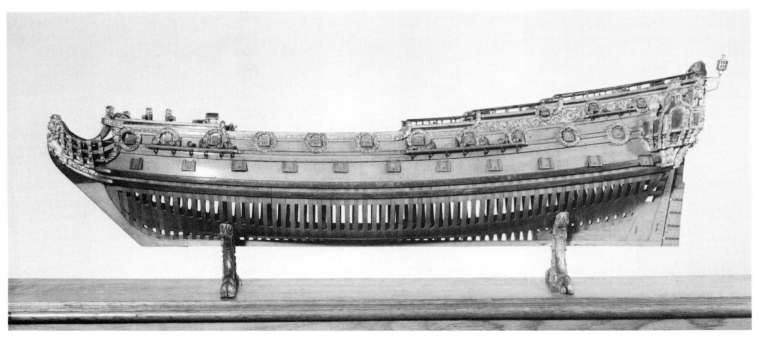

Plate 55 *This is a fine example of the lavish stern decoration of a ship from the later part of the Charles II period. The date is elaborately painted in four of the panels between the two tiers of lights, with the plumes of feathers in the centre panel. The lanterns are early examples of the hexagonal- and parallel-sided type that became fashionable towards the end of the seventeenth century. Author.*

The plumes of ostrich feathers prominently displayed on the quarter galleries and stern suggest a connection with James, Duke of York, and Lord High Admiral of the Navy. The badge is seen on several other seventeenth-century models of a date no later than 1685, when James became King, a notable one being the famous First Rate *Prince*, 1670. Popularly known as the Prince of Wales Feathers, the device is properly that of the Heir Apparent, and being the brother of King Charles who had no natural son, James was entitled to the badge. James formed a collection of ship models which were seen by the Grand

Plate 56 *View of the head and the splendid lion. As on a few other models of this period, there are no bollard timbers or 'knight heads' at each side of the stem head. Author.*

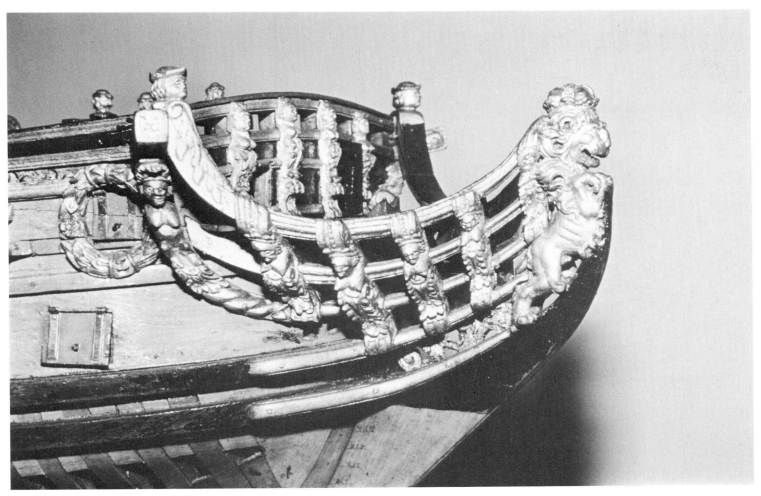

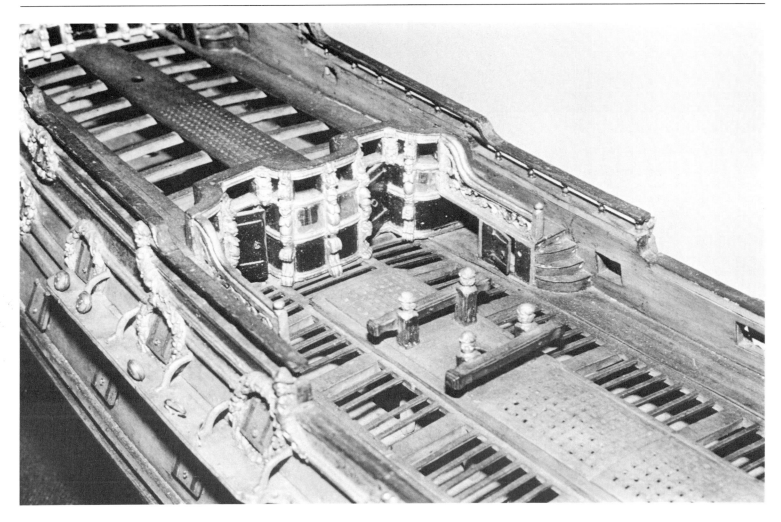

Duke of Tuscany who described them as 'remarkable objects', and 'beautifully executed after the designs of His Royal Highness'.[1] Whether the models actually were designed by the Duke of York is uncertain. It is feasible not so much that he designed the hull lines but that only the layout and decoration were from his hand, which may not have been incorporated in a ship that was built. Perhaps this model was included in the Duke of York's collection and specially made for him, and while the hull itself may have been built from an existing draught, it was completed to the designs of His Royal Highness.

Hull construction

As on the *St Michael*, 1669, the floor heads are cut off horizontally athwartship. The floor heads are very uneven and many of the sharp ends are filed off square to a greater or lesser extent to perfect the rising line. In the hold, a pair of footwales are fitted each side, one just below the floor heads and the other flush with the futtock heels. These strakes are fastened with treenails at ¼in intervals to each of the floors and futtocks, but the gun deck clamps are fastened with small brass nails. Several floor riders, a little shorter than the length of floors, are spaced along the hull. An extra-broad rider, at about 3ft 0in fore and aft, doubles as the main mast step. A number of other unrigged models are fitted with mast steps, complete with mortices, and it seems that they were fitted as a matter of course so that masts could be fitted later if required. All deck beams are let down on the clamps about half their depth. Draught of water marks are indicated by Roman numerals on the port side of the stern post and starboard side of the stem. The marks are spaced in feet at an accurate scale of 1/48, and show a maximum draught of 14ft 0in forward and 15ft 0in aft. The construction of the model appears to be mostly of apple wood.

Plate 57 *Upper deck in the waist showing the quarterdeck bulkhead, stairs and bitts, etc. Note the simulated grating on the quarterdeck, with the holes simply punched through the deck plank, and with no coamings.* Author.

Outboard construction

The mainwales, which are fastened in a similar manner to the internal footwales, are 1ft 3in broad, 10½in thick and spaced 12in apart. The chainwales are 9in broad, 6in thick and 9in apart. The top side plank is laid in full-width pieces which are fastened with treenails in straight rows to each of the top timbers. The fore and main channels are 2ft 0in broad with the inner edges the same thickness as the breadth of the chainwale, and the outer edges about 6in thick. Rudder hangings, port lid straps, chain plates and other metal fittings are made from brass with a natural finish.

Inboard details

The internal construction is much the same as other seventeenth-century models, except that the side gangways from the stairs to the quarterdeck and poop are unusually enclosed below by lockers, or perhaps they were intended to be tiny cabins for the ship's boys. Stairs and gangways are also fitted leading from the waist to the forecastle which are seldom seen except on models of three-deckers. The jeer capstan in the waist is unfortunately missing, but at this time it would probably have been a drumhead type.

Decoration

The style and extent of the decorative work, which can mostly be seen in the photographs, is remarkable for a Fourth Rate, and compares with that on the prestige three-deckers. The frieze design at the top of the side is painted in gold picked out with black on a pale red background. The elaborate and florid designs painted in compartments of the counter, stern and quarter galleries are in gold on a black background.

Colour scheme

Black: Mainwales; plank sheer and fife rails; narrow frieze at top of the side; knee of the head above waterline; inner sides of the head rails, and head timbers; bitts; roof of belfry; stairs.

Red: Inside of port lids; inner sides of the bulkheads; muzzle, ears, and inner part of the crown of the lion figurehead.

Gilt: All carved work; moulded rails of the broadside and stern; outboard edges of plank sheer and fife rails; head cheeks; head rails; cat heads; hand rails of the stairs; lanterns; cradles.

Footnotes

1. Extract from 'Travels of Cosmo the 3rd, Grand Duke of Tuscany, through England', *The Mariner's Mirror*, Vol 4, p157.

9. Coronation, Second Rate of 90 guns 1685

Location: **Kriegstein collection**
Scale: **1/51**

Dimensions			Gun ports	
	Model	*Ship*	Lower deck	26
Gun deck	160ft 3in (37.7in)	160ft 4in	Middle deck	26★
Breadth	45ft 0in (10.6in)	45ft 4in	Upper deck	26
Keel	–	132ft 0in	Quarterdeck	10
Depth	–	18ft 3½in	Poop	4
Tonnage	–	1442	Total	92

Ship dimensions from Dimension Book B (PRO). ★ Includes one port each side, forward of the cat supporter.

The *Coronation* was one of nine Second Rates of 90 guns included in the 'Thirty New Ships' instigated by Samuel Pepys, Secretary of the Admiralty, in 1675. They were all built in the period 1677–1685, and the *Coronation* was the last to be launched. This coincided with the accession to the Throne of James II in 1685, and the ship was named to commemorate the occasion. Prominently displayed on the quarter galleries and tafferal of the model are large crowned monograms of James, along with other Royal insignia. On this evidence, the model has been identified as the *Coronation*, as this ship was the only Second Rate launched during the reign of King James. Henry Culver measured the model many years ago, and the dimensions I have given are his. This is another example where the scale, at 1/51, must be calculated from the dimensions of the ship the model represents rather than the other way round, whether or not it works out at an apparently odd one. For instance, if this model was measured at the so-called 'normal' scale of 1/48, it would turn out to be something like 10ft 0in too short and 2ft 6in too narrow for any of these Second Rates. The *Coronation* was built at Portsmouth Dockyard by Mr Isaac Betts, and the model is reputed to have been made by him. It is a very fine and beautiful example of a seventeenth-century three-decker. The rigging is not original, and was added by Dr R C Anderson.

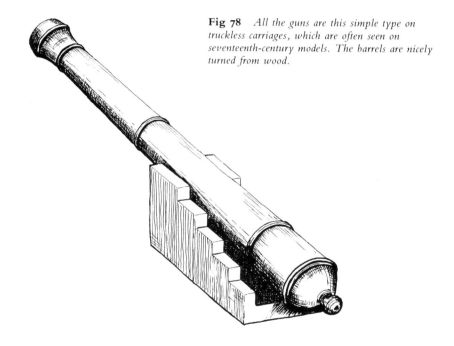

Fig 78 *All the guns are this simple type on truckless carriages, which are often seen on seventeenth-century models. The barrels are nicely turned from wood.*

Hull construction

The hull framing is the standard type, and the whole of the construction appears to be a dark variety of pear wood that is a particularly lovely golden brown colour. The deadwood aft is rather low, and to make up for this there are more transoms than usual on a model of a large ship of around this date.

Outboard fittings and details

The plank of the top sides is laid with single wide pieces between the three pairs of wales, and are scored to represent the seams. This plank is secured by scattered fastenings, but in contrast, the wales are fastened by many treenails, in a precise staggered formation, one up and one down, in every futtock and top timber. The 'black strake'

above the mainwales is indicated by a band of black paint. It looks as though the modeller had a little difficulty in positioning the main channel. While the forward end of the channel is in its correct place, on the upper of the two chainwales, and should retain this position the whole length of the channel, the aft end has been forced down to avoid encroaching on the ports. This has resulted in some of the chain plates being at an impossibly low angle. The mizzen channels are in an unusually low position, being below the upper deck ports. A few ships are known to have had the channels here instead of above the ports, notably the *Royal Charles* (ex-*Naseby*, 1655), but no

other contemporary model has been seen with the channels in this position. The fore and main channels are braced above by the typical arched 'spurs', four on the fore channel and six on the main. Very conspicuous below the upper wales is the row of scuppers that drained water from the upper deck. One or two other models of this period have scuppers, but these seem to be unique as they are decorated with lion mask 'gargoyles', which were common on Gothic buildings for shedding rain water. There is an ornate entry port to the middle deck, both to port and starboard. This is probably the earliest model of a three-decker to show the upward extension of the quarter

Plate 58 *Port broadside. This view shows well the great height above the waterline of these large ships with three decks. Kriegstein collection.*

galleries, allowing a third tier of lights at the level of the quarterdeck. At the stern is a single open stern walk at the level of the upper deck. The stern lights are glazed with mica, which is scored on the inside to represent the necessarily small panes in use at this time. The panes are indicated as diamond-shaped in the stern and rectangular in the quarter galleries. The large central lantern is made up of something like forty small panes. It shows an all-round light and has a representation of a small door on its forward side. The smaller lanterns at the quarters show a stern light only. Of interest at the head is the manner of securing the bowsprit. It appears to be a transitional arrangement showing the emergence of the timbers each side of the stem, but before they were extended upwards and carved with the 'knight', or 'noble', heads to become bollards.

Inboard details and fittings

Ninety guns are fitted, and fill all the ports except the luff port on the middle deck, forward of the cat supporter. A belt of planking is laid at the sides of all the decks, of just sufficient width for the guns to stand

on. The upper jeer capstan in the waist and the single main capstan are very early examples of the drumhead type invented by Sir Samuel Morland some time in the 1670s. Morland was a somewhat eccentric inventor and was still attempting to protect his ideas, which also included a chain pump, as late as 1786 by petitioning the King to prevent his rival, Sir Robert Gordon, from imitating his inventions.[1] The main capstan is on the lower deck, and like the jeer capstan in the waist, is fitted with ten bars. Its position is halfway between the main and mizzen masts. Of great interest on this model is a very rare example of a fully working whipstaff, which was the steering arrangement before the introduction of the wheel in about 1702. It is illustrated in Appendix V.

Decoration

The quality of the carved work on this model, and the extent of it, is quite exceptional, and can be compared with that on the famous model of the *Prince*, 1670, at the Science Museum. But there is one area that shows a complete contrast with the *Prince* and other models of the seventeenth

Plate 59 *Starboard quarter. Points of interest here are the unusually low position of the mizzen channel and the decorated scuppers. Also seen is the aft end of the main channel, where it has been forced down out of place by the port. The monogram of King James on this side is curious, as it is reversed. Kriegstein collection.*

century. This is the beak bulkhead, where
there is no decoration whatsoever, just two
moulded rails. Neither are there the usual
'knight-heads' carved on the bitts or timber
heads. Of the inboard carvings, the decoration of the quarterdeck bulkhead is the
most notable. The central doorway is
flanked by large female caryatids which
support an arched canopy with a lion head
each side. Above this is a huge Trophy of
Arms consisting of a drum, a visored helmet,
flags and a wheeled field gun. In the centre

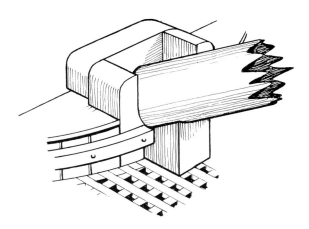

Plate 60 *Starboard bow. The foremost lower
deck port is much wider than the rest, presumably
to allow the gun an increased arc of fire, which
would be quite considerable. The lack of decoration
on the beak bulkhead is conspicuous. Kriegstein
collection.*

Fig 79 *Detail at the stem head. The cross piece,
which helps to prevent the bowsprit from lifting, is
directly against the beak bulkhead, and there is
only a very small platform forward of the*
*bulkhead. There is a step down to the gratings
between the head rails, which are normally level
with the platform.*

of this group is a small tablet bearing the incised initials JR, for James Rex. This bulkhead, and the one at the forecastle, is of open framed construction with no doors. The lion figurehead is a particularly splendid 'beast' and beautifully carved. He stands dignified and proud, with a naked child clinging to his mane. It is difficult to realise that it represents a carving some 15ft high. In the frieze at the top of the side towards the stern are several carved and gilded stars, which are probably those of the Order of the Garter. These stars also appear at the ends of the cat heads. The carvings of the tafferal are cut clear through, and the openings on the forward side have been carefully chamfered off. In the centre compartment, below the upper tier of stern lights, is the small but finely carved Achievement of Arms of the Stuarts.[1]

Colour scheme

Red: Inner side of gun port lids; gun carriages; muzzle of the lion figurehead and inner part of the Crown.

Black: Main- and chainwales; the 'black strake' above the mainwales; plank sheer and fife rails; beak bulkhead; stair cases; capstan; bitts; gun barrels; frieze at the top of the side.

Gilt: All carved work; moulded rails of the head, stern and broadside; cheeks of the head; edges of the plank sheers and channels; stern lanterns.

Plate 61 *Some idea of the inboard decoration can be gained from this view. The upper end of the whipstaff can just be seen protruding through the upper deck, aft of the mizzen mast. The long side gangways from the quarterdeck and poop lead to the typical winding staircases of this period. These are repeated also at the forecastle deck. Kriegstein collection.*

Footnote

1. Arthur Bryant, *Samuel Pepys, The Saviour of the Navy*, 1938, p 136.

10. Fourth Rate of 50 guns c1691

Location: **National Maritime Museum**
Scale: 1/48

Dimensions★			*Height to the lower edge of the mainwales*	
Gun deck	126ft 3in		At the stern	19ft 0in
Breadth	33ft 6in		Midships	12ft 0in
Depth	13ft 0in		At the stem	14ft 9in
Keel (touch)	108ft 6in, 648 tons			
Keel (calculated)	105ft 3in, 628 tons		*Gun ports*	
Timber and room	2ft 1in		Lower deck	22
Rake of the stem	16ft 9in at the harpin		Upper deck	22
Rake of the stern post	3ft 3in at the main transom (10°)		Quarterdeck	10
Draught of water	13ft 9in forward		Total	54
	15ft 0in aft			

The monograms of William and Mary on the stern clearly define the date of this model to the short period of five years between 1689 and 1694 when Queen Mary died. There are no particular features about the model which suggest an identification,

Plate 62 *Starboard broadside from aft. This view, and that of the port side, illustrates the lovely curve of the rising line of floor heads. The small square tuck has produced very fine lines to the hull at the stern. NMM.*

unless the carved figures on the quarter pieces and above the quarter galleries are of any significance. These are attired in Roman-style military dress which is not uncommon on seventeenth-century models, but in this case, it suggests a tentative connection with the *Centurion*, 1691. The dimensions of the model, which was probably made to an accurate scale of 1/48, almost exactly agree with those of several of the many Fourth Rates built in the 1690s,

particularly the *Centurion*, as the following table shows:

	Model	*Centurion*
Gun deck	126ft 3in	125ft 8in
Breadth	33ft 6in	33ft 2in
Depth in hold	13ft 0in	23ft 5in
Keel (calculated)	105ft 3in	105ft 0in
Tons	628	614

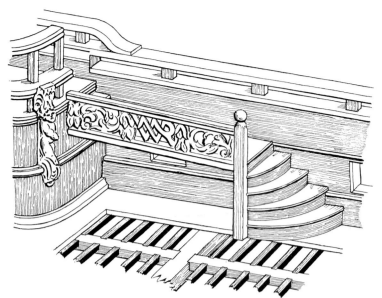

Fig 80 *The 'winding stairs' and gangway to the quarterdeck at the port side. The combined monogram of William and Mary is incorporated in the carving below the handrail of the gangway.*

Plate 64 *Unlike larger ships, these Fourth Rates of the late seventeenth century are notable for the sharp fine lines of the bows, which can be clearly seen here by the slight curve of the mainwales. The missing upper end of the main head rail brings into view the seat of easement with its shaped back rest. No bollards, or 'knightheads', are fitted at the stem, which is not uncommon on some models of this period. NMM.*

Plate 63 *Port broadside, from forward. NMM.*

This in itself does not prove the identification, but the model probably represents a ship that was built, and the *Centurion* appears to be the most likely. In comparing the full-sized dimensions, it is interesting to note that only a few inches' difference in breadth and length of keel produces an increase of no less than 14 tons for the model. Unfortunately, there is some damage at the head, and some of the guns and carvings are lost, but this does not detract from the model. It is beautifully made, and its craftsmanship, particularly the carved decoration, is superior to the quality which

was generally achieved by the 1690s.

Hull construction

The hull appears to be made from pear wood and is basically the standard type, except that the stern has the distinctive square tuck. This type of stern was probably quite common on Fourth Rates of the end of the seventeenth century. Relatively few models of Fourth Rates for this period exist, but of these at least four, dated 1687 to 1703, have a square tuck stern, which

certainly suggests that this type of construction was not unusual. The sided dimensions of the hull timbers indicate a timber and room of 2ft 1in, which yet again agrees exactly with that specified for Fourth Rates at this date. The draught of waterline is marked on the hull, giving a depth forward of 13ft 9in and 15ft 0in aft. In midships the waterline corresponds to the lower edge of the upper mainwale.

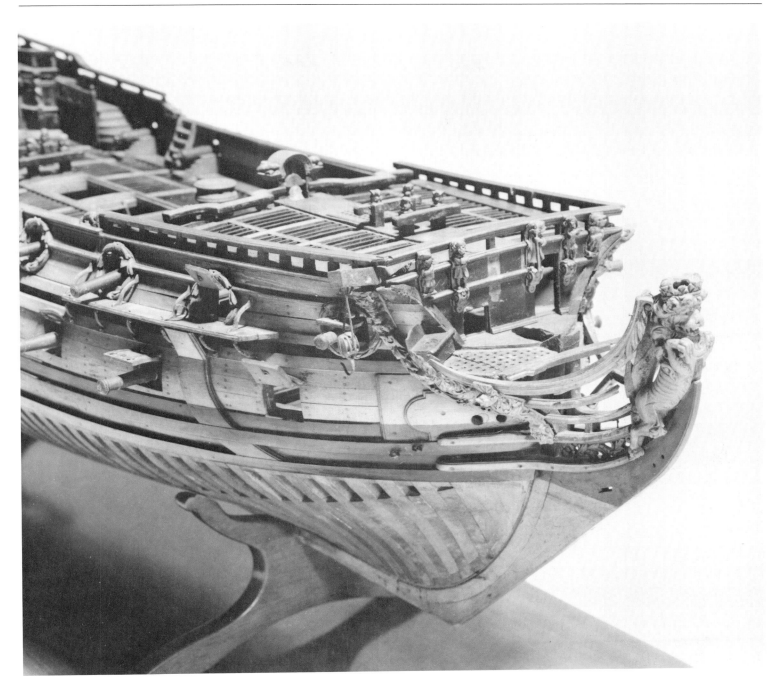

Outboard fittings and details

The mainwales are 12in broad, 9in thick and 1ft 3in apart. Above the wales is the 'black strake', a single plank of about 6in thick. This is one of the earliest models seen with the top side plank laid on in separate strakes. These are double fastened with treenails, in neat straight lines, into every top timber. The strake between the chainwales is left out, showing the top timbers, which always looks nice on a model. Simple curved and moulded rigols are fitted above the lower deck ports which are 2ft 8in broad and 2ft 4in deep. Two details connected with the bowsprit rigging are of interest, as neither is believed to have been introduced until the early eighteenth century: the knee of the head is bored for double bob stays, and there are two large eyebolts in the upper mainwale for bowsprit shrouds. The hawse holes were misplaced at first, as all four were filled in with a cross-grained plug, then rebored slightly outboard of the original holes. This is curious, as the holes have been shifted only about the equivalent of 6in, and the modeller must have been very particular to go to such trouble. The beak bulkhead has one door to port and a single chase port to starboard. Stern and quarter gallery lights have been fretted out from thin sheet metal.

Inboard fittings and details

The upper deck is completely planked except for the waist, where it is framed in

gesso and gold paint) the superb quality of it is more readily apparent. At the stern, the tafferal carvings depict male figures seated in two wheeled scallop shells, drawn by two sea horses. This carving is cut clear through, and the fore side is decorated with a simple design which follows the contours of the main carvings. The friezes between and below the stern lights are fretted out and carved from single pieces of thin wood, which are glued to a black painted backing; the figures that divide the intricate designs are added afterwards. The row of five human heads at the touch of the counter are remarkable carvings, and with their gentle and expressive features, they are in complete contrast to the grotesque animal mask heads that were prevalent in the seventeenth century. Figures standing at the quarters and seated above the quarter galleries are in Roman military dress. All rails of the stern, broadside and head are beautifully moulded in a number of different forms. The gun port wreaths are carved in a simple and elegant design of laurel leaves.

Colour scheme

Black: Mainwales, including the strake between, and the 'black strake'; plank sheer, and rails at the top of the side; breast rails, and stantions of the forecastle and quarterdecks; bulkheads; bitts; gun barrels; deck ledges; spirketting of the bulwarks on the upper and quarterdecks; string in the waist.
Red: Inside of port lids; capstan; stairs; gun carriages; bulwarks of the quarterdeck; quick work of the bulwarks in the waist.
Pale blue: Upper part of the counter; friezes at the top of the side.

Plate 65 *The beautiful and delicate carvings of the stern on this model are among the very finest examples of the seventeenth century. The Garter Stars on the square tuck are often shown on models with this type of stern. William and Mary's monograms are seldom seen apart, as these are, and are most often merged together.* NMM.

a distinctive pattern, with the beams and carlings in natural wood and jet black ledges. An oddity is that the forecastle and quarterdecks are also framed with two tiers of carlings each side, and again with black ledges, which is not seen at all on other models of any period. The guns are the simple type, with turned wood barrels on truckless carriages, which are glued to a narrow strip of deck plank at the side. The upper jeer capstan in the waist is a normal drumhead type, the lower one being just a warping, or veering, drum with no whelps. The capstan is made from a single piece of wood, probably turned to profile first, then the areas between the whelps, and the sockets for the bars cut out afterwards.

Decoration

All the carved work is left in the natural varnished wood, and perhaps because of this (the carvings not being obscured by

II. Boyne,
Third Rate of 80 guns
on two decks 1692

Location: **National Maritime Museum**
Scale: 1/48

Dimensions*				Height to lower edge of mainwales		
	Model	*Ship*		At the wing transom	23ft 3in	
Gun deck	157ft 0in	157ft 0in		In midships	16ft 3in	
Breadth	40ft 9in	41ft 3in		At the stem	19ft 3in	
Keel (touch)	130ft 6in, 1153 tons	128ft 2in, 1160 tons		*Gun ports*		
Keel (calculated)	128ft 7in, 1136 tons			Lower deck	28	
Timber and room	2ft 5in			Upper deck	28	
Rake of the stem	22ft 6in at the harpin			Forecastle	6	
Rake of the stern post	6ft 6in at the main transom (13°)			Quarterdeck	14	
				Poop deck	4	
				Total	80	

The *Boyne* was built at Deptford Dockyard in 1692 by Mr Fisher Harding. One of the most certainly identified of all models, this model of the *Boyne* is one of the very few examples of a Third Rate of 80 guns on two decks. Another, at the Naval Academy Museum, Annapolis,[1] may be a model of the *Sussex*, 1693, a ship of the same class as the *Boyne*. This model, incidentally, is an unusual example of a two-decker with an entry port on the upper deck. The dimensions of the model agree almost exactly with those of the *Boyne*, and on the break of the poop deck is the following inscription: 'YE BOYNE Bt BY MR HARDING DEP SA...'. The last part of this is difficult to make out. DEP is an abbreviation for Deptford, and there are one or two more letters after SA, but what this signifies is not obvious. Prior to Dr R C Anderson's identification of this model as far back as 1912, it was known as the *Winchelsea*, 1694, a small ship of 32 guns.[2] An old photograph of the model clearly shows the label bearing this description in place on the stand. It seems scarcely possible that an error of this magnitude would have been made, even in those days, when there were many uncertain identifications, and a likely explanation is that it was simply a case of a mix-up of labels at some early period. Where the model that could be identified as that of the *Winchelsea* is, is difficult to determine. This model was in the collection of King William IV, and was given by him to Greenwich Hospital in

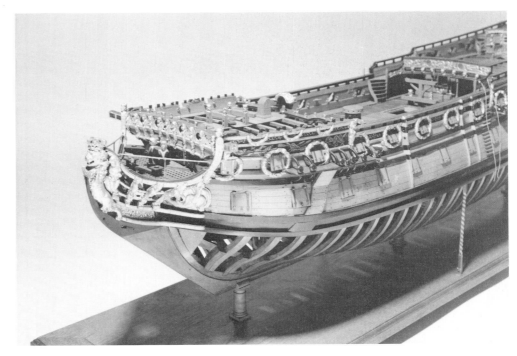

Plate 66 *Port side from forward. The large carving surrounding the hawse holes is uncommon, and there are a greater number of carved brackets on the forecastle bulkhead than usual.* NMM.

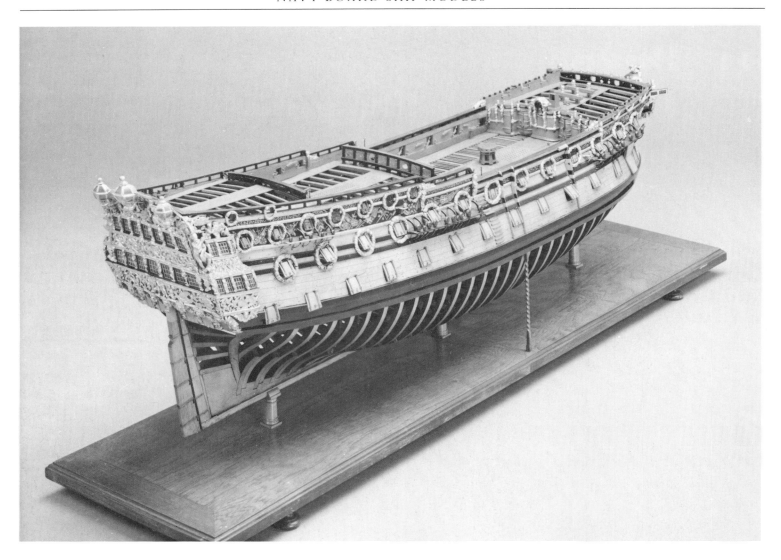

1830, then, via the Royal Naval Museum to the National Maritime Museum on its establishment in 1937.

Hull construction

The distinctive open framing of this model affords a clear view of the interior of the hull. Of interest here are the riding bitts, or 'carrick bitts' as they were generally known in the seventeenth century. Instead of the bitt pins being straight, with their heels stepped on the ceiling, these curve in towards each other at about the level of the orlop deck and unite to form a common step on the keelson. Like all ships with a single main capstan on the lower deck, the barrel of it is taken down and stepped on the orlop deck. This deck is not fitted on the model, but for the purpose of stepping the capstan, a fore and aft beam has been

fitted between two pillars standing on the keelson. A single footwale is fitted each side, with its upper edge level with the floor heads. This strake is about 1ft 6in broad and 6in thick. The lower deck beam clamps are very large: about the equivalent of 2ft 0in broad and 1ft 0in thick. They are bearded back on the lower edges to half the thickness. Each of the lower deck beams is let down in the clamps to a depth sufficient for the thinner ledges to rest on the clamps and remain flush with the upper side of the beams. All the fore and aft strakes in the hold are treenailed into every timber of the frame. The precise nature of this internal work, which cannot normally be seen, is impressive, particularly the way in which the beams have been let down into the clamps, with all the variations of angle that this entails.

Plate 67 *Starboard side from aft. NMM.*

Outboard fittings and details

Each of the two mainwales is 13½in broad and 12in thick, with a thinner strake of 2ft 3in broad between them. The chainwales are 10in broad and 9in thick, with 10in between them. The plank between the two pairs of wales is laid on in one broad piece, and is deeply scored and inked in to represent the seams between five planks. Brass pins have been used as fastenings, two in each plank, at each timber. The fastenings

Plate 68 *The stern. This view shows well the open framing of hull. It is the same as on a 'normal' model, except that every other floor and futtock has been left out. NMM.*

extend up in line with the futtocks, showing that the heads of these timbers reach up at least as high as the chainwales. A small bolster is fitted to the top of the side, aft of the chesstree, to take the chafe of the main course tack. Two minor features at the head are interesting as they show an early appearance on this model. The first of these is the 'false rail', which was an extra smaller timber fastened to the upper side of the main head rail. This example is very plain, and was probably fitted originally to take the chafe of the various ropes that would be used in this area for catting the anchor, etc. The false rail developed considerably in later years, with the addition of two or more fair-leads and a decorative upper end. The second feature is the 'berthing rail', for supporting a tarpaulin spread across the beak head. Those on models up to about the mid-eighteenth century are invariably of rope, taken up at the aft end by two small deadeyes and a lanyard, but this example is metal. It is simply an iron bar hooked into an eye bolt abaft the figurehead, and another at the upper end of the main head rail. The rail is supported in the centre by a single iron stantion. At the stern, the frames and glazing bars of the lights are made from very thin strip metal, about $\frac{1}{16}$in wide, and soldered at the intersections. The lights are glazed with mica. An interesting note on the glazing of ships of this period is given in the contract-specification for the *Humber*, 1693, an 80 of the same class as the *Boyne*.[3] The contract gives an early example of the use of 'stone ground' glass instead of mica, which had been usual, and specifies the minimum and maximum sizes of the panes: 'Noe more than 12in one way and 10in the other. Nor less than 9in by 7in'. These sizes are virtually the same as those on the model.

Inboard fittings and details

The upper deck in the waist has a somewhat unusual construction, as there is no outer tier of carlings and therefore no short ledges. Instead, closely spaced and substantial half beams have been placed between the side and the carlings at the sides of the hatches. Although the contract for the *Humber* calls for two tiers of carlings, the deck on the model has not been simplified as it probably shows an alternative way of doing it. The carlings that make the sides of the hatches are large, and the full length of the waist. They are let down in the beams about half

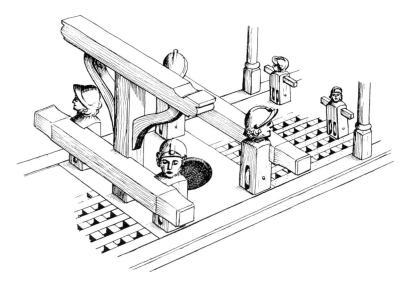

Fig 81 *Detail of the main jeer, top sail sheet bitts and gallows, from forward. The grating abaft the bitts has double fastenings marked in at the intersection of the ledges and battens.*

Fig 82 *Aft end of the poop deck, showing one of the very small trumpeter's cabins, complete with cot. Note the finely shaped end to the athwartship bench seat. The sheave set into the carving on the rail, above the cabin, is for the main brace.*

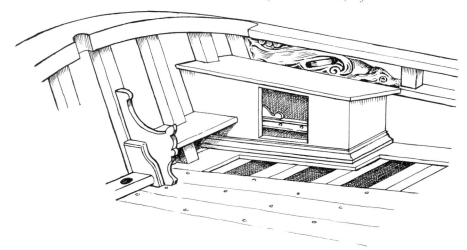

their depth, the upstanding part forming the coamings. This does agree with the contract, as it specifies that 'the long coaming carlings shall be 12in square'. The lower deck is framed in the conventional manner, with two tiers of short carlings each side. The gratings are the 'pierced' type and particularly well made. On some of them, the modeller has carefully marked in double fastenings at the intersections of the battens and ledges. On each deck is a narrow belt of planking at the side, scored to represent the seams of three strakes. It is fastened with scattered treenails.

Below each port on the upper deck a shallow recess the same width as the port has been cut out across the breadth of the spirketting. Except for a few at the bow and stern, these recesses have been carefully

filled back in and painted over. This is intriguing, and the only explanation I can offer is that it may have been intended originally to fit guns, and the recesses were cut out to locate the simple truckless carriages that were common on models of the seventeenth century. The gallows, for supporting the ends of the spare top masts and spars, is the earliest example I have seen. It is also the only example where the cross piece is supported on a single, central, post. On all others either the jeer or the topsail sheet bitts are extended upwards to take the cross piece. With a gallows like this, it is not difficult to understand how the term originated. The quarterdeck bulkhead illustrates another change that took place at about this date. It is quite plain and set back under the deck about 6ft, unlike

Fig 83 *Two of the many different designs of Trophies of Arms that are painted in the friezes at the top of the side.*

Fig 84 *The inscription at the break of the poop deck. The last part of it is not clear enough to be absolutely certain as to what it represents.*

Plate 69 *The forecastle bulkhead and belfry. Details here are the 'piss-dale' on the starboard side, and the doors of the bulkhead, and the cabins at the side. The absence of an outer tier of carlings on deck can also be seen. Author.*

the bulkheads of earlier models that were lavishly decorated and set directly under the break of the deck. The bulkhead is actually in much the same position as previously on ships of comparable class, and the overhang is mostly due to an increased length of the quarterdeck. In the centre of the roundhouse bulkhead, just above the deck, is a six-paned light providing a lookout for the helmsman on the whipstaff, who would be on the deck below. Aft of the bulkhead, and enclosing the light, is a small box-like structure with a grating above. Directly below this 'companion', and set in the upper deck, is the pivot, or 'rowle', for the whipstaff. A few other models show a rowle, but this one is particularly interesting as the surround to the rowle has an angled recess each side for the whipstaff when laid over to its full extent (see Appendix V).

At the aft end of the poop are the two trumpeter's cabins, one on each side. The contract mentions four cabins, and in this case the extra two would probably be athwartship and take the place of the bench seats against the tafferal. These cabins are very small, and in each of them is a finely made cot — a rare illustration of sleeping arrangements on models. The cat tails at the forward end of the forecastle deck are united by a well fitted, long hooked scarph.

Decoration

The carved work is typical of the decoration of ships during the reign of William and Mary. Notable at the head is the large carving surrounding the hawse holes and the greater than usual number of brackets on the beak bulkhead. At the stern the intertwined monogram of William and Mary is shown between the tiers of lights on the starboard quarter gallery, but on the port side the monogram is that of William alone. The frieze at the top of the side is painted with many different and bold designs, of Trophies of Arms. Some are of shields, with flags and gun cleaning

implements, and others of crossed muskets and pistols, with drums, swords and spears. The friezes are painted in gold on a black background. Much of the inboard work is painted red, and with the black details and the gilt of the carvings, the result is a brilliantly colourful model. It may have been even more so, as there is some evidence that it was once fitted (or perhaps it was intended to fit them) with flag poles and flags that decorated a ship at the launching ceremony. There is a step and bracket aft of the figurehead for a jack staff, and moulded turnings on the decks at the positions of the masts. These are bored out with a quite small hole, and are typical fittings on models that display these flag poles.

Colour scheme

Red: All inboard works, except for the decks; inside of stern lanterns; the ground

of the stern carvings; inside of port lids.
Black: Main- and chainwales; channels and spurs; rails at the top of the side; quarterdeck port lids; inside of head timbers; false rail; seats of ease; lower part of the beak bulkhead; stern light surrounds; the ground of the carvings on the upper counter.
Blue: Lower counter; panels of the beak bulkhead.
Gilt: All carvings; stern lanterns; port wreaths; belfry; moulding rails; head rails and cheeks; edges of channels.

Footnotes

1. Henry Huddleston Rogers, *Collection of Ship Models, USNA Museum* (Naval Institute Press, Annapolis).
2. *The Mariner's Mirror*, Vol 2, pp 264–6.
3. NMM SPB/8, contract for the *Humber* or *Newark*.

12. Lizard,
Sixth Rate of 24 guns 1697

Location: **Pitt-Rivers Museum, Oxford**
Scale: 1/48

Dimensions				Gun ports		
	Model	*Ship*		Main deck		22
Gun deck	95ft 0in	95ft 0in		Quarterdeck		8
Breadth	25ft 0in	25ft 0in		Total		30
Depth	–	10ft 10in				
Keel (for tonnage)	–	79ft 4in				
Tons	–	263¾				
Timber and room	1ft 10in	–				

Dimensions of the *Lizard* are from Dimension Book B.

This attractive little model is believed to have been made by the Master Shipwright Robert Shortis. It has been identified as the *Lizard* on the evidence of the dimensions, the initials RS and the date, '97, both of which are carved on the ornamental cradles.

The *Lizard* was built by Shortis at Sheerness Dockyard and was launched in 1697. Dr George Clarke gave this model and two others to the Ashmolean Museum, Oxford, at some time between 1719 and his death in 1736.[1] All three were subsequently trans-ferred to the Pitt-Rivers Museum in 1886,[2] where they have remained ever since, in a

Plate 70 *Port broadside.* Pitt-Rivers Museum.

very large display case, along with a number of other models. Dr Clarke was a prominent figure in the Navy, and was Secretary to the Admiralty, 1702–05, and a Lord of the Admiralty, 1710–14. He was also Secretary to Prince George of Denmark, the husband of Queen Anne, for several years until his dismissal in 1705.[3] It is interesting to note this connection, as Prince George, no less a person than Lord High Admiral of the Navy, is known to have been an enthusiastic builder of ship models.[4] Nineteenth-century

Plate 71 *Port stern quarter. The Royal Arms on the standard are in the reversed position from this side.* Pitt-Rivers Museum.

catalogues of the Ashmolean Museum list the model as 'a model of the Royal Yacht'.

Hull construction

This model is one of two that have been seen with the numbered and lettered station lines marked on the starboard side of the keel. Also marked are the intermediate spacings of the timber and rooms, which give a dimension of 1ft 10in and agree perfectly with those given in several contract-specifications for Sixth Rates of the 1690s.[5] The heels of the futtocks terminate 1ft 0in from the keel and have a scarph with the floors of 5ft 0in, giving a length of floors in midships of 13ft 0in, or a little over half

the breadth. This hull is a good illustration of how the rising lines of the floor heads, as they would appear on the body plan, can differ considerably between the fore and aft bodies. From the stern it is clear that the 'diagonal' of the rising line is almost vertical, but from the bows it is very much less so. In the hold are wide fore and aft strakes made of pine, equal in width to the scarph of the timbers, and with edges flush with the ends of the futtocks and floors. The keelson is scored down on the floors about 3in and all the mast steps are fitted. Except for the pine strakes in the hold, the hull is constructed from pear wood.

Plate 72 *Detail of the port side, showing the quarter 'badge'. The decorative frieze is in gold on a black background.* Author.

Outboard fittings and details

The top side plank is deeply scored and inked to represent the seams and butts between the individual strakes. Chain plates are the short curved type, and bolted to the upper mainwale. They are made from brass, as are the port lid straps, ring eyes and other metal fittings. The channels are braced above by small spurs, four on the fore channel, five on the main and three on the mizzen. The stern lanterns are made from solid glass around which the base, finial and framework of lead, or perhaps pewter, is assembled and soldered. All three show a stern light only. The aforementioned contracts specify oar ports: 'To cut out and fix so many Oar Scuttles between the ports as shall be thought convenient by the Surveyor of the Navy'. But it is evident that in the case of this model it was not thought to be convenient. Unfortunately, a contract for the *Lizard* itself is not included among the five that exist for Sixth Rates of the 1690s. These are all dated 1694, for named ships, and are copies of the same specification for sending to the various yards. Apart from the absence of the oar scuttles, the model differs in a number of respects from these contracts, and it is possible that the specification was amended for the *Lizard*, of a slightly later date. On the other hand, shipwrights were known to have made considerable departures from the specifications, and these differences may not be particularly relevant.

Inboard fittings and details

The main deck is framed with a single tier of carlings each side, which form the sides of the hatches, and the partners for the capstans and masts. There are three small hatches in the waist, one forward of the jeer capstan and the other two fore and aft of the main mast. The gratings are the pierced type, with a much greater camber than usual. These are set in deep coamings which are mitred to the cambered head ledges. The jeer capstan is made from a single piece of wood, and is 4ft 0in high, with a diameter at the drumhead of 3ft 0in. The capstan is fitted with ten bars which are 6ft 0in long. Partners for a main capstan are shown between the quarterdeck bulkhead and the aftmost hatch, but the capstan is missing or perhaps was never fitted. The single pair of riding bitts are in the open waist, directly abaft the forecastle bulkhead, where the anchor cables would lead through two doorways. The bulkhead is full width, with a small cabin each side. This differs from the contracts, as they specify 'a very slight bulkhead without cabins, fit only to shelter the fire hearth from the weather'. This mention of the fire hearth is interesting, as it goes on, 'To build on *each inside* within the bulkhead, one small fire hearth for a double kettle, lining the *side* in the wake thereof with double white plates' (author's italics). Whether this actually means one each side is not clear, but it certainly appears that the fire hearth was intended to be at

the side of the ship instead of in the usual place, at the middle of the bulkhead. This is confirmed by the model, as there is a fire hearth on the starboard side, between the first and second gun ports. It is quite a simple thing, made from a block of wood, with two openings in the top for the 'kettles' and a recess below to represent a fire door. At the port side is another small structure that looks as though it may be a separate oven. Neither of these show any indication of a chimney. If the measurements can be trusted, there would be very little headroom

for the cook below the forecastle, as it is only 5ft 0in plank to plank, which would give about 4ft 3in in height below the beams. The height below the quarterdeck is 6ft 0in plank to plank. The quarterdeck bulkhead is set back under the break of deck about 3 to 4ft, and has small cabins each side. Like the forecastle bulkhead, it has two pairs of doors. One door of each pair is about twice as wide as the other, and contains a small port with a side hung lid. At the aft end of the quarterdeck are two grilled hutches for small livestock. These would have to be portable, as they obscure two circular ports pierced in the stern. Steering is by tiller on the quarterdeck, which engages with the rudder head inside a small casing between the hutches. The tiller is brass (specified as iron in the con-

tracts) and about 14ft long. The forward end is turned up about 3ft and terminates in a small ball end.

Decoration

The centre of the tafferal is taken up by a crowned cartouche, containing the Arms surrounded by the Garter, of William III. Cherubs each side suspend a mantling draped behind the Arms. In the centre

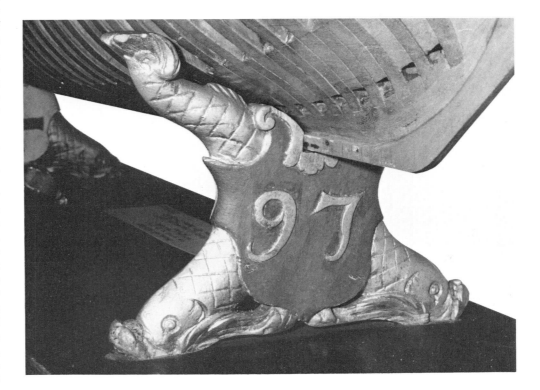

Plate 73 *The forward cradle showing the date of the model. The dolphins and the date are gilt, with the centre shield in red. At the aft side of the cradle, the shield is painted white with a red St George's Cross. The aft cradle is the same, but with the initials RS.* Author.

compartment between the stern lights is another Crowned Arms, probably of a Peer such as a Duke or an Earl who had a connection with the Admiralty. The Arms are simply carved, and contain a single large Lion Rampant, but with no detail that would enable the Arms to be positively identified. One Peer whose Arms were mainly a single Lion Rampant was John Egerton, Third Earl of Bridgewater, who achieved high positions in the Admiralty and was First Lord by 1700.[6] The Earl's Arms included three small Pheons, or arrow heads, and it is just possible that those on the model are his, but the carver has not included what would be very small detail. It is a pity that, in all these illustrations of Heraldry, they are not finished in the correct tinctures instead of being all gilded, which would greatly help in identification. Prominently displayed at the position of the main mast is the flag pole flying the Royal Standard. Instead of bearing the Arms of William III, as it should for this date of 1697, they are those of the Stuarts in use 1603–89 and 1702–07. A probable explanation for this is that the Standard has been exchanged by mistake with that on another

of Dr Clarke's models, a galley-frigate, dated 1702, which does bear the Arms of William. The Standard is beautifully painted, in white, red and gold, and if contemporary, as it appears to be, is a rare and early example. The model as well is equally uncommon, as very few Sixth Rates of the seventeenth century are known to exist.

Colour scheme

Black: Wales; plank sheer; rails at the top of the side; breast rails and stantions at the break of the decks; bitts; stairs; bulkheads; inside of head timbers; flag poles.

Red: Inside of gun port lids.

Gilt: All carved work; moulded rails; lanterns; belfry; trucks of the flag poles.

Footnotes

1. P B Duncan, *A Catalogue of the Ashmolean Museum, Descriptive of the Zoological Specimens, Antiquities, Coins and Miscellaneous Curiosities*, (Oxford, 1836).
2. Manuscript Catalogue, Ashmolean Museum, 1886.
3. *Dictionary of National Biography*.
4. David Green, *Queen Anne* (1970), pp116, 202.
5. PRO Adm 106/3070 and 106/3071.
6. *Dictionary of National Biography*.

13. First Rate of 96 guns c1702

Location: **National Maritime Museum**
Scale: 1/60

Dimensions* (at a scale of 1/60)		Gun ports	
Gun deck	169ft 4in	Lower deck	28
Breadth	48ft 8in	Middle deck	26
Keel (calculated)	138ft 8in, 1746 tons	Upper deck	26
Keel (touch)	140ft 4in, 1767 tons	Quarterdeck	10
Timber and room	2ft 5in	Forecastle	4
Rake of the stem	27ft 6in at the harpin	Poop	2
Rake of the stern post	4ft 0in at the main transom	Total	96

This unidentified three-decker is one of those puzzling models where the dimensions calculated from an even scale can be misleading. At a scale of 1/60 ($\frac{1}{5}$in), the dimensions are very close to those of a First Rate, but the number and arrangement of gun ports is more suggestive of a Second Rate. There are a total of 96 broadside ports, which does not include a further one each side taken up by the very unusual secondary entry ports on the upper deck. Whether guns would be employed in entry ports is not entirely clear, but if the model is of a First Rate – which would have to carry up to 100 guns – it could only be done by placing a gun in every port, with another two on the poop. Very few models of First Rates exist from around the turn of the eighteenth century to enable a comparison, but one of the *Royal Sovereign* rebuilt in 1701 has no fewer than 112.[1] The Second Rate 90s built during the period 1678–85 were specified to have 94 ports, without any on the poop.[2] On the Gun Establishment of

Plate 74 *Port broadside from aft. The unique second entry port to the upper deck can be seen here. On other models that have an entry port on the middle deck, the access is invariably from forward instead of aft, as on this one. The absence of the vertical skids on the ship's side is noticeable, and is a surprising omission. The jeer capstan in the waist is farther forward than on ships with two decks to clear the bars of the second capstan on the middle deck, which was usual on First and Second Rates. NMM.*

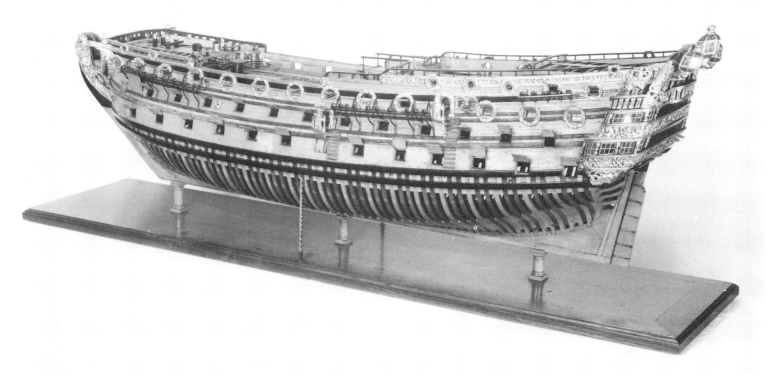

1703, Second Rates were classed as ships of 86/96 guns, and therefore had to have at least 96 ports. It is probable, then, that the model represents a Second Rate, in which case the dimensions would have to be calculated from a ratio of at, or very close to, 1/57. This would not be unusual considering the odd scales often used by early modelmakers. As a matter of interest, the dimensions at 1/57 are 160ft 10in on the gun deck, with a breadth of 46ft 3in, but this is of no real value for identification purposes.

to the monogram, we have to bear in mind that, although the figurehead must have been carved in the first year or two after the accession of Queen Anne in 1702, the model may have been made over quite a long period and actually begun in the late 1690s.

Seven Second Rates were built or rebuilt in the period 1697–1702. The new ships were the *Association*, the *Barfleur* and the *Namur*, all launched in 1697, and the *Triumph*, 1698. Rebuilt ships were the *Prince George* and the *St George*, both in 1701, and

it to Greenwich Hospital.

Hull construction

The distinctive pattern of the light and dark wood used for the hull framing can be clearly seen in the photographs. This is more than mere decorative work, as the futtocks made from the light wood almost certainly indicate the positions of the 'station lines', or body profiles. In midships,

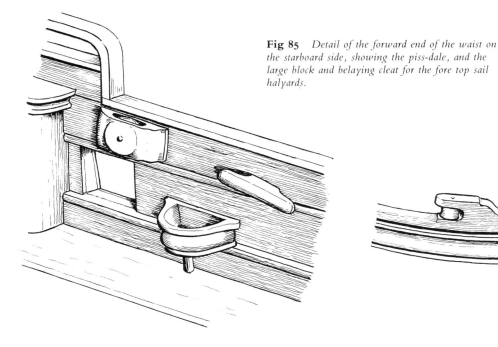

Fig 85 *Detail of the forward end of the waist on the starboard side, showing the piss-dale, and the large block and belaying cleat for the fore top sail halyards.*

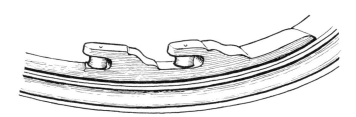

Fig 86 *The fair leads on the main head rail. No other model has been seen with the fair leads fitted with rollers.*

The apparent date – at approximately 1702 – is suggested by the monogram of Queen Anne on the figurehead, and the lavish decoration, which was ordered to be greatly reduced by the Admiralty in 1703. Other indications of date are the fore and main channels in the raised position above the middle deck ports, a change that was introduced generally in the first few years of the eighteenth century, and the 'round-houses' or latrines each side of the beak bulkhead, an innovation of around the same time. It seems fairly safe to say that the date is no later than 1703 due to the decoration, but as features and monograms are not an infallible guide, it is possible that the model represents a ship built before then, perhaps in the late seventeenth century. There is no reason to suppose, because the new features were only generally introduced in the early eighteenth century, that they were unknown a few years earlier. With regard

the *Royal Katherine*, 1702. There is no particular evidence to suggest which ship the model represents, and the figurehead – although a very distinctive one – appears to have no connection with the names of any of the above ships, unlike those on some other three-deckers of the time. It is unlikely, however, that the model is not of a named ship, and there is probably a connection with one of the Second Rates built at the time if we did but know it. Whatever it is, the model is an interesting one for illustrating the transitional features that suddenly appeared at around the turn of the eighteenth century. In addition to those mentioned above, the central gang-way from the quarterdeck to the main mast is shown, and perhaps most importantly, the windlass and rope steering system is fitted which superseded the old whipstaff.

The model was in the collection of King William IV until 1830, when he presented

there are three light futtocks, spaced at two timber and rooms apart, and the foremost of these is marked on the aft side with the usual symbol for midships, a cross within a circle. The position of this midship bend is marked up to the top of the side with a scribed line. This initial group probably represents 'dead flat', or the length of the hull that did not change its shape. From thereon, towards bow and stern, the light futtocks are spaced at every third timber

Plate 75 *The small balcony at the level of the quarterdeck may have been an afterthought, as there is no access to it from the accommodation. The circular apertures each side of the balcony and below the breast rail of the gallery below, although glazed, are probably loop holes for small pieces of ordnance. NMM.*

and room, which was quite usual for the spacing of the station lines of this period. The futtocks are either numbered or lettered on the sides, in pencil on the light ones, but to make it more clear on the dark wood they have either been incised or dotted in with a sharp point. The timber and room, at 2ft 5in, would be a usual dimension for a large ship of the early eighteenth century.

Fig 87   *The bell hung on simple metal brackets instead of in a belfry is highly unusual. The curved metal bar on the cross beam is for the bell rope, which would hang down to the deck below.*

Outboard fittings and details

The immediate result of raising the fore and main channels on ships with three decks was that the chain plates became more efficient. They are shown on this model as still slightly curved, but much longer, and fastened to the side with separate, double bolted preventer plates. The channels are braced above by large serpentine-shaped spurs. On the upper deck, the three aftmost ports are fitted with four paned glazed lights, and the next one forward of these is taken up by the entry port. This is in addition to the one in the usual position on the middle deck, and the model is probably the only one known with two entry ports on each side. The ports, except for those sheltered by the channels, have nicely shaped rigols fitted above them. Of interest at the head is a narrow athwartship cat walk consisting of gratings supported by a moulded rail. Each end of the cat walk rests on the tops of the roundhouses. The fair-leads on the false rail of the main head rail are fitted with small rollers. Normally the false rail just had several small projections on the upper side, that have sometimes

Fig 88   *Quarterdeck gangway and stairs. The plain and simple construction of the stairs is in complete contrast to the elaborate winding staircases of the seventeenth-century First and Second Rates.*

been associated with the bumkin, but this evidence of the rollers certainly suggests that they are fair-leads, probably for handling the ropes used to assist in catting the anchors. At the stern are recessed open galleries at the level of the middle and upper decks, and a curious semicircular balcony at the quarterdeck. Also at this level are small balconies on the quarter galleries, with direct access to the cabin beneath the poop deck. The attractive stern lanterns are the short-lived parallel-sided type that was

Fig 89   *The steering windlass is on the quarterdeck abaft the position of the mizzen mast, and is the earliest known evidence of a steering system worked by rope.*

the fashion between the globular ones of the seventeenth century and the tapered lanterns that became standard in the eighteenth century. The lanterns are glazed with thin glass, and the glazing bars are simulated, like all the rest of the stern lights, by cut-out paper glued on the glass.

Inboard fittings and details

The upper deck in the waist is framed with long and short carlings. The long ones that form the sides of the hatches are the full length of the waist, and are let down in the deck beams about half their thickness, enough remaining above the beams to provide the coamings for the gratings. These carlings are grooved on their outboard edges to take the athwartship ledges between there and the outer tier of short carlings. The gratings are the pierced type. Two of them, one on the quarterdeck and one on the forecastle, are rather strangely set in an oval-shaped ventilation hatch. The forecastle bulkhead is set deeply under the break of the deck, and the centre part of it is taken up by a low glazed companion to provide light to the galley, which would be on the middle deck below. The bell, on its simple iron stand, is a complete anomaly on this highly decorated model, and difficult to understand compared with the usual elaborate belfries. A small contemporary alteration was made to the fore top sail

sheet bitts on the forecastle. These bitts, forward of the fore mast, were first placed on the fore side of a beam, but were then shifted to the aft side. The scores in the beam, and the holes in the deck where the bitts originally stood, have been very carefully filled in. This alteration has also been seen on another model, a Fourth Rate of about 1710, and it must have been considered important to have gone to this trouble. The early example of the central gangway from the quarterdeck is made from a grating between fore and aft beams, which are supported by the cross piece, or 'gallows', of the jeer bitts aft of the main mast. This is unlike the usual arrangement, as invariably, the gallows are on the top sail sheet bitts, and in these cases the gangway extends forward and encloses the mast. The grating of the gangway is large and made

from a single sheet of wood which is pierced with some 400 perfectly squared out holes. At the aft end of the poop deck are two athwartship hutches, with a pivoting step for lowering the ensign staff between them. Perhaps the most important feature on this model is the steering arrangement, for it is believed to be the earliest known, showing the rope steering system that superseded the whipstaff. It also shows the forerunner to the wheel that was introduced about 1703. The steering is worked by an athwartship rope drum with a cranked handle at each end and mounted on a simple iron stand. This windlass is on the quarterdeck, aft of the mizzen mast. Models rarely have the steering rope actually fitted, as on this one, which is fortunate on this early example, as the rope can be followed down to below the middle deck, where it is taken to the

Plate 76 *The head. Points of interest here are wreathed chase ports of the forecastle deck and the attractive decoration of the head timbers. The figurehead appears to depict the legend of Europa and the Bull. Note the scattered treenails in the plank of the side. NMM.*

tiller via sheaves in large knees fastened to the side. The geometry of this is illustrated in Appendix V.

Decoration

One of the most notable aspects of the decoration on this model is internal. Between the gun ports on the upper deck, in way of the aft accommodation, is a

a rosette. The port wreaths are carved with a number of different floral designs. At the stern, the carvings of the tafferal depict a warrior with a shield to port, and a female figure to starboard, also bearing a shield, which contains a grotesque head. This group suggests Perseus and Athene. In classical mythology, Perseus slew the Gorgon, Medusa, and gave the head to Athene, who placed it on her shield. The areas of the counter, and between the galleries, are covered with a profusion of small carvings in shallow relief, of trophies, cherubs and swans. The whole effect of the decoration on this model is rather gaudy, and does not have the refined quality usual at this period.

Colour scheme

Black: Wales; channels; chain plates, spurs and deadeyes; plank sheer and fife rails; timber heads; beak bulkhead; lower counter; capstan; hatch coamings; galley chimney; belfry; bitts; stem head and bollards; seats of ease; false rail of the main head rail.

Red: Inside of gun ports and port lids; forward side of the tafferal; hutches on the poop deck; cat tails; ground between the stern and quarter gallery carvings.

Blue: Quarterdeck, poop and forecastle bulkheads; deck heads of the open stern galleries; panels at top and bottom of the stern lanterns.

White: Glazing bars and frames of the lanterns and stern lights.

Gilt: All carved work; moulded rails of the side, stern and head; the bell; head cheeks; base and finials of the lanterns.

Footnotes

1. This model of the *Royal Sovereign* is believed to have been given to Peter the Great, Czar of Russia, by King William III, and is now in the Naval Museum, Leningrad, USSR.
2. See Brian Lavery, *Ship of the Line* (London 1983) Vol 1, p196.

Plate 78 *Bow framing. The fore side of the stem is scribed in, and there is a finely fitted stem/keel scarph.* Author.

remarkable series of large mural paintings. They have not been seen clearly enough to describe them, but they are beautifully executed in bright colours, and seem to be of scenes from classical mythology. The paintings, and also the gun ports in this area, are contained within gilded frames. The figurehead is a fine group consisting of a female figure and a double-headed bull, with a cupid hovering above, which apparently depicts the legend of the abduction of Europa by Zeus. The head timbers are decorated with double twist turned columns, connected at top and bottom by shell-like ornaments, and in the centre by

14. Third Rate of 70 guns c1702

Location: **Kriegstein collection**
Scale: 1/48

Dimensions		Gun ports	
Gun deck	153ft 0in	Lower deck	26
Breadth	40ft 0in	Upper deck	28
Keel (touch)	129ft 0in, 1098 tons	Quarterdeck	14
Keel (calculated)	127ft 6in, 1085 tons	Total	68
Timber and room	2ft 4in		

With the number of changes that were taking place in the first two or three years of the eighteenth century, models which date from that time are of particular interest. Several other Third Rate 70s exist of the 1690s and after about 1705, but this fine and very early Queen Anne model is probably the only one known of the transitional period, and as such, is an important link in the development of the class. Although the dimensions are similar to a number of Third Rates that were built or rebuilt in the late seventeenth and early eighteenth centuries, there are no particular features allowing the model to be identified. This does not detract from the model, as it is a lovely example, and interest lies in the number of features that were going out of fashion, and others that have appeared for the first time which became standard in later years. The design is interesting for the arrangement of gun ports and the very short poop, which is little more than half the length of those on other models of Third Rate 70s of both earlier and later dates. The normal 70s of the time were pierced with twenty-six ports on each of the two main tiers, with twelve on the quarterdeck, and would be armed with four guns on the forecastle and four on the poop, which did not require ports.

With the extra two ports crowded into the quarterdeck and two more on the upper deck, it appears that the model may be an early design for 70 with no armament at all on the poop, as they were in later times. The model was originally in the possession of Thomas Herbert, Earl of Pembroke. The Earl was Lord High Admiral in 1701, and again for a short period following the death of Prince George in 1707.[1]

Plate 79 *Port broadside. The very short poop and the closely spaced ports on the quarterdeck are noticeable. Models of 70s normally have six a side until after the gun establishment of 1716. Kriegstein collection.*

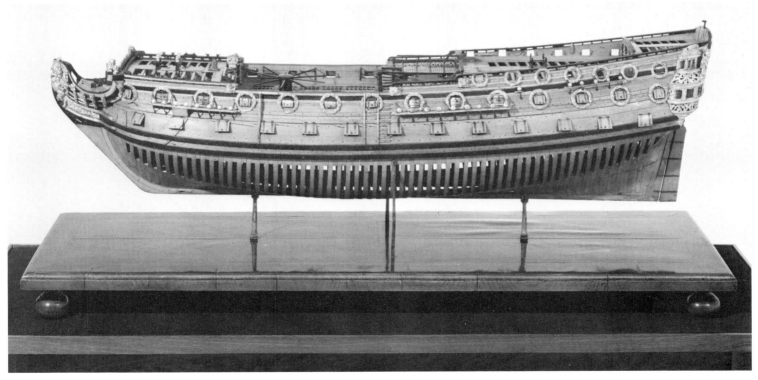

Hull construction

The hull framing, which appears to be made from pear wood, is finely built and conventional, except for the series of vertical timbers between the transoms, which are seen only on a very few other models.

Outboard fittings and details

Compared with Third Rates of an earlier date, there is little change in the fittings and general outward appearance, except for the quarter galleries. A great difference can be seen here, with the galleries taking on a basic form that was retained for many years. The galleries are much smaller and a rounded shape, quite unlike the bulky and angular affairs that were common previously. A small balcony appeared on the upper tier, which is normally only seen on models of a few years later when there was access to it from an open stern gallery on the quarterdeck. On this model, with no stern gallery at the same level, the access to the balcony is via a pair of small doors between the lights of the gallery itself. The port lids above the fore and main channels are split in two, with each half side hung. This is often seen on models, but it was evidently not a standard practice, as many have whole lids which are top hung in the normal way. It probably depended on the breadth of the channels and the position of the shrouds in relation to the ports. Lids are still fitted to the ports on the upper deck in the waist, but the practice was generally discontinued during the first 10 years of the eighteenth century.

Plate 80 *The stern. The motto SEMPER EADEM (always the same) was previously that of Elizabeth I, and Queen Anne adopted it when she came to the throne in 1702. A bust of Anne is carved in the centre of the tafferal, flanked by her personal badge of a Rose and Thistle springing from a single stalk. The seated female figure to port is holding either a palm or an olive branch, the emblems of Peace or Victory, and the one to starboard is cradling a Cornucopia, symbolising Prosperity and Plenty. The quarter figures are holding a cross staff to port, and an anchor to starboard. The friezes are carved in relief, but the tafferal is cut clear through and covered on the forward side by raised panels. Note the fine jointing of the vertical timbers between the transoms. The frames and bars of the lights are made from thin round wire. Kriegstein collection.*

Plate 81 *Stern framing. The rising timbers are unusually deeply recessed into the deadwood and fitted with precision. Some of the futtocks are numbered in pencil on the sides. Numbers 23 and 28 can be seen here, both prefixed by the letter L for larboard. Author.*

Plate 82 *Bow framing. The deadwood extends aft to just forward of the keel support. Between here and the deadwood aft the futtocks are longer, with the heels terminating about a foot from the keel. The 'touch' is well defined, and in this case, is to the forward end of the keel/stem scarph. Author.*

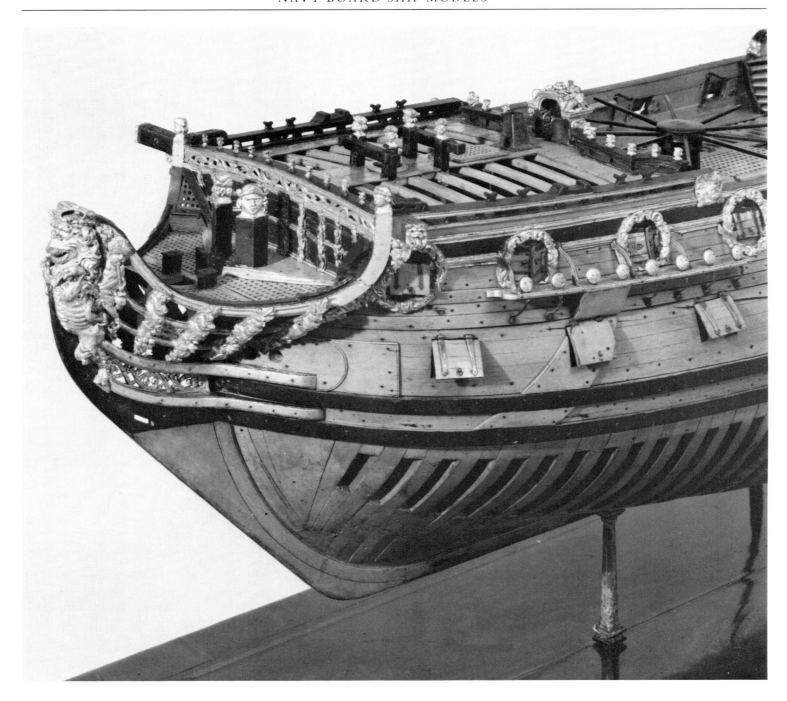

Inboard fittings and details

An innovation at the beginning of the eighteenth century was the long central gangway from the quarterdeck. It was a prominent feature, and one of the earliest examples is shown on the model. The fore and aft beams of the gangway are supported at the forward end by the gallows on the main top sail sheet bitts, with a large grating between which terminates just aft of the

position of the main mast. The moulded guard rails are supported by stirrups at the upper ends of four tapered metal stantions. In the waist three brackets are fitted to the bulwarks each side for gangways. The brackets are simply made of metal, with an upturned end to retain the gangboards, and are fixed in position by an eye bolt at the upper and lower ends. This is surprisingly early evidence of the use of side gangways, and it not seen again until many years later. The jeer capstan in the waist has six whelps,

Plate 83 *View of the head and forecastle. Many carved heads can be seen here, with those on the bollard timbers unusually large. The trail board is delicately carved in a design of interlaced strapwork. Kriegstein collection.*

and is fitted with ten bars. The large hatch abaft the capstan is fitted with a ladder way down to the lower deck. A grating is fitted to the hatch, but has two openings, about 2ft 6in square, to allow access to the ladder without removing the whole grating. The forecastle bulkhead is one of the last of the old type that is entirely flush with the break of the deck, with a projecting central bay, rounded cabins each side, and gun ports in the two pairs of doors. Other details include a single span shackle for the fish davit on the forecastle deck, a flight of bell stairs leading down from a companion on the quarterdeck, and the usual array of cleats, knights and kevels fitted to the bulwarks.

Decoration

The fine carved decoration of the model is an interesting example of the fashion for a very short period immediately prior to the great changes which took place in 1703. Compared with models of the previous decade, heraldic symbols have completely disappeared, and so have the familiar brackets and mask heads of the lower counter, but the ubiquitous winged head of a cherub is still retained as the lower finishing of the quarter galleries. At the bulkheads and between the quarter gallery lights, carvings of figures have gone except for a pair that support the ornate belfry, and lighter carvings decorated with simple designs of flowers and foliage have taken their place. The whole of the head shows little change from earlier years, but a small development in the evolution of the lion figurehead has taken place, as the 'beast' now sports a tail! Perhaps there are exceptions, but of some fifteen seventeenth-century examples noted, none of them has a tail, then they suddenly appear on all lions soon after the turn of the century. The hances are unusually decorated with square panels at the sides which are carved with small boys and mythological sea creatures. The model

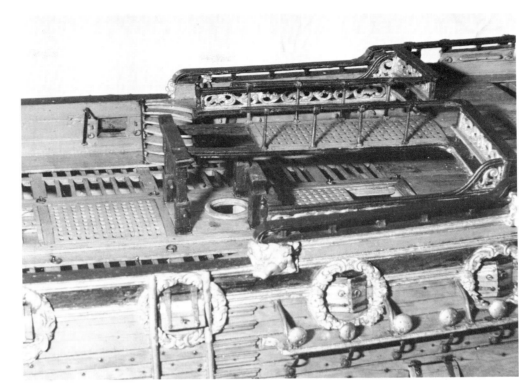

is one of the very latest still to be equipped with gun port wreaths on the upper deck.

Colour scheme

Black: Mainwales; knee of the head above waterline; plank sheer and drift rails; lower frieze; lower counter; inside of head timbers; bollard timbers; seats of ease; all bulkheads; bitts; capstan; breast rails at the breaks of the decks; ground between the stern carvings.
Red: Bulwarks; upper friezes; forward side of tafferal; interior of stern gallery.

Plate 84 *View of the aft end of the waist, showing the quarterdeck gangways and bitts. One of the brackets for the gangways at the side can be seen on the bulwarks.* Author.

Gilt: All carved work; moulded rails at the top of the side; edges of plank sheer, drift rails and channels; deadeyes; head rails; cheeks of the head.

Footnote

1. *Dictionary of National Biography.*

15. Galley-frigate of 32-40 guns 1702

Location: **Pitt-Rivers Museum, Oxford**
Scale: 1/64

Dimensions★ (at a scale of 1/64)			At 1/65
Gun deck	128ft 0in	(130ft 4in)	130ft 0in
Breadth	28ft 8in	(28ft 10in)	29ft 0in
Depth	8ft 8in	(9ft 0in)	8ft 10in
Keel (touch)	116ft 0in, 507 tons	(118ft 0in)	117ft 0in
Keel (calculated)	111ft 8in, 488 tons	(114ft 0in)	113ft 5in
Keel (tread)	119ft 0in, 520 tons	(124ft 0in)	120ft 10in
Timber and room	1ft 5in		

(The dimensions in brackets are of the *Charles Galley*, and taken from Dimension Book B for the gun deck, breadth and depth. The keel lengths are from an early draught of the ship, for comparison with the model.)

Height to the lower edge of the mainwale
In midships   9ft 8in

Height to the top of the side
In midships   22ft 0in

Oar scuttles   1ft 4in square
Upper deck gun ports   3ft 0in broad, 2ft 4in deep

Gun ports
Lower deck	4 + 2 + 4
Upper deck	22
Quarterdeck	6
Total	38

Height of decks (plank to plank)
Below upper deck	6ft 0in
Below quarterdeck	6ft 4in

Several old labels are displayed with this model, which give conflicting opinions as to which ship it represents. No scale or dimensions are given except that it is 27in long overall. The earliest of these indicates that it is a 'Model of the Royal Yacht, date 1702, given by Dr Clarke, All Souls, 1719' (for Dr Clarke, see Model No 12). Another label describes it as a 'Model of a Ship of War, showing construction, date 1702'. The third, and probably the latest, gives the description as a 'Model of a Fourth Rate of 44 guns, date 1702, probably an unrealised design'. The one certain thing these various descriptions have in common is the date, which is clearly carved on the decorative cradles, along with the initials IE, which could also be taken for JE. When initials are shown on cradles, or on the model itself, they can usually be related to known Master Shipwrights of the period, but in this case no shipwright has been noted with either of these initials. At first sight, even before the dimensions are known, it is apparent that the model has extraordinary proportions, being very narrow and of shallow depth compared with the length. No ships were built in the eighteenth century with anything like these proportions, and this is evidently the reason for the proposal that the model was a preliminary design which was not carried out. This suggestion is quite

Plate 85 *An early draught of the* Charles Galley, *1676. This draught, and the later eighteenth-century one, are the only illustrations of the ship that clearly show two forward gun ports on the lower deck. The inscription reads, 'The draught of his Maties Shipp the Charles Galley Friggott built by Mr Pett at Woollwich'. This is probably one of the earliest known draughts of a named ship. NMM.*

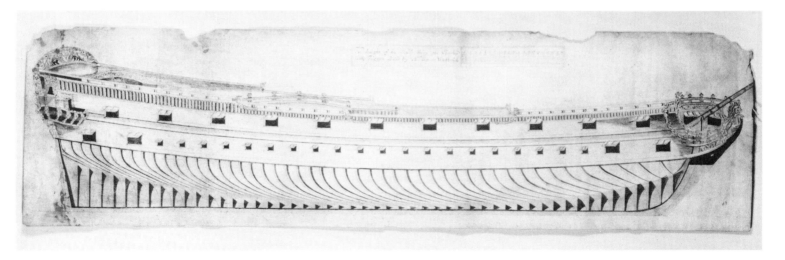

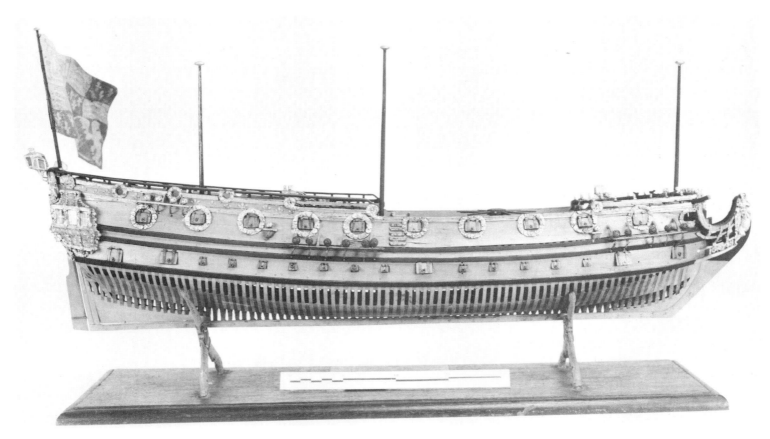

possible, but on the other hand a simpler explanation may be that the model is of a ship that already existed in 1702. There does not appear to be any reason why a model should not be built to represent an earlier ship, and if this is the case, there was only one that in appearance and dimensions can be reasonably considered. This was the *Charles Galley*, an oared galley-frigate launched in 1676 which had quite unique proportions, and there is enough evidence to suggest that the model is indeed of this ship, but as she was around the turn of the eighteenth century. Originally a Fourth Rate of 32 guns, the *Charles* was made a Fifth Rate in 1691, and was rebuilt in 1693 with similar dimensions. Another rebuild in 1710 gave the ship completely different proportions, with dimensions similar to a normal Fifth Rate at that time. The final end of the *Charles* came when she was 'surveyed 2nd May, 1726, found to want rebuilding, fitted with jury masts, sailed to Sheerness to be sunk for breakwater. Drove out her chain bolts, scuttled her bottom and sunk for breakwater'.[1] The ship was still known as the *Charles* during the so-called rebuild, but was renamed the *Torrington* at the launch of the new ship in 1729.

The model is quite a small one, and it is impossible to say exactly to what scale it was built, but it is probably at, or very

close to 1/64. At that even scale, the dimensions are close to those of the *Charles Galley*, except that they are all a little smaller. As these small scales can be suspect and imprecise, it may be that the true scale is 1/65, which provides dimensions that almost exactly agree with those of the ship. Two draughts exist for the *Charles Galley*. One is evidently seventeenth-century, and may have originated from the time the ship was first built, or perhaps it was for the 1693 rebuild. The other draught appears to be a late eighteenth-century copy.[2] From the scale on both draughts, other dimensions can be compared, such as the heights to the wales and top of the side, both of which agree very closely with the model.

In appearance, the model can be compared with several contemporary portraits of the ship, in addition to the draughts. Most of these differ from each other in some respects, and depict the *Charles* at various times in her long career. Two of the portraits,[3] and the early draught, are virtually identical and show the ship in her original state with no ports on the quarterdeck, a single mainwale and a small open balcony forward of the quarter gallery. Another drawing of unknown date is similar but with the addition of three ports on the quarterdeck and a different stern. A drawing dated 1708 shows the *Charles* with

another change to the appearance of the stern and apparently not equipped with oars.[4] The later eighteenth-century draught shows a number of differences. Four ports appear on the quarterdeck, the mainwales are double, and the balcony of the quarter gallery has disappeared, but the stern is much the same as the early portraits.

All these illustrations, except the drawing of 1708, show twenty or twenty-one oar scuttles a side, whereas the model has twelve. A reason for this may be that the number of oars were reduced by the time the model was built and, if the drawing can be trusted, done away with altogether by 1708. The *Charles* is depicted in a skirmish with several French galleys in a flat calm off Nice. Coming up astern are the galleys, all bristling with oars, but the *Charles* cannot bring her broadside to bear as she is shown with no oars at all. No scuttles are shown either, but the midships port on the

lower deck can be seen, as it is on the model. All the evidence suggests that this model *may* be the *Charles*, but whether it is or not, it is an interesting one, and probably the only example of its type. The craftsmanship is not up to the standard generally achieved by this time, and the model may be the work of an amateur, rather than an official one.

General construction

The hull is notable for the unusually small timber and room, which has produced many narrow sided and closely spaced frames. At every fourth timber and room, the station lines are numbered and lettered on the starboard side of the keel, with the midships bend indicated as just forward of the port on the lower deck. Pear wood has been used for the whole of the construction, except for the floors which are a darker wood. The stern is framed with a series of vertical timbers between the transoms, which are seldom seen on models. The single mainwale is most unusual. The

inboard work is not particularly well detailed, and of simplified construction, for example the gratings, which are just holes punched in the deck plank, and the stairs carved from a block of wood. The forecastle bulkhead has a small cabin each side and two doors, each containing a gun port

Fig 90 *Midship section of the model, showing the very shallow depth in proportion to the breadth. The drawing is based on heights to the wales and top of the side, height between decks,*

Plate 87 *An undated portrait of the* Charles. *This seems to be the only illustration of the ship that shows three gun ports on the quarterdeck, as they are on the model. The stern is shown with a square tuck, probably in error. NMM.*

breadth and the distance outside the frames from the keel to the lower edge of the mainwale. The hatched areas indicate the length of scarph between the futtocks and floors.

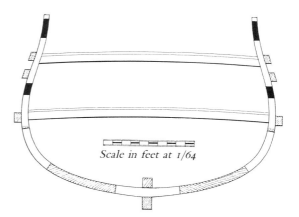

Scale in feet at 1/64

Plate 88 *The Royal Standard of William III. The Arms are those of the Stuarts, but with the addition of William's paternal shield of Nassau – gold billets and a lion rampant on blue. From this side of the standard, the Arms are in the reversed position. Author.*

with a top hung lid. At the break of the quarterdeck the bulkhead is the same but without cabins.

Decoration

Prominently displayed on the tafferal is a very large Achievement of Arms, complete with the Lion and Unicorn supporters, in the fashion that had virtually died out altogether by the 1680s. The Arms are those of William III, which are repeated on the break of the quarterdeck. Queen Anne's monogram appears in two compartments below the Arms, which were probably hastily added on completion of the model in 1702, at the death of King William. The quarter pieces are inverted lions, with their hind legs supporting the ends of the tafferal. Other carved work is much the same as usual on models of the period, with a nice lion figurehead, floral port wreaths and carved heads on the bitts and timber heads. The frieze at the top of the side is painted with Fleur-de-Lis motifs on a pale blue background. Although the Royal Standard is described in one of the old labels as being that of Prince George of Denmark, it is in fact a perfect and rare example of the Arms of William III (see Model No 12). The attractive cradles are in natural wood, with the fins and tail of the dolphins picked out in red. The centre tablet is black with a red border, and the initials and date gilt.

Footnotes

1. Progress books, Vol 1.
2. NMM Draught Room (reproduced in Howard, *Sailing Ships of War*), 1979.
3. NMM Nos 538 and ? (Both these portraits are reproduced in Fox, *Great Ships*, 1980).
4. This drawing is reproduced in the *Journal of the Royal United Services Institute*, June 1909.

Plate 89 *The aft cradle, with the enigmatic initials. The date, 1702, is on the other side of the cradle. Author.*

16. Fourth Rate of 46-54 guns c1703

Location: National Maritime Museum
Scale: 1/48

Dimensions★		Height to lower edge of mainwales	
Gun deck	128ft 6in	At the main transom	19ft 3in
Breadth	33ft 6in	In midships	12ft 6in
Keel (touch)	111ft 9in, 667 tons	At the stem	14ft 3in
Keel (calculated)	107ft 3in, 640 tons		
Timber and room	2ft 0in	*Gun ports*	
Rake of the stem	15ft 6in at the harpin	Lower deck	24
Rake of the stern post	3ft 3in at the main transom (10°)	Upper deck	22
		Quarterdeck	10
		Total	56

Large numbers of Fourth Rates were built in the late seventeenth and early eighteenth centuries with dimensions very similar to those of this attractive and decorative model. Although the model cannot be identified with any particular ship, it is interesting to make some speculation on the evidence of the initials IL or JL, and the date of 1701, both of which are contained in a small carved cartouche on the stern. The monogram of Queen Anne is also displayed at the stern, which conflicts with the date, as she did not succeed to the throne until March the following year. This is of no great significance, however, as the model clearly represents a ship of the William III period. If we take notice of the initials, assuming them to be of a known shipwright, it suggests that the model is of one of the Fourth Rates built in the 1690s, the date 1701 being that when the model itself was completed. Of all the shipwrights who built Fourth Rates in this period, only two had suitable initials. John Lock was Master Shipwright at Plymouth in the early 1700s, and although he built the Fourth Rates *Pembroke*, 1710, and *Bristol*, 1711, it is unlikely that a model would be prepared as a design some 8 years before. But in all

Plate 90 *Port broadside. The line of the top timber heels has a much greater sheer than the wales, and the ends of the timbers disappear behind the wales at bow and stern. This is frequently seen at the bows, but rarely also at the stern.* NMM.

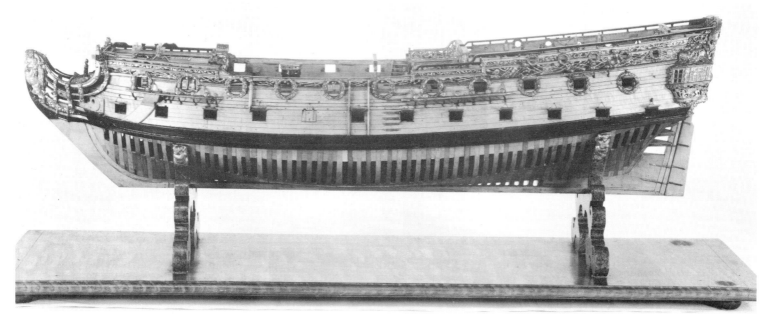

Fig 91 *Companion on the quarterdeck. The stantions and rails are made of metal, soldered together and painted black. An athwartship flight of 'bell stairs' leads down to the upper deck.*

Fig 92 *The steering wheel. The box-like structure, with a small light in its forward side, is for the use of the helmsman operating the whipstaff on the deck below. Note the staggered slots in the top for the steering rope.*

Fig 93 *The tafferal carvings. Triple crowns are sometimes seen in contemporary illustrations of the Achievement of Arms of William III, with the usual one above the visored helmet, and one each side, symbolising his Kingship over England, Scotland and Ireland. The sword crossed with a baton bearing a fleur-de-lis behind the crowns is also connected with William, and seen on almost all models from his reign, usually at the ends of the upper counter, but never after 1702, when Queen Anne succeeded to the throne.*

probability Lock would previously have been Assistant at Plymouth under Mr Waffe, who built the *Anglesea*, 1694, and the *Carlisle*, 1698, and he may very well have made a model of one of these two ships. The other Master Shipwright was Mr Lawrence of Woolwich, who built the Fourth Rates *Chester*, 1691, *Portland*, 1693, and *Lincoln*, 1695. Of these five ships, the dimensions of the model agree closest with those of the *Lincoln*, taking into account the usual increase in length and breadth over the design dimensions. The *Lincoln* had a length on the gun deck of 130ft 7in, breadth of 34ft 3½in and a keel of 108ft 4in. This is all conjecture, of course, as the initials may be those of a person of whom we have no knowledge, but nearly all dated and initialled models can be related to known shipwrights, and in most cases, to a particular ship.

Hull construction

The hull framing is conventional but, although the overall effect is quite good, it is clear that whoever made it was inexperienced in this type of construction. In much of the midships part of the hull, the sided dimensions of the timbers vary widely. Some of the timbers are too thick in their siding, others are too narrow, with some of them tapered, and numerous packing pieces have been inserted in the scarphs of the floors, futtocks and top timbers. In a few places, in order to improve the appearance, the thick futtocks have been reduced in their siding, but only between the floor heads and the heels of the top timbers. This sort of thing is rarely seen on models, and it is interesting to see that towards bow and stern, the framing becomes much more evenly spaced, as though the craftsman improved his technique as he went along. The hull, and most of the rest of the model, appears to be made from apple wood.

Outboard fittings and details

The mainwales are 9in thick, 12in broad and spaced 1ft 3in apart. There is no strake between this pair of wales, and the exposed hull timbers are painted black. The lower deck ports are 3ft 0in broad and 2ft 3in deep, with those on the upper deck 2ft 6in broad and 2ft 0in deep. The port lids are rabbeted on their edges and retained in the open position by single lifts made of thin twisted wire. There were originally intended to be twenty-four ports on the upper deck, but one each side, just abaft the cat supporters, have been filled in with a small piece of plank. The alteration would scarcely be noticed, and it is only from the inboard side that the port can be seen, which is framed with upper and lower cills carefully jointed into the frame timbers. All the ports on the quarterdeck are circular and very small, only about 1ft 3in in diameter. The model is probably one of the

earliest to show the absence of lids to the ports in the waist on the upper deck, a practice that became standard on ships with two or three decks from about 1700. The port lid straps, rudder hangings, chain plates and other metal fittings are made from brass with a natural finish.

Inboard details and fittings

The decks are of usual construction, except that the plank is much more extensive than on other models of this period, which has left only quite narrow gaps at each side. Fine lines are scored on the plank to represent the seams and butts. On the forecastle and quarterdecks the beams are alternately black and natural wood. The hatch coamings are very shallow and bevelled on their outer edges, almost down to the deck plank. Gratings are the pierced type, but well made. Compared with Fourth Rates of a slightly earlier date, a few changes have

taken place. The main top sail sheet bitts have been extended upwards to take the cross piece, or 'gallows', and the quarter-deck is longer, overhanging the bulkhead below, which is in about the same position as previously. With the lengthening of the quarterdeck, the side gangways have reached farther forward and the dual-pur-pose stairs have come into use, providing access to the waist both from the gangway and the entering place over the side. An oddity at the break of the quarterdeck is that there is a central gap in the breast rail, about 5 to 6ft wide. This does not seem to serve any useful purpose, unless there was an original intention to fit a central gangway to the gallows, a feature that appears on models from about 1700. The double jeer capstan in the waist is the normal type, with no drumhead on the lower one, but it is considerably larger than those on other models of the period and seems to be out of scale. It has a maximum diameter at the drumhead of 5ft 0in, which is also the height. Both upper and lower capstans have

Plate 91 *Quarter view from the bow. The filled in gun port on the upper deck aft of the cat supporter can just be seen.* NMM.

five whelps and the drumhead has sockets for ten bars. The main capstan is a single drumhead on the lower deck, abaft the main mast. A radical change in steering arrangements was taking place in the first few years of the eighteenth century, with the new wheel and rope system taking the place of the older whipstaff. Both are shown here, with the 'rowle', or pivot, for the whipstaff fitted on the upper deck, and the steering wheel directly above, on the quarterdeck. The model is the earliest known to be fitted with a wheel, but whether it is original is not certain. The exact date of the introduction of the wheel is not known, but bearing in mind the primitive steering windlass on the three-decker of about 1703, it is difficult to believe that this 'modern'-looking example is the first of its kind, and is probably an addition of a slightly later date.

Plate 92 *Quarter view from the stern.* NMM.

Decoration

The whole of the decoration is typical of the 1690s, and shows no trace of the subtle developments that took place prior to the major change of about 1703, when most of the carved work disappeared. No fewer than ten large birds are incorporated in the carvings. Except for eagles that appear each side and abaft the lion figurehead, all the birds have long legs and beaks, with outspread wings, and seem to depict water fowl of various kinds. Four are displayed on the upper counter, the others above and below the quarter gallery lights. The stern and quarter gallery decoration is carved in relief, with the ground between the carvings painted black, except for the tafferal, which is pierced through.

Colour scheme

Black: Mainwales; plank sheer and drift rails; knee of the head above the wales; all bulkheads; head timbers; breast rails at the breaks of the forecastle and quarterdecks; jeer capstan, except for the drumhead; friezes.

Red: Inside of gun ports and port lids; top of jeer capstan; ends of cat heads; muzzle, ears and inside the crown of the lion figurehead.

Gilt: All carved work, except for the knightheads on the bitts; head rails; moulded rails at the top of the side; cheeks of the head; deadeyes; frieze decoration; outer edge of the capstan drumhead.

17. Marlborough, Second Rate of 90 guns 1706

Location: **Kriegstein collection**
Scale: 1/72.

Dimensions			Gun ports	
	Model	*Ship*	Lower deck	28
Gun deck	161ft 5in	162ft 8in	Middle deck	28
Breadth	47ft 8in	47ft 4in	Upper deck	28
			Quarterdeck	10
			Total	94

The *Marlborough* was rebuilt from the remains of the *St Michael*, 1669, by Johnson at Blackwall. The rigging of the model is not contemporary, and was added by Dr R C Anderson.

The *Marlborough*, and the *Blenheim*, 1709, of the same Rate, were both named to commemorate the victory over the French forces at the Battle of Blenheim in 1704. John Churchill, 1st Duke of Marlborough, was the commander of the British troops, and there is much evidence amongst the decoration of the model connecting it with him. The figurehead depicts the Duke on horseback, riding roughshod over Marshall Tallard, the defeated French commander, and a large M is carved on the saddle cloth. At the stern, the Heraldic Arms of the Churchills is displayed on the upper counter, and the Crest of these Arms is worked in with the decoration of the quarters. There is also an intertwined monogram, JC, for John Churchill, incorporated in the fretted decoration of the frieze below the breast rail of the lower stern gallery. Few models of the early eighteenth century have been positively named, and the identification of this one, on the evidence of the dimensions and the number of references to Marlborough, can be considered quite certain. The craftsman made no concessions to the small scale of the model; the work is equally as detailed and executed as those of a larger scale.

General construction

The finely built hull appears to be made from pear wood and is the standard type. An unusual stem/keel scarph is shown, which is illustrated in Chapter II. The wales and top side plank are fastened with many hundreds of treenails to each top timber, in precise straight lines, unlike the random fastenings used on most models of this period. In addition, the mainwales are fastened to the futtocks as well. Timber standards, or knees, make an early appearance above the channels, instead of the arched spurs that were universal until about this time. The chain plates are straight and double fastened, with the lower bolt in the upper chainwale. Rigols are fitted above some of the lower and middle deck ports, but only where there is a clear space for

Plate 93 *The starboard broadside.* Kriegstein collection.

them, without encroaching on the wales. Compared with the three-decker of about 1702, the stern shows a change in the arrangement of open galleries. While the lower gallery has been discontinued, a full width one at the quarterdeck has been added and, in effect, the two galleries have simply been shifted up one deck, which became the usual arrangement for First and Second Rates. The galleries have a considerable overhang, which has allowed the lower to reach out to the side of the quarter galleries, unlike the earlier ones.

Decoration

The limitation of carved work and lack of other decoration on this model is typical of the early period of Queen Anne, and shows a complete contrast with those of only two or three years earlier. At the broadside, the absence of gun port wreaths is most noticeable, but there is a vestigial remnant of them shown on the quarterdeck ports, where circular moulded rings have been fitted instead. At the stern, the attractive and unusual decoration below the gallery breast rails can be seen. Some idea of this

Plate 94 *Detail of the starboard quarter. The lion bearing the banner containing a hand is the Crest from the Achievement of Arms of Marlborough. Kriegstein collection.*

Plate 95 *The stern. Queen Anne's monogram is incorporated in the fretted decoration of the upper gallery, and the monogram of Marlborough is shown in the lower one. The lanterns illustrate a small change in their evolution, and have now become slightly tapered. These stern views give a good idea of the diagonal of the rising line of the floor heads. The stern lights are made from wire soldered together. Kriegstein collection.*

Plate 96 *View of the bow, Kriegstein collection.*

Plate 97 *This figurehead, representing the Duke of Marlborough, is a very fine carving considering the small scale. Note the M carved in relief on the saddle cloth. The absence of carved decoration on the head timbers, compared with models of a slightly earlier date, is apparent.* Author.

fine work can be gained from the fact that the designs are fretted out from strips of thin sheet brass, little more than half an inch wide. The Coat of Arms of Marlborough displayed on the upper counter is quite a remarkable piece of work too. In this very small area, the Arms are minutely detailed and encircled by the motto of the Order of the Garter. But the carver made one small error. When carefully cutting in the minute letters of the motto around the Garter, 'HONI SOIT QUI MAL Y PENSE', he ran out of space and could not include the last two letters! The whole of the exterior of the model, including the carvings, is left in natural varnished wood, except for the mainwales which are black.

18. Third Rate of 70 guns 1706

Location: **Pitt-Rivers Museum, Oxford**
Scale: **1/48**

Dimensions (at a scale of 1/48)		Gun ports	
Gun deck	150ft 5in	Main deck	26
Breadth	41ft 2in	Upper deck	28
Depth	17ft 3in	Quarterdeck	12
		Total	66

Model dimensions were taken from the label.

This is the third, and last, of Dr Clarke's models, which he gave to the Ashmolean Museum in 1719, and which were subsequently transferred to the Pitt-Rivers Museum in 1886. The history of the model can be traced back in unusual detail, and it is probably the earliest existing example where we know both the name of the modelmaker and the purpose for which it was made. In the Book of Benefactors[1] at the Ashmolean, an entry in Latin records the occasion of Dr Clarke's gift to the Museum. The translation is as follows:

AD1719

George Clarke LLD, Fellow of All Souls College and several times Member of Parliament for this University had, in Queen Anne's reign, the post of Lord Commissioner of the Admiralty. Being very fond of well made things, he commissioned a model of a warship with all its masts, sails, rigging and equipment and decreed that it should be allowed to come to port in this most excellent of harbours. By rights one ought here to remember also William Lee Esq who made the little ship so beautifully.

The mention of sails is probably an error in translation, as the model was certainly never fitted with them. A manuscript catalogue of 1886[2] lists the model as 'with full rigging, but no sails'. Both this catalogue and an earlier printed one of 1836[3] list the model as a ship of 64 guns. This evidence of a model being privately commissioned leads one to speculate on just how many of them were constructed for this purpose, and nothing whatever to do with the Navy Board. It is frustrating and rather disappointing to be able to trace the model this far back and find that there is still no

indication of the ship it represents or the actual date it was made, which would be so valuable to us. However, the monogram of Queen Anne on the stern dates it at between 1702 and 1714, and the decoration of the head and the carved wreaths on the quarterdeck ports suggest that it is of the early part of this period. The Royal Arms on the stern would indicate the date as being before or after 1707, but it is difficult to see, being as usual partly concealed by the stern lantern and its support; a close examination would no doubt reveal which Arms these are. This early example of contemporary rigging is of some importance, and shows a high level of execution. The absence of preventer stays and bowsprit shrouds and the shape of the tops suggest the rigging that was in use prior to 1706.[4] There was a Master Shipwright of the same name as the builder of this model. This was William Lee, who was building at Woolwich Dockyard in the early years of the eighteenth century until, in 1706, he was appointed joint Surveyor of the Navy along with Daniel Furzer, a post he held until 1713.[5] Lee built one Third Rate of 70 guns at Woolwich, the short-lived *Resolution* of 1705. It is tempting to assume, if this is indeed the same William Lee, that having been commissioned to build a model for Dr Clarke, he would choose as a subject a ship that he himself had built, and that this model may be of the *Resolution*. It is an interesting speculation, but of course it will probably never be proven.

The 1705 *Resolution* was a pre-Establishment ship, but had dimensions that were virtually the same, with a gun deck of 150ft 10in, breadth of 40ft 11in and depth of 17ft 1in, which compares closely with the dimensions of the model. The model received some attention in 1940 when a

limited restoration was carried out, mainly to the original rigging. All the running rigging was removed, dressed with oil and replaced. The top-gallant masts were straightened by steaming, and slack in the standing rigging was taken up. A few replacements were needed, such as the main top-gallant stay, mizzen vangs and a few ratlines and deadeye lanyards. Work on the hull was confined to steaming and straightening the gratings, and treating the wood with oil and shellac. The guns were also removed and cleaned, and the gilt work touched up with nine carat gold ground in gum. At the same time as this restoration, a series of small electric lights were fitted in the hull, as it was considered that the interior was so finely finished.

Hull

Entirely made from pear wood, the construction of the hull is of a singular nature, which has not been seen on any other model and which may very well be unique. It nearly escaped notice, as it was initially put down as having an unusually long scarph between the floors and futtocks! This hull is illustrated in Chapter II, but briefly, the difference between this and usual models is that the heels of the futtocks butt directly on to the floor heads, with a 'naval timber' lying alongside and overlaunching the butt, giving scarph to both the floor and futtock. The principle of this construction is of considerable interest, as it closely follows the one commonly specified in contracts of this period. Nothing has been noted of the interior of the hull, but it can be seen that orlop deck clamps are fitted.

Outboard details and fittings

The top side plank between the two pairs of wales is laid in separate strakes. No fastenings at all have been used in this plank or the wales, which illustrates a new technique that became common in the early eighteenth century, when glue only was relied on. A refinement rarely seen on models is the 'black strake' above the main-wales. It is a single strake, of a thickness halfway between that of the wales and the ordinary plank above. The five aftmost gun

ports on the upper deck are fitted with glazed nine pane lights, which is apparently the arrangement for 'peace at home and war abroad' when 62 guns were carried on a Third Rate of 70 guns, with none in the main accommodation.[6] Despite this, the modeller has made 68, and placed six on the poop where there should be four, six on the forecastle, also where there should be four, and two in the chase ports of the beak bulkhead. The guns are beautifully made, with brass barrels on properly made carriages, and well detailed, but no tackles are fitted. There are only two sizes of guns:

Plate 98 *Starboard broadside. The unusual style of the framing has almost filled the hull with timber. The upper limit of the solid work is formed by the heads of the naval timbers, and not the floor heads as might be supposed.* Pitt-Rivers Museum.

those on the lower deck and all the rest. While those on the lower and upper decks are probably accurate, the guns on the forecastle and quarterdecks are oversized, and those on the poop very much so. The absence of gun port lids on the upper deck,

in the waist, is noticeable on this model. These started disappearing about 1705, and the trend was universal by about 1715 according to models. The channels are braced above by arched spurs and the chain plates are the short curved type with a single bolt in the lower chainwale. Of interest at the head are the early round-houses, used as latrines by the junior officers. They are much larger than later ones and are farther outboard, with the sides resting on the main head rail. A fish davit is rigged out to port, with all its associated tackle for stowing the anchors. The inner end of the davit is held down by a single span shackle. Like most models fitted with this shackle, the retaining bolt is taken down and fastened to one of the upper deck beams. The fish hook pendant is taken forward to the snatch block for the cat fall inboard of the cat head. This would be feasible, as the cat

fall being already belayed, the snatch block would be free to be used for another purpose, but it is not obvious where the pendant leads to from here. Other models with this gear show that the pendant is led aft in various ways, to the jeer capstan in the waist. The stern has two open galleries which became quite common on Third Rates of 70 guns from the beginning of the eighteenth century until about 1730, when the lower one was filled in with a tier of lights. Frames and bars of the stern and quarter gallery lights are delicately made from metal wire, which is soldered at the intersections.

Inboard fittings and details

As far as can be seen, all the upper deck beams are fitted with lodging and hanging

Plate 99 *The head. A surprising omission on this detailed model is the doubling of the plank, or 'Naval Hoods', in the way of the hawse holes, and the absence of the bolster. Not often seen are the outlet chutes from the seats of ease. The anchor cables are beautifully made with the correct left-hand lay. Author.*

knees. The jeer capstan in the waist is a conventional drumhead type, and has ten bars which are fitted with the seldom-seen rope 'swifter'. The rope is reeved through holes bored in the ends of the bars, then a single round turn outside the standing part and on to the next bar. On the quarterdeck, immediately aft of the mizzen mast, is the steering wheel. It is quite small, and set on the forward end of the steering drum. Below the drum, and against the round-house bulkhead, is a long and low com-

Plate 100 *This view shows well the two open galleries, each with an inset screen bulkhead, in what is otherwise a flush stern. Later models than this invariably have an overhanging upper balcony. The tapered and hexagonal lanterns are the form that was retained through much of the eighteenth century. A small detail is the athwartship retaining pin in the end of the tiller. The over-large guns can be seen on the poop.* Pitt-Rivers Museum.

panion, which is glazed on its forward side. This was for the convenience of the helmsman working the whipstaff on the upper deck, and the model is an interesting transitional example for illustrating evidence of the earlier steering arrangement as

well as the wheel and rope system which appeared around the turn of the eighteenth century. The whipstaff itself is not in place, and it is difficult to see whether the pivot, or 'rowle', for it is fitted on the upper deck, but the typical cranked fitting for the whipstaff is shown at the forward end of the tiller. Some of these early eighteenth century models have attractive little bench seats fitted in various positions on the open decks. This one has a seat in the centre of the forecastle bulkhead, about 8ft long and facing aft. There are also two more at the break of the quarterdeck, one each side of the central gangway facing aft.

Decoration

This model is an excellent example of the transitional nature of the decoration soon after the radical Admiralty Order of 1703 which severely restricted the amount of carved work and other embellishment.[7] The head itself, with the carved 'brackets' on the head timbers, the carved and pierced trail board and the typical figure on the cat supporter, is virtually the same as those on models of many years earlier. The port wreaths on the quarterdeck are also retained, although those on the upper deck have gone. On the other hand, except for the quarter pieces at the stern and the tafferal, all other carvings have disappeared. Instead, panels, mouldings and pillasters adorn the bulkheads and stern. Volutes also appear at the hances, and the bitts, etc, have plain timber heads. In all, it is a quite remarkable transformation and it is useful to compare this model with the Third Rate of about 1702 (Model No 14). The quarter figures are large and fine representations of Zeus/Jupiter, with the god's attribute, a large eagle, at his feet. In the centre of the tafferal are the Arms of Queen Anne, flanked by reclining female figures blowing long trumpets. The painted friezes of the side, quarter galleries and stern are in gold on a black background. An elaborate and intertwined AR, the monogram of Anne, is painted in the centre of the upper counter.

Footnotes

1. Ashmolean Book of Benefactors, Ashmolean Library, AMS2, 1683–1766. Reproduced as Microfiche No 1 in A McGregor, *Tradescant Rarities* (Oxford, 1983).
2. Ashmolean Manuscript Catalogue, 1886.
3. P B Duncan, *Printed Catalogue of the Ashmolean Museum, descriptive of the Zoological Specimens, Antiquities, Coins and Miscellaneous Curiosities* (Oxford, 1836).
4. James Lees to the Author. See *Masting and Rigging of English Ships of War, 1625–1860* (Conway, 1979).
5. R D Merriman, Editor, *Queen Anne's Navy*, Navy Records Society, Vol 103.
6. Robert Gardiner, 'Gun Establishment of 1703', *Model Shipwright* 20, June 1977.
7. This Order is reproduced in *The Mariner's Mirror*, Vol 3, pp 20–1. Also in L G Carr-Laughton, *Old Ships' Figureheads and Sterns*, (London, 1925).

19. Fourth Rate of 44-50 guns c1710

Location: **Kriegstein collection**
Scale: 1/48

Dimensions (at a scale of 1/48)		Gun ports	
Gun deck	115ft 0in	Lower deck	22
Breadth	32ft 6in	Upper deck	24
		Quarter deck	6
		Total	52

This model originated from the large Cuck-field Park collection, formed in the late seventeenth and early eighteenth century by Charles Sergison, Clark of the Acts at the Admiralty, 1690–1719. At the scale of 1/48, the dimensions are very close to those of a few unusually small Fourth Rates built in the first decade of the eighteenth century, which had lengths on the gun deck of 115ft 0in to 118ft 0in, and breadths of 31ft 6in to 33ft 0in. The date of the model can be determined to the period 1707–14 on the evidence of the portrait bust and motto of Queen Anne on the stern, and her badge, of a crowned rose and thistle on the upper finishing of the quarter galleries, which Anne adopted on the occasion of the Act of Union with Scotland in 1707.

Hull construction

The hull construction is of the usual pattern, but the rising line of the floor heads is uncommonly low at the bow and stern. In the hold, a number of square pillars stand on the keelson to support the lower deck beams, and all mast steps are fitted. The model seems to be made entirely from pear, or perhaps apple, wood.

Outboard fittings and details

The gun ports appear to be in the 'peace at home, war abroad' configuration, when 44 guns were carried, with the aftmost four ports on the upper deck fitted with nine

Fig 94 *This charming figure of a winged merchild forms the lower finishing of the quarter galleries.*

Plate 101 *The port broadside.* Kriegstein collection.

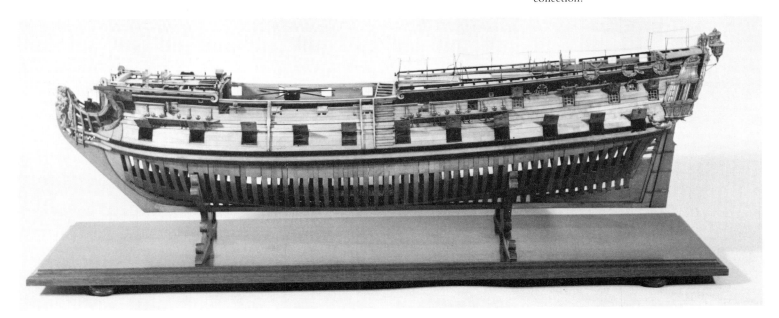

paned glazed lights. Between these are two glazed scuttles, surmounted by shell-like canopies supported on shaped brackets. Single paned scuttles also appear in the side to light the small cabins at the forecastle and quarterdeck bulkheads. No fastenings have been used in the top side plank, which is in separate strakes. Timber 'standards', or knees, make an early appearance on the fore and main channels, instead of the arched spurs that were universal until about this time. But three small spurs are retained on the mizzen channel. No hances or drifts are shown aft of the one at the waist, which has resulted in the top of the side towards the stern being abnormally low. This has produced a very low 'snug' stern, with no part of it protruding above the poop deck. Rarely seen on models of any period are the hammock cranes aft, and the guard rail stantions surrounding the forecastle deck. A small detail at the head is the shaped brackets each side of the gammoning slot,

Plate 102 *The stern. Queen Anne's portrait bust is partly concealed by the lantern. Below, between heads of cherubs, is the motto of Anne, SEMPER EADEM. The flanking figures are the Greek god Apollo with his lyre, and a warrior god, probably representing Ares. The quarter pieces appear to be of Britannia. Kriegstein collection.*

Plate 103 *View of the head from the port side. The lion, with his attractive little female companion, is a particularly good example. Kriegstein collection.*

Plate 104 *View of the quarterdeck showing the hammock cranes and steering wheel. The glazed lights fitted in the gun ports have circular openings, similar to those on the Third Rate of about 1705. Author.*

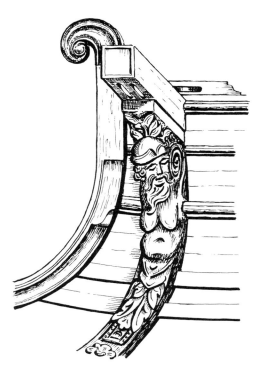

Fig 95 *Cat head supporters carved with figures were common during the previous century, but were generally discontinued around 1702. This example is probably one of the last of its type. The distinctive volute scroll at the upper end of the main head rail is most unusual.*

which has been seen only on a few early eighteenth-century models.

Inboard fittings and details

Much of the inboard structure and fittings can be clearly seen in the photographs, but a few details are not readily apparent: there is no breast rail at the break of the quarterdeck, just a rope supported on metal

Plate 105 *The waist and forecastle. The central gangway to the main mast is shown on this model, but not all Fourth Rates were so fitted. At the forecastle bulkhead, the bench seat can be seen. Kriegstein collection.*

stantions, which extends round the central gangway to the mast; a single span shackle for the fish davit is fitted on the forecastle deck, with its retaining bolt taken down and fastened through an upper deck beam; and lastly, a feature that seems confined to the early years of the eighteenth century is the bench seat with high decorative ends, fitted at the forecastle bulkhead.

Decoration

Although the carved work is greatly reduced compared with earlier models, there are remnants of the old style, such as the cat supporter and lower finishing of the quarter galleries. The ungilded carvings are of exceptional quality, which always seems to be enhanced when left in natural wood. At the stern, the tafferal is carved in deep relief, with the ground stippled with a point. The quarter figures have been cleverly designed to fit the awkward space caused by the stern lights.

20. Fourth Rate of 50 guns c1715

Location: **National Maritime Museum**
Scale: 1/48

Dimensions★ (at a scale of 1/48)		Gun ports		Breadth	Depth
Gun deck	130ft 0in	Lower deck	24	2ft 9in	2ft 4in
Breadth	35ft 9in	Upper deck	24	2ft 3in	2ft 1in
Depth in hold	14ft 0in	Quarter deck	10		
Timber and room	2ft 3in	Total	58		

Models of complete hulls 'in frame', illustrating the technical methods of construction, are relatively uncommon, and except for this one are confined in date to the second half of the eighteenth century. The later examples are of great value, but we know from many other sources, such as 'disposition of frame' plans and other detailed drawings, and works on Naval Architecture, exactly how the frame was constructed. This was not quite the case in the early eighteenth century, however, as in a number of respects it is a somewhat grey area, with hardly any constructional drawings existing, and the meaning of the written word very often difficult to interpret. Several basic changes were taking place at this time, and this early framed model is of particular interest as not only does it show the construction in considerable detail, it is also evidently an experimental one, with the framing to port being that then in use, and the framing to starboard showing proposed improvements. The dimensions of the model agree with those laid down for a Fourth Rate of 50 guns in the 1706 Establishment, except that there is a small increase of 9in in the breadth.

Construction of the port side

The principal timbers are double up to the mainwales, with the joint lines corresponding to the station lines at every fourth timber and room, which was not uncommon on early eighteenth-century draughts. Between these double timbers are six single filling frames, except for aft of the midships bend (which is clearly marked on the wales) where there is the usual odd number, seven being fitted here. The framing of the top sides is comparatively slight, with many of the frames terminating at the heads of the third futtocks, about 2ft above the mainwales. At this period the station lines, and the intermediate timber and rooms, did not conform with the disposition of gun ports as they did from about the mid-eighteenth century, to allow the timbers to be taken straight up to the top of the side. On this model, considerable modifications have been made to the top side framing to overcome this problem. Some of the timbers are leaning, others are cut into, and many short timbers have been scarphed in to form the sides of the ports. At the bows, two wide hawse pieces are fitted, with the hawse holes bored in the centre of each. This agrees with those specified in the 1719 Establishment when two were called for, or alternatively, four 'as can be conveniently had'. When two were fitted, each piece was to be 2ft 3in broad, which corresponds exactly with the breadth of those on the model. The hawse pieces, inside and outside, are thickened in way of the holes to form the 'boxing' which was flush with the plank. The mainwales are double, with each strake 12in broad and 8in thick. Simple scarphs

Plate 106 *The port broadside. NMM.*

150

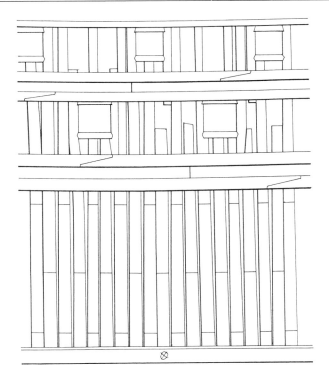

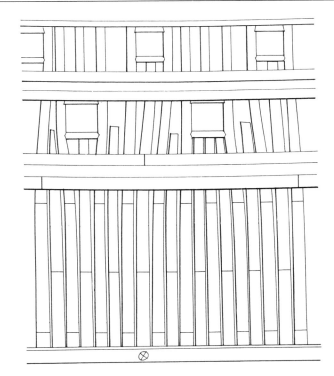

Fig 96 Framing in midships on the port side. With a very few exceptions, all timbers are straight in the upper works, and have been modified extensively to form the sides of the ports.

Construction of the starboard side

Fig 97 Framing in midships on the starboard side. The sides of the ports are framed by the use of curved timbers. Beneath every other lower deck port, three timbers have been crowded in with either one or two beneath the rest.

are marked on the wales at intervals of about 24ft. The thinner strake between the wales has square butt ends. The chainwales are also double, with strakes 10in broad and 6in thick, and scarphed as the mainwales. All these strakes are fastened with many treenails.

Except for having the same number of stern transoms, the framing on this side is different in every way from that to port, although at first sight it appears basically the same. All frames are apparently single, but this probably means that the principal timbers are intended to be double, and bolted together with spacing chocks, which are not shown on the model. Much use of curved timbers can be seen in the top side framing to form the sides of the ports.

Perhaps the most interesting feature of the model is the early evidence of the use of cant frames at bow and stern, and the method of construction. In later years, the canting of the frames was gradually increased by reducing the siding of the timbers at the deadwood. But here it is a quite different principle, with either one or two wedge-shaped timbers intoduced at

Plate 107 *The starboard broadside. NMM.*

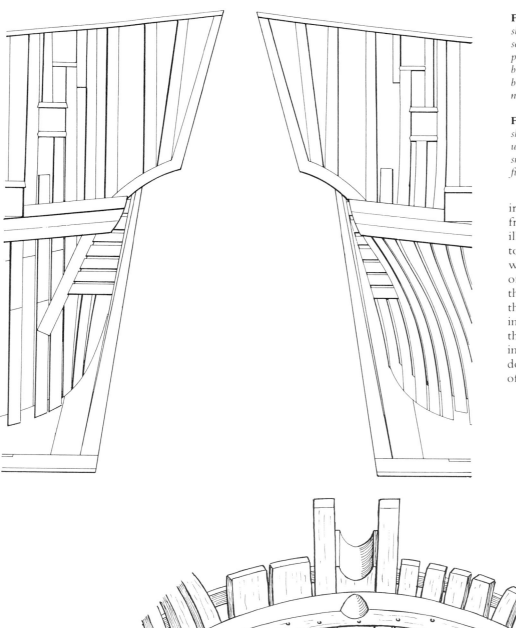

Fig 98 *Stern framing on the port side. The short, straight 'fashion piece' shown here is often seen on early eighteenth-century draughts, and is probably a good indication that the ship was to be built with all square frames. The wide space between the top timbers is for the gallery doors, but no cills are fitted on the model.*

Fig 99 *Stern framing on the starboard side, showing the typical profile of the fashion piece when cant frames are used. Note that there is a small difference in the way the transoms have been fitted to the stern post compared with the port side.*

irregular intervals to 'fan out' the cant frames to the required angle. This is a good illustration of how models are so valuable to us, as if it were not for this one, we would almost certainly have no knowledge of this particular method of constructing the cant frames. Another early feature on this side is the flush mainwales, which are in three strakes, each 12in broad and 8in thick. These strakes have plain butt ends instead of scarphs. The chainwales are still double, but filled in flush at the positions of the main and fore channels.

Fig 100 *Inboard view of the bow structure showing the different arrangement of the hawse pieces. The lower deck breast hook has been* *carefully made from one piece, and there must be a very good reason why the port side of it has been stepped down, but no explanation can be offered.*

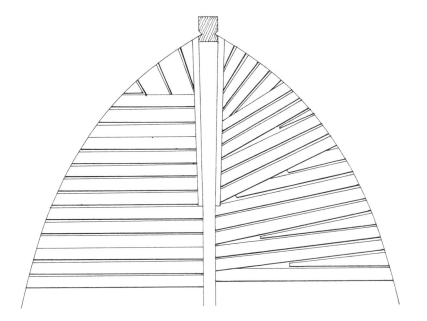

Inboard work

The keelson is fitted, with a single footwale, 12in broad and 6in thick each side at the floor heads. All lower deck beams and a few on the upper deck are in place, which are let down in the clamps about half their thickness. No carlings or ledges are fitted. A single standard, or vertical knee, is shown above the wing transom against the side counter timber, at the starboard side only. From the inside it can be seen that the heels of the first futtocks meet on the centre line,

Fig 101 *Plan of the bow framing showing the all square frames to port and the way the cant timbers have been angled by the use of short tapered timbers that do not reach the deadwood.*

except for three forward of the midship bend, and two aft, which terminate 1ft 6in from the keel.

This model clearly shows the authentic construction and disposition of timbers in the framing of early eighteenth-century ships, and a considerable amount of careful work was evidently involved in making it.

Plate 108 *View of the bow, showing the 'boxing' in way of the hawse holes. The hawse pieces are fayed close together at the boxing, with a space for air above and below. The flush mainwales can be seen on the starboard side, with the double ones to port. NMM.*

This type, with separate and unconnected frames, was probably built up solid initially, in a similar manner to the partially completed one illustrated in Chapter II. After being marked out, the hull would be sawn up to provide the individual frames, which were then erected separately on the keel.

21. Lion,
Fourth Rate of 60 guns 1738

Location: **Kriegstein collection**
Scale: 1/60

Dimensions			Gun ports	
Length of the gun deck	144ft 4in		Lower deck	26
Breadth	37ft 10in		Upper deck	24
			Quarterdeck	12
			Total	62

The *Lion*, launched at Deptford Dockyard by Mr Richard Stace in 1738, was a rebuild from the remains of the *Lion* originally built at Chatham in 1709, and was again rebuilt at Portsmouth in 1777.

This fine model is identified as the *Lion* on the evidence of the name of the ship, which is contained in a small label incorporated in the painted decoration of the upper counter. Except for the numerous 'solids' that exist, named models of this period are extremely uncommon, particularly when they represent rebuilt ships. An excellent box wood model of the 1777 *Lion* is also known, which has the distinction of being possibly the very latest with a lion figurehead, and is on display at the Dorset County Museum, Dorchester.

Plate 109 *Starboard broadside. The white strake below the mainwales is a distinctive feature.* Kriegstein collection.

Hull construction

The hull framing is of usual construction, of the type where the futtocks have a fairly short scarph with the floors and terminate short of the deadwoods. In the hold, the orlop deck clamps, beams and carlings are fitted, but no plank is laid.

Outboard fittings and details

The mainwales are wrought in three flush strakes, with one strake of ordinary plank below. This lower strake is unusually painted white, the line of which is continued on round the knee of the head and wing transom. The chainwales are still in two projecting strakes, with one thinner strake between. The top sides between the wales are laid with plank in separate strakes. No fastenings have been used in any of this outboard work. The edge of the fore channel is parallel with the centre line, which has resulted in the forward end being considerably wider than at the aft end. The channels are braced above by timber standards, with five on the fore, six on the main and three on the mizzen. The chain plates, which are made of brass, are serpentine-shaped in profile, and double bolted to the side below the lower chainwale. A small

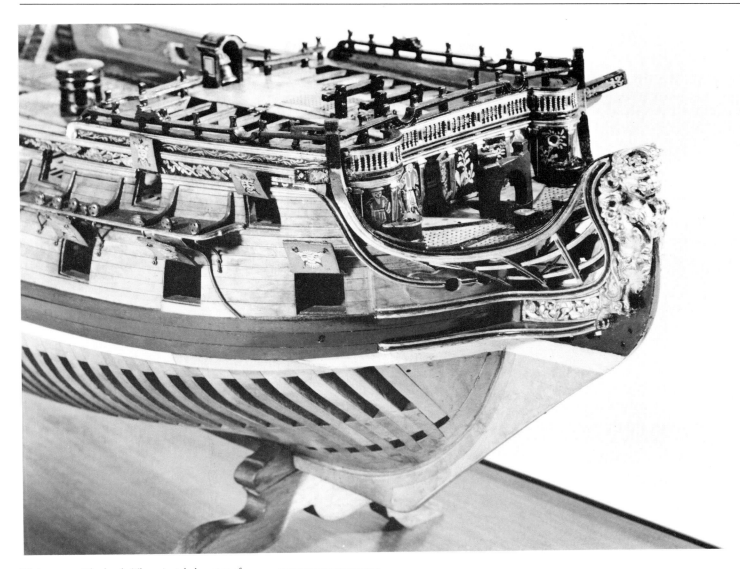

Plate 110 *The head. The oriental character of the painted decoration can be seen on the port lids and roundhouses.* Kriegstein collection.

feature that has not been mentioned, but which appears on many eighteenth-century models, is a half round bolster fitted to the top of the side abaft the chesstree, to take the chafe of the main course tack.

Inboard fittings and details

Changes in the arrangement of capstans were taking place in the 1730s, when the double drumhead main capstan was introduced, and a drumhead also appeared on the lower jeer capstan. Models of this period often illustrate either the main or jeer capstan of the new type, with the other in the earlier manner. This model is fitted

Fig 102 *One of the painted heads on the port lids. There are 42 of them, each one with a quite different expression.*

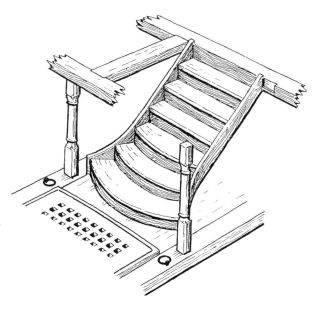

Fig 103 *The 'bell stairs' leading down from the forward end of the quarterdeck to the waist. Quite a lot of careful work would be involved in making this little flight of stairs. The height between decks is only about 1⅜in. The gratings are the pierced type*

155

with an early example of a double main capstan, but with the lower jeer capstan still lacking a drumhead. Another change that occurred in the 1730s was that the steering wheel generally became double, and shifted from its old position aft of the mizzen mast to forward of the mast. During the changeover period, a few models are seen fitted with a double wheel still aft of the mast, and others with the wheel in its new position but still single, as in this case. One advantage of the wheel forward of the mast was that it allowed in turn an increase in the area of the Captain's accommodation. This can be seen on the model, where the bulkhead has been moved forward to directly below the break of the poop. It is surprising to see that there is no central gangway from the quarterdeck to the gallows on this model. A fire hearth is fitted in the usual place on the upper deck, just forward of the forecastle bulkhead. The fire

hearth is simply made from wood, with the two coppers set into a brass top, and no chimney is fitted. Two square span shackles for the fish davit are fitted on the forecastle deck, one each side and aft of the ventilation grating above the fire hearth.

Decoration

The model is noted for being one of the few decorated in the oriental fashion known as Chinoiserie. The beak bulkhead and the lower counter are painted in lacquer and depict Chinese-style figures in a rich combination of red and gold on a black background. The upper frieze at the top of the side towards the stern is decorated with an unusual zig-zag design in black and gold, with a narrow band of red at top and bottom. Tendrils of foliage are painted in the narrow frieze, with the broad frieze below containing Trophies of Arms, again in the eastern style. The inner sides of the port lids are curiously painted with mandarin-like heads in gold, and defined in black on a red background.

Colour scheme

Black: Mainwales; upper part of the knee

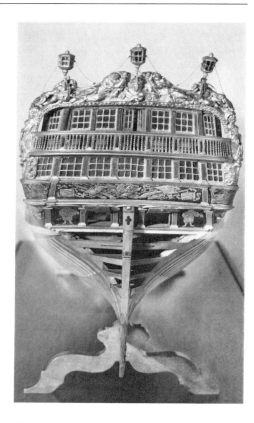

Plate 111 View of the poop and quarterdeck. Features of interest here are a flight of bell stairs leading down to the waist, the wheel in its new position forward of the mizzen mast, and a pivoting step for lowering the ensign staff. The deck of the Captain's cabin is laid in a diagonal pattern of small black and white squares. A finely carved monogram of King George II appears on the upper finishing of the quarter gallery. Kriegstein collection.

Plate 112 The stern. The open stern gallery extends round the quarters to form a tiny balcony, a practice that was generally discontinued during the next decade. The delicate twist turned balusters beneath the breast rail are repeated between the lights of the quarter galleries, and above the beak bulkhead. The modeller has taken the trouble of reversing the hand of the twist at the centre line, for perfect symmetry. Note the stays that brace the lanterns. Kriegstein collection.

of the head; plank sheer and fife rails; timber heads; knightheads; seats of ease; jeer capstan; bitts; breast rails at the breaks of the decks.
Red: Inside the port lids; port linings; bulwarks; all internal plank at the sides above the upper deck.
Gilt: All carved work; moulded rails of the stern, quarter galleries, broadside and head; upper and lower edges of the head cheeks; frames and bars of the stern lights; balusters.
White: Strake below the mainwales.

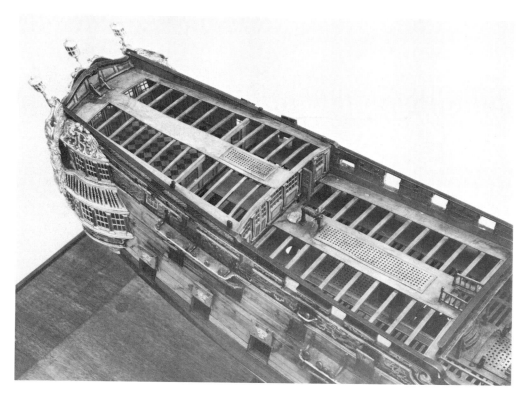

22. Second Rate of 80 guns c1740

Location: **National Maritime Museum**
Scale: 1/48

Dimensions*			Gun ports	
Gun deck	160ft 0in		Lower deck	28
Breadth	45ft 0in		Middle deck	28*
Timber and room	2ft 3in		Upper deck	28
Length of forecastle	28ft 0in		Quarterdeck	6
Length of poop deck	38ft 0in			—
			Total	90
Heights of decks				
Below upper deck	7ft 0in			
Below forecastle	6ft 3in			
Below quarterdeck	7ft 0in			

* Includes one each side on the upper deck forward of the cat supporter.

One of the more puzzling eighteenth-century models, this superbly made three-decker with the name *Barfleur* painted on the stern is a complete mystery. Although models of this period can usually be dated within fairly close limits, it is very difficult to determine with any accuracy in this case due to a number of apparently anomalous and contradictory features. The full-width open stern galleries, the long rake of the stern post, the type of chain plates, and the paired chain- and sheer wales could be of any date from early in the eighteenth century to around the 1740s. On the other hand, the long projection of the shallow head, the raised position of the cheeks to one below and one above the hawse holes, the deeply concave profile of the cut-water, and the style of the figurehead all suggest a date of not earlier than the 1750s. Also of this later date are the permanent side gangways in the waist, and the long quarter-deck which has reached and enclosed the main mast. The model certainly dates from around the mid-eighteenth century, but the timber and room, or room and space, of the hull framing suggests that it was made

Plate 113 *Port broadside from the stern. The canted stern frames can be seen from this view.* NMM.

157

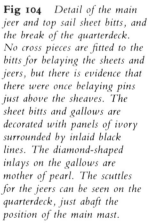

from a much earlier draught with station lines spaced at multiples of 2ft 3in. After 1719 at the latest, the timber and room of a large ship would normally be at least 2ft 6in, and by the 1750s as much as 2ft 8in or 2ft 9in. Another oddity is the length of poop deck, which at 38ft 0in is well over twice as long as the 16ft 0in specified in the Establishments of 1719 and 1745 for a ship of 80 guns. The length of the forecastle deck on the model, at 28ft 0in, is also non-standard compared with the 10ft 4in specified in 1719, and 36ft 0in in 1745.

The name painted on the stern, in the fashion that became commonplace on ships following an Admiralty order in 1772, is difficult to relate with a ship named *Barfleur*, but there is a possible explanation. The *Barfleur* was originally built in 1697 as a Second Rate of 90 guns, with a length on the gun deck of 162ft 10½in and a breadth of 46ft 4in. She was rebuilt in 1716 with similar dimensions but reduced to 80 guns, and the ship was hulked in 1764. A new *Barfleur* of 90 guns was laid down at Chatham in 1762, and the ship was launched in 1768 with a length on the gun deck of 177ft 6in and a breadth of 50ft 3in. The model has no connection with this *Barfleur* as the dimensions are far too small, and the port arrangement, stern and other details

Plate 114 *Starboard broadside from the bow, showing the deeply concave profile of the cut-water, and the shallow head rails caused by the* raised position of the cheeks, with the upper one above the hawse holes. NMM.

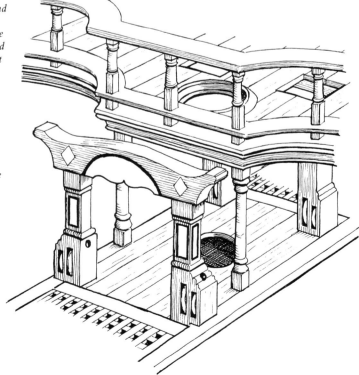

Fig 104 *Detail of the main jeer and top sail sheet bitts, and the break of the quarterdeck. No cross pieces are fitted to the bitts for belaying the sheets and jeers, but there is evidence that there were once belaying pins just above the sheaves. The sheet bitts and gallows are decorated with panels of ivory surrounded by inlaid black lines. The diamond-shaped inlays on the gallows are mother of pearl. The scuttles for the jeers can be seen on the quarterdeck, just abaft the position of the main mast.*

Fig 105 *The ladder leading up to the side gangway in the waist on the starboard side. The gangway is intended to be a permanent structure, and is supported on three large timber knees. Note the fancy little platform for the ladder to stand on.*

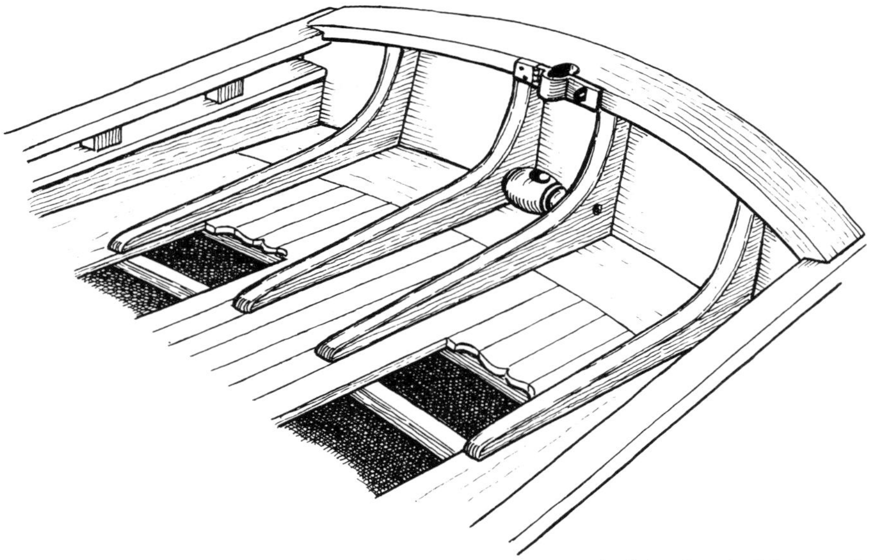

are quite different to the finalised draught for the ship. As a matter of interest, the original draught for the 1768 *Barfleur* was a radical and highly unusual design for a three-decker without a poop, and with two-tier quarter galleries and a single open stern gallery similar to a two-decker. But an amended draught was sent to Chatham in 1766, and the ship was completed with a poop and a normal stern.[1]

Nothing certain can be said about this model, but considering the name on the stern, the dimensions and the fact that it was probably made at some time around 1750–60, it is feasible that it represented the 1716 *Barfleur* as she was towards the end of her long life. She would have been well known at the time, and there is no reason why a model should not have been made of a ship built some 30 or 40 years earlier. This might explain some of the apparently anachronistic features about the model, which would reflect changes in the appearance of the ship over a long period due to alterations and repairs. It is possible that the hull itself was built from the original draught for the *Barfleur*, and this would account for the small timber and room of 2ft 3in which was quite common for big ships in the 1690s, and specified in contracts of the time.[2]

The profusion of intricate inlaid ornament suggests that the model was probably

not made in a Dockyard, but rather by an independent craftsman, either as a commission or one for sale, and of a ship which was already in existence. Although there may have been others, we know of only one such modelmaker who was working in the eighteenth century. This was Allen Hunt of Southwark, and one of his trade cards has survived which illustrates Hunt proudly indicating three models of large ships he had made, and the card is inscribed, 'Models of Ships, Cutters, and Boats Built by Draft and Scale in the most accurate manner by Allen Hunt, Ship Modeller; No 7 Kings Lane, Horsleydown, Southwark. Models ? and clean't'. Nothing is known of Hunt's models except for one of the steam yacht *Dolphin* which he made in 1822 at the age of 81, but being in business for that purpose he probably made many in the second half of the eighteenth century which exist today. As Hunt was born in 1741, it is conceivable (though merely speculation) that he made this one of the *Barfleur* when in his early twenties. Models made by craftsmen working on their own account would no doubt be of equal quality in construction to those produced in the Dockyards, but perhaps they would not worry unduly if their interpretation of the ship was not entirely accurate in every respect, and this too might explain anomalous features.

Hull construction

The well built hull is one of the very few examples of the Navy Board type which are constructed with cant frames. The cant-

Fig 106 *Detail of the aft end of the poop deck showing the very large standards against the tafferal. Pivoting steps for lowering the ensign staff such as this one are seen on many models from the late seventeenth century onwards. The securing bracket is hinged, and fastened with a hasp and staple arrangement.*

ing at the bow is not all that great, but at the stern it is more noticeable and was achieved by a slight increase in the siding of the futtocks at the breadth, with a reduction in the siding at the deadwood. The most interesting constructional details are in the hold. The well, surrounding the main mast up to the level of the lower deck, is fitted. This is built with horizontal planking between rabbeted corner posts up to the level of the orlop deck. Above this, the well is filled in with diagonal lattice work. Three heavy floor riders, the same length as the floors, are equally spaced in midships, with one each side of the well and another one forward. Three pairs of 'pointers' are fitted. These are diagonal braces, rising up and inwards from the heads of the floor riders to below the lower deck beams where they turn inwards and scarph together. The pointers are about 12in square, and exactly agree with the number and construction for an 80 that was specified in the 1719 Establishment, four pairs being required for a ship of 90 guns. All the rest of the lower deck beams are supported by 9in square pillars standing on the keelson. The riders, pointers and pillars are stop-chamfered on their edges. This internal work is very carefully constructed, considering that it is hidden away and difficult to see.

Outboard details and fittings

The mainwales are in three flush strakes, 4ft 0in overall in width and 9in thick. Above the wales is the 'black strake', which is 12in broad. None of the wales, or the ordinary plank between, is fastened in any way. The chain plates are double bolted to the hull and made of brass, like all the rest of the metal fittings. The channels are braced by closely spaced standards, with six on the fore, nine on the main and six on the mizzen.

Inboard fittings and details

All capstans are the drumhead type, but not fitted with bars. A single jeer capstan is fitted on the upper deck in the waist, with the barrel taken down and stepped on the middle deck. Aft of this, at a sufficient distance away for the bars to clear the barrel of the jeer capstan, is a double capstan, but

one deck lower and stepped on the lower deck. The main capstan is on the lower abaft the main mast. A double steering wheel is situated forward of the mizzen mast position, and is supported on fancy ivory pedestals with an intricate design picked out in red. The spokes are ivory and the rims, which have an unusual serrated inner edge, are painted red. Although the poop deck is long, the accommodation area in the roundhouse below is very small, and only about one-third the length of the deck. The bulkhead of the cabin is placed about halfway between the quarter gallery and the aftmost gun port on the quarterdeck. The deck of this cabin is laid in parquetry, with a design of small and irregular geometrical shapes, in several different coloured woods. In the accommodation on the upper deck, the deck is laid with diagonal black and white squares. The gratings in the waist are made of wood, but those of the forecastle, quarter- and poop decks are ivory. No bulkhead is fitted at the forecastle but there are small cabins each side with

Plate 115 *No suggestion can be made as to what this figurehead represents, but it is a superb example of miniature carving. The inner ends of the boomkins are secured to the stem head, and are restrained from lifting by metal bars instead of the usual rope shrouds. Note how the boomkins can have no connection with the raised projections on the main head rail.* NMM.

doors opening on to the waist, and a small square light. In the centre, between the cabins, is an enclosed area, leaving an open access each side into the forecastle. The pillars supporting the upper deck beams are wood and painted red, with those below the forecastle and quarterdecks made from ivory. Like some other models of this period, the two poop ladders are placed beneath the break of the deck and have access to the poop deck via small square scuttles.

Decoration

The craftsman who made this model was certainly fond of inlaid decoration, and the extent of it is considerable. In the three levels of the aft accommodation, the bulkheads, doors, partitions and the ship sides are profusely inlaid with panels of ivory or mother of pearl, all edged with triple lines in black and different woods. The cabins beneath the forecastle are similarly treated, and even the cat heads and top of the jeer capstan are inlaid with mother of pearl. At a conservative estimate, there are well over a hundred of these tiny inlays, a daunting task indeed, and perfectly executed. The stern carvings, moulded rails and other small details, such as the deadeyes, are finished in a thin yellowish brown paint and brightly varnished. At the breaks of the forecastle and quarterdecks the mouldings are painted in the same colour, but with the centre member of the moulding picked out in red. The friezes are painted in shades of buff, highlighted in white, on a rich deep blue background.

Fig 107 *Although of a quite simple basic structure, this belfry is remarkable for the fine inlaid decoration. The panels in the top and sides, and the bases and capitals of the corner columns, are ivory surrounded by double black lines, and triple black lines are inlaid in the columns. The bell is polished brass and the inside of the belfry is painted red.*

Colour scheme

Red: Capstan; ladders; bulwarks; inside of port lids; port linings; steering wheel rim and rope drum; tafferal standards.
Black: Mainwales; plank sheer and drift

rails; hatch coamings; breast rails; timber heads; bitts; boomkins; bollard, or knight heads; seats of ease; false rail of the main head rail.

Footnotes

1. NMM Draught Room. Draughts of the *Barfleur* (1768).
2. NMM SPB/8. Contract for the *Newark* (1695).

Plate 116 *Some very fine and delicate work is evident in this stern. The popular 'draped curtains' on the lower counter are painted in different shades of blue, with the cords and tassels in gold. The ship's name is in gold on a black background. The lower finishing of the quarter galleries is hollowed out, with the design pierced through and painted red inside. The inlaid decoration at the rudder head is repeated at the sides, but in a diamond shape. Even the deck heads above the open galleries are inlaid with a double row of ivory panels, all surrounded with double black lines. It is unusual for a large ship to have only two gun ports in the counter. NMM.*

23. Third Rate of 70 guns c1740

Location: **National Maritime Museum**
Scale: 1/60

Dimensions★				Gun ports	
	Model	*Yarmouth*		Lower deck	28
		(from draught of ship)		Upper deck	30
Gun deck	161ft 10in	160ft 0in		Quarterdeck	12
Breadth	43ft 10in	44ft 3in			
Keel (touch)	135ft 6in	135ft 6in		Total	70
Timber and room	2ft 5in	2ft 5in			

Although this exquisite model has long remained unidentified, it almost certainly represents the Third Rate *Yarmouth* built at Deptford and launched in 1748. On the tafferal, partially concealed by the centre stern lantern, is the Coat of Arms of that town, and by comparison with the original draught of the *Yarmouth*, the model agrees in all respects. The *Yarmouth* was an odd ship as she was not built to the design or dimensions laid down in the Establishment proposals of 1741. According to the draught, the *Yarmouth* was originally supposed to be a ship of 70 guns, but she is listed in Dimension Book B as a 64, with a note in brackets ('6 foot longer than off.'),[1] the abbreviation presumably being for 'official'. The dimensions given in this list are the same as those indicated on the draught.[2] There is a discrepancy of 1ft 10in in the length on the gun deck between that of the model and the ship, and a smaller difference in the breadth, but it is insignificant considering the fairly small scale. The touch keel and rake of the stern post, at 12½ degrees, agree exactly with the draught, which indicates that the difference in length on the gun deck lies in the model having a slightly increased fore rake of the stem. The arrangement and number of gun ports agrees precisely with the draught. The layout is unusual, as there are four more ports than on a normal 70, and with the usual four guns on the forecastle the ship could actually carry 74. The port arrangement of the *Yarmouth* is the same as for the first Third Rate 74, the *Culloden*, 1747, and all the later classic 74s, except that the quarterdeck is not long enough to take seven ports and therefore has six each side. To make up the 74, an extra one is placed in the gap between the cat head and the foremost upper deck port. An intriguing question is whether the *Yarmouth* was originally intended to be an early design for a 74. The draught of the *Yarmouth* is dated 1745, the same year in which a proposal was made to build 74s, but the new design found little favour at the time and was rejected.[3]

The model is of superb craftsmanship, and the rigging is mostly contemporary.

Hull construction

The hull is framed in the usual way, but the length of floors in midships is shorter than most and the line of floor heads rises steeply towards bow and stern. From the stern it can be seen that the rising line of floors would appear on the aft body plan as a straight and almost vertical 'diagonal'. The timber and room, at 2ft 5in, is the same as that specified for a Third Rate of 70 guns on the 1719 Establishment, and agrees with the spacing of the station lines on the draught of the *Yarmouth*. In the hold are strakes of thick stuff fitted at the floor heads and heels of the futtocks. The keelson is fitted, and there are square pillars on the centre line beneath every other gun deck beam.

Outboard fittings and details

The mainwales, although appearing to be double due to the black paint, are unlike the earlier projecting ones in that the upper

Fig 108 *The Heraldic Arms of the town of Yarmouth (now Great Yarmouth).*

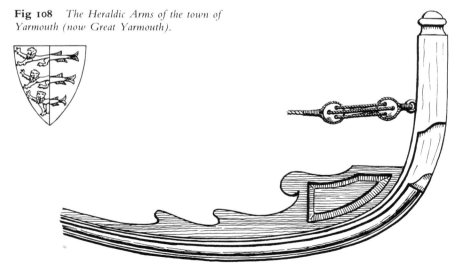

Fig 109 *Detail of the main head rail, showing the fair leads on the false rail, and also the feature at the upper end that became common from about* this date. *The deadeyes take up the slack in the berthing rope.*

and lower strakes are broader and less thick, and the strake between is almost flush. The channel wales are laid in single broad pieces representing three strakes, but the remaining top sides are laid with separate planks. No fastenings were used for any of this outboard work. The model is one of the latest two-deckers where the fore and main channels are still in the old position below the upper deck ports. The channels are placed in the middle of the channel wales, unlike the usual position at the upper edge of the wale. Again the model can be compared with the draught of the *Yarmouth*, as it not only confirms the position of the channels, but also the exact number and spacing of the deadeyes, and their position in relationship with the ports. This may not be particularly relevant, but models, and also draughts, often show considerable differences in the number of deadeyes on ships of similar rate and period. For instance, on this model there are seven deadeyes on the mizzen channel, whereas there were normally five or six. The channels are braced above by timber standards, six each on the fore and main, and four on the mizzen. The chain plates are slightly curved and double fastened, except the short ones above the ports, which have a single bolt. Like all the other metal fittings on the model, the chain plates are brass with a natural finish, and beautifully made. A good example of this fine work can also be seen in the hangings of the rudder, as the braces, complete with their gudgeons and pintles, have been entirely fashioned from solid brass. This is not all; as the braces of the rudder are quite thick and are let in so that they are almost flush, with no room for error. Modellers will probably know the difficulties encountered in lining up seven gudgeons and pintles, but on this model it has been achieved with absolute precision. A fish davit for stowing the anchors is rigged out to port, with its inner end held down by a single, centrally placed span shackle. The fish hook pendant is taken aft over the top of the side in the waist, to a tackle secured to the coaming abreast the main hatch. From here, the hauling part is taken direct to the jeer capstan.

The lanterns are six-sided, the forward three sides panelled and the rest glazed with very thin glass. The panes of glass are mitred together and it looks as though these, and the panels, have been assembled first, then set into grooves in the top and base of the lantern. Finally, small mouldings were fitted to the intersections of the glass, but these are now missing. Another impressive

illustration of the fine work on this model is the stern and quarter gallery lights. At this small scale, the lights are no more than ¾in deep and ⅝in broad, but all are divided into twelve panes and have been fretted out of very thin sheet wood. The glazing bars are very fine and rounded off on the edges.

Inboard fittings and details

A total of 50 guns are fitted, including two in the stern ports on the lower deck. Although they have no tackles, the guns are very detailed and have finely turned brass barrels. Both the jeer and main capstans are the double drumhead type. None is fitted with bars. Double pawls are shown on the deck, forward of the upper jeer capstan. The steering wheel is double and

Plate 117 *Port side from forward. NMM.*

aft of the mizzen mast, which is a late example of the wheel in this position. Gratings are properly made, with thin battens let into the athwartship ledges. A flight of bell stairs leads down from the hatch at the forward end of the quarterdeck. This deck is not as long as they generally became by the 1740s, and still has the long central gangway to the main mast.

Decoration

The Coat of Arms on the stern is contained in an elaborate cartouche in the centre of the tafferal. On each side are large Tritons, blowing conch shells and holding flags bearing the monogram GR. Outboard of

Plate 118 *Starboard side from aft. NMM.*

Plate 119 *Detail of the port side showing the rigged out fish davit, the anchor buoy lashed to the shrouds, and the manner of stowing the anchor. NMM.*

these are small figures with shields containing a cross. The ground between all these carvings is stippled with a sharp point. Each of the quarters are embellished with three small figures standing one above the other and decorated with flowers. The balusters beneath the breast rail of the balcony, and the pillasters between the stern lights, are made from ivory. This material has also been used internally for the spokes of the steering wheel, and pillars below the deck beams. The upper counter is painted with various fabulous sea creatures and seaweed, in shades of yellow and ochre on a ground of mid-blue. The lower counter is painted in similar colours, with the popular design of draped curtains tied back with tasseled cords. At the bows, the false rail, on top of the main head rail, shows an early example of the distinctive feature that appeared on its upper end at about this time. Although decorative, it was also practical, as it was always adjacent to the seats of ease, and was probably introduced as protection for the seamen. The lion figurehead is a fine piece of work, and like the rest of the carvings,

is left in natural varnished wood.

Colour scheme

Black: Mainwales; plank sheer and rails at the top of the side; anchors and anchor buoys; timber heads; bollards; stem head; inside of head timbers; false rail of the main head rail; fish davit; bitts; chocks between the whelps of the capstans; rim of the steering wheel.

Red: Gun carriages; muzzles of gun barrels back to the first astragal; inside of gun ports and port lids; inside of stern lanterns; inside of quarter galleries.

Footnotes

1. PRO. A list of HMRN dated 25 June 1742, corrected to 1748.
2. NMM, Draught Room, Box 21.
3. Brian Lavery, *Ship of the Line* (Conway, 1983) Vol 1, p91.

24. Fourth Rate of 52 guns c1740

Location: **Pitt-Rivers Museum, Oxford**
Scale: 1/48

Dimensions*		Gun ports	
Length of gun deck	146ft 6in	Lower deck	22
Breadth extreme	41ft 0in	Upper deck	24
		Quarterdeck	6
		Total	52

The earliest known record of this model is contained in a nineteenth-century catalogue of the Pitt-Rivers Collection,[1] which is brief in the extreme, and gives a fuller description of the contemporary display case than it does of the model. The entry reads, 'A model of a ship in a glass case, on a mahogany stand'. A later label with the model identifies it as a Fourth Rate of 52 guns of about 1740, but this date is obviously much too early. In every respect, the model agrees in dimensions, gun ports, details and general appearance with the existing draughts of the Portland class Fourth Rates built between 1770 and 1790.[2] One of these was the *Leopard*, 1790, and judging by the number of leopards incorporated in the decoration, the model is almost certainly of this ship. The *Leopard* was an

Plate 120 *Port broadside. The extension to the slipway is resting on a table, but it would normally be supported by the hinged board that can be seen below the slip.* Pitt-Rivers Museum.

unusual case, as she was originally laid down at Portsmouth in 1776, but her frames were taken to Sheerness 9 years later, where the ship was completed and launched in 1790.[3] The dimensions given on the draught of the *Leopard* are 146ft 0in on the gun deck and 40ft 6in in breadth, compared with the model at 146ft 6in × 41ft 0in. This can be considered accurate as the discrepancy in both dimensions is only $\frac{1}{8}$in on the model. The scale of 1/48 is confirmed by the draught of water marks, in feet, on the stem and stern post, which are at exact intervals of $\frac{1}{4}$in. These are always of value when shown on a model, as apart from determining the scale, the load waterline (LWL) depth is known. In this case, the LWL of the model agrees with that of the *Leopard*, as taken from the draught of the ship, at 18ft 0in forward and 19ft 0in aft. This draught is an 'as built' one, and as such shows the stern carvings, figurehead and other details of the decoration. In this respect the model does not agree with the

draught, and the stern carvings are totally different, but common to both are carved leopards on the trail boards. At the stern, the draught shows the name of the ship in large letters on the upper counter that was introduced in 1772,[4] but in its place the model has a painted leopard. The figurehead is a similar type except that the figure on the draught is holding a pair of cymbals, whereas the one on the model is carrying a horn in her left hand, and perhaps there was also something else in her right, which has broken away. But these differences are not too relevant, and it would not be reasonable to assume that the carvings on the ship as built would turn out to be the same as on the model. What is important is the depiction of leopards in the decoration, to suggest the name of the ship.

When and where the model was actually made is not clear, but it was probably Portsmouth, and the absence of the name on the counter suggests the early 1770s, or a little before, as the first design draught for the Portland class is dated 1767. If this is so, there is an anachronism in the flags, as these certainly date from no earlier than 1801. The Arms on the Royal Standard are those in use from 1801 following the Act of Union with Ireland. The Union Flag also dates from the same time and is in its finalised form, with the addition of the Cross of St Patrick. As the Royal Arms were changed again in 1816, it can be assumed that the flags were added, for some reason, in the period of these 15 years. With the model is a comprehensive list of some 130 items describing the parts of a ship, which correspond to numbered labels on the model. The date of this list is unknown, but it is possible that it is contemporary with the flags. It seems to be later than the model, as several items refer to details that were old-fashioned at the time the list was compiled. For instance, item 31 describes

The detailed slipway is evidently intended to be of practical use, to demonstrate the launch of a ship, as the cradles are fitted with small concealed brass wheels to allow the model to run freely down the ways, which show evidence of considerable use. It is logical to believe that the slipway, and therefore the display case, are contemporary with the undoubted date of the flags, and made at some time between 1801 and 1816, but the discrepancy between the apparent date of the model itself and this period is difficult to understand. A possible explanation is that a model was needed for instructional purposes in the early nineteenth century, and this earlier one was taken, the case and slipway made, the flags added and the list of parts compiled. A School of Naval Architecture was established in Portsmouth in 1811,[5] and as the model may have originated from there, it is quite possible that there is a connection with that School.

Another link with Portsmouth — although a tenuous one – is that in style and quality of workmanship, the model is remarkably similar to a fine example of the Third Rate *Lion*, 64 guns, at the Dorset County Museum, Dorchester. This *Lion* was launched at Portsmouth in 1777, and it is likely that both models were made at that Dockyard by the same craftsman.

Hull construction and outboard details

Although it cannot be seen, the hull of this planked model is probably solid or hollowed out pine up to the level of the lower deck, and built on the 'lift' or 'bread and butter' method, as were the common block models of the eighteenth century. Separate top timbers would then be erected on the hull to form the top sides. The hull planking, in finest quality box wood, is a superb example of the modeller's art. Not a single fastening was used, and the way in which the strakes are expanded at the lower end of the stern post and diminished at the wing transom is nothing short of perfection. To achieve the necessary expansion at the post, only one stealer was needed which is inserted directly above the garboard strake. The planking was very carefully set out, with strakes of the correct length, and all the butt ends, where they come on the same line, are separated by three strakes. As on many models, the knee of the head is fitted to a separate stem. These usually show a perfect fit, which would be quite difficult

Plate 121 *Stern. The outer windows of both tiers are dummies, known as the 'mock lights', and are not glazed. A point of interest is the bracket for the ensign staff, which was necessary on these ships with a low tafferal. The painted leopard can be seen in the centre of the upper counter. Pitt-Rivers Museum.*

the deadeye chains and adds in brackets, '*At the present time* a solid bar of iron takes the place of the linked chain'. And under the section 'Parts of the rudder', we find, 'In the *old* wooden ships, with square headed rudders, *as in this case*, the helm port was necessarily large so as to allow the rudder

to turn freely' (author's italics). Although it does not say so, the comparison is with the round headed rudder that came into general use in the early years of the nineteenth century. Some interesting and uncommon terms appear on the list, such as 'caboose' for the galley stove, and the 'woodlock', which was a piece of wood nailed in the gulleting of the upper rudder pintle to prevent the rudder being unshipped. Those wishing to learn the authentic terminology relating to ships of this period would do well to go and have a look at this model.

to achieve on a long curved joint. But on this model, the task was eased, as the grain of the wood indicates that the stem was bent to shape, probably by steaming. The rudder is made up of two pieces, with the joint corresponding to the upper hance, and a separate backing piece and sole are fitted, both about 6in thick. For some reason the backing piece is grooved on the after side. Pintles and gudgeons are finely made of brass, and the braces are fastened with tiny, closely spaced brass pins, with up to twelve in the longer ones. Only the lower deck ports are fitted with lids. These are much thicker than on most models, where the lids are the same thickness as the plank of the side, and are rabbeted at the sides and lower edges to allow them to lie flush. Each lid is marked on the inner side with small incised Roman numerals.

Inboard fittings and details

These later eighteenth-century models are generally shown with much more deck planking than formerly. On this one, the lower deck is fully planked and all the rest just have a few strakes left out each side. Despite all this planking, the work below decks is remarkably detailed and can only be seen by peering through the gun ports. On the lower deck, one can see the rows of standards and pillars, bitts, capstans, ladders and also the chain pumps, with the pump dales rigged out to starboard. The upper deck is fully framed with carlings and ledges, and the beams are all fitted with lodging and hanging knees. Of interest in the waist are the gangboard brackets, made of brass. There are four each side and they are detachable. The lower end fits into an eye bolt and the upper part is slotted over an eye plate, where it is retained by a wedge secured to the side with a small piece of chain. Standards, or vertical knees that brace the decks to the ship's side, are rarely seen on models of any period. They are shown here on the lower and upper decks, between each port. Although the knees are generally known as standards, they are given in the list of parts as stanchions to the bulwarks. The finely made and detailed galley stove beneath the forecastle deck is made of brass and set on a fire hearth of small squares of bone. This material has also been used for many of the small details such as the steering wheel, belfry, pillars, and balusters and pillasters of the stern galleries. The bulkheads of the accommodation below the

Fig 110 *Detail of the fore end of the launching cradle at the port side. The chock to release the cradle is hinged, and held in position by a small spring. The cord from the chock emerges at the head of the slipway, where it forms a loop and returns to the chock at the starboard side. In use, a* pull on the cord releases both chocks simultaneously, and allows the cradle to run down the ways. A similar method would be employed in full-sized practice, but with the chocks held in place by wedges, which would be knocked out at the moment of launch.

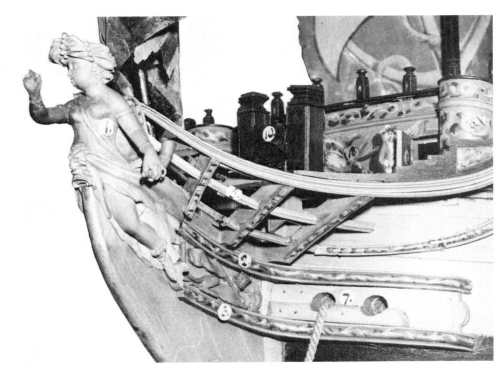

poop are framed in wood, with panels of bone. A nice little touch in the Captain's cabin is a beautifully made and gilded couch.

Decoration

The stern carvings relate entirely to the cult

Plate 122 *Detail of the head. The carved leopards on the trail boards are carrying flags, which are incised with a single G on the starboard side and an R to port. The middle and lower head rails are in short pieces, and fitted between the head timbers. Author.*

Plate 123 *Upper deck in the waist. The gangboard brackets are extended upwards to provide supports for the athwartship beams, which carried the boats and spare spars. Shot racks are fitted between the ports.* Author.

of the Greek god Dionysus and his retinue. Among other things, Dionysus was god of wine and merriment, and always associated with him were the god Pan, Satyrs and various female followers such as Maenads and Bacchantes. The particular attribute of Dionysus was the leopard, and two are shown here in the centre of the tafferal, drawing the god in a shell-like chariot. Either side of this are Satyrs each holding a drinking cup and a Thyrsus. The quarter figures are of Pan, and above the quarter lights is a basket of flowers to starboard and group of musical instruments to port, consisting of a horn, tambourine and pan pipes. If this model is indeed of the *Leopard*, the theme of the carvings may well have been inspired by the name of the ship. The figurehead is more difficult to identify, but it too is perhaps associated with Dionysus, and may be a representation of a Maenad or a Bacchante. A large trophy of arms is painted on the beak bulkhead flanked by military figures in uniform, holding muskets. The lower stools of the quarter galleries are painted with a design of a lion's head with a rose, and a unicorn's head with a thistle. Models with the full array of contemporary flags are relatively uncommon, and these are probably some of the best examples. Beautifully painted, they are in the correct sequence. From forward they are the Union Jack, Board of Admiralty

Plate 124 *Launching cradle aft. A peculiarity shown by other models is that the base of the cradle, which slides on the ways, is made of coarse-grained pine compared with the fine wood used for the rest of the cradle. In this case there is a separate sole fitted to the underside. The small wheels can be seen. Note that there are also horizontal ones running against the sides of the ways.* Author.

Plate 125 *Launching cradle forward.* Author.

Flag, Royal Standard, Union Flag and the White Ensign. All the painted decoration is in exceptionally bright and unfaded colours, no doubt due to the rather dark conditions in which the model is displayed.

Slipway

For the purpose of taking the photographs, the model was 'launched', but not quite in the correct way, as the keel blocks were temporarily stuck to the keel, which has caused the aft end of the cradles to lift off the ways. The keel blocks are all attached to a thin slip of wood, which would normally be removed before the launch to allow the cradle to sit firmly down on the ways. Cables lead from the hawse holes of the model which are made up on bollards at the head of the slip, and are of just sufficient length to check the cradles at the end of the extension to the slipway. An alteration was made to the cradles, as there were originally two more spurs aft and one more forward, but these were removed at some time and the screw holes stopped up. When not in use, the slipway extension and its folding support are stowed in a compartment below the base of the display case.

Colour scheme

Black: Mainwales; deadeye chains; knight heads; timber heads; bitts on forecastle and poop; plank sheer and fife rails.
Red: Insides of port lids and ports; inside of hawse holes; sides of deck beams and ladders; standards; main jeer and top sail sheet bitts.
Blue: Insides of the timbers and rails of the head.

Footnotes

1. Black, *Catalogue of the Pitt-Rivers Collection* (1875) p72a.
2. NMM Draught Room.
3. J J Colledge, *Ships of the Royal Navy, an Historical Index* (1969), Vol 1.
4. Carr-Laughton, *Old Ships' Figureheads and Sterns* (London, 1925).
5. *The Mariner's Mirror*, Vol 2, pp363–4.

25. Royal Oak, Third Rate of 70 guns 1741

Location: **National Maritime Museum**
Scale: **1/48**

Dimensions*	Model	Ship 1713 rebuild	Ship 1741 rebuild	Gun ports	
				Lower deck	26
Gun deck	150ft 3in	150ft 0in	151ft 0in	Upper deck	26
Breadth	40ft 10in	41ft 4½in	43ft 5in	Quarterdeck	14
Depth	16ft 8in	17ft 4in	17ft 9in		
Timber and room	2ft 2in	—	2ft 7in	Total	66

Royal Oak, 1713. Rebuilt at Woolwich Dockyard (Mr Ackworth). *Royal Oak*, 1741. Rebuilt at Plymouth Dockyard.
The dimensions of the ship are from Dimension Book B, except for the timber and room which has been taken from the draught.

One of the most beautiful of all eighteenth-century Third Rates, this model of the *Royal Oak* is of exceptional interest. From the name on the counter, and the theme of oak leaves incorporated in the decorative work, there is no doubt that the model is of the *Royal Oak,* but whether it represents the ship as rebuilt in 1741 is open to question. The manner of construction, features, fittings and general appearance of the model all strongly suggest that the hull dates back to the early eighteenth century. A small medallion at the port side of the tafferal contains what could be taken for either a single R or a combined AR. It is difficult to be certain, but a single R appears to be meaningless, and it is probably the monogram of Queen Anne, and not later than 1714. Although the rigging is original, it is believed to be of a date no earlier than the 1719 Establishment, and may not be contemporary with the hull.

There is one apparent anomaly. From the early eighteenth century until about 1730 at the latest, Third Rates normally had two open stern galleries, while the model has only one at the level of the quarterdeck. The accommodation forward of the screen bulkhead on the quarterdeck is divided into cabins for the officers, which indicates that the Captain's quarters were on the upper deck, as was usual until the lower gallery was discontinued. But why is there no upper deck gallery on this model? It would be inconceivable for the officers to have the advantage of one and not the Captain. The answer is that there *was* originally a lower gallery, as it can be

seen that the screen bulkhead was removed and the opening in the hull filled in with a flush tier of lights. The only external evidence of this is that the small decorative pillars between the lights are of a different design and rather better made than the original ones at the side, and the gallery

balusters are painted instead of being made as on other models. But from inside it is quite clear. There are two entrance doors through the hull into the quarter galleries, and it is obvious that a bulkhead was once

Plate 126   *The broadside.* NMM.

fitted between them, and the paint is a different colour each side of where it used to be. Another oddity is that in the upper and below the gallery breast rail, there are four small gun ports at each level, all with painted lion heads on the inside of the lids. These areas are covered up externally with what appears to be thick paper, on which is painted the gallery balusters and the name of the ship. Except for the ports, the stern of this model in its original state would have been very similar to that on the Third Rate of about 1705 (see Model No 18).

When and why all this alteration took place can only be a matter of conjecture. It is tempting to believe that if the hull is indeed of the 1713 *Royal Oak*, it was altered in connection with the rebuilding of the ship in 1741, but that does not make a great deal of sense. The type of stern that the model now has was quite normal for a mid-eighteenth-century two-decker, and there would be little point in making the alteration – which was, after all, a considerable amount of work – just to illustrate a stern with one gallery instead of two. Perhaps it is simply one of the many mysteries of Navy Board models.

The craftsmanship in construction and rigging is of a very high standard, and the model illustrates a number of interesting features and fittings. The model is known to have been in the possession of King George II who gave it to his brother, the Duke of York. It was later obtained by Trinity House, Leith, and was acquired by the National Maritime Museum in 1974.

Hull construction

The rising line of floor heads on this model is unusually low at bow and stern, and would be shown on the body plan as 'diagonals' of considerable curvature. The hull is one of the few where the futtock

Plate 127   *Quarter view from forward. NMM.*

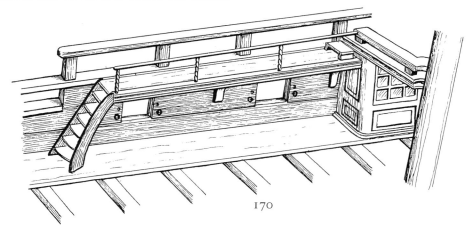

Fig 111   *The very long side gangway leading forward from the poop deck. It is supported by three timber knees.*

heels meet on the centre line instead of stopping 2 or 3ft short of the keel. There are fewer transoms than usual, and two short vertical timbers are fitted where there would normally be a further one or two lower transoms. In the hold is a heavy fore and aft strake each side about a scale 4ft 0in broad and 9in thick, with the outer edges a little below the floor heads. These two strakes are fastened with hundreds of treenails, and the modeller must have been very careful with the depth of drilling as there is no trace of any on the outside of the timbers. Beneath each of the gun deck

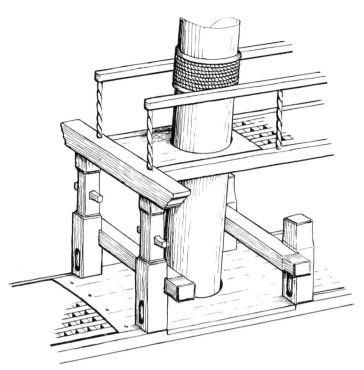

Fig 112 *Detail of the main mast at the upper deck showing the main jeer, main top sail sheet bitts and the central gangway from the quarterdeck.*

Fig 113 *The small single steering wheel aft of the mizzen mast. Models rarely have the steering rope fitted as on this one.*

beams there are 9in square stop-chamfered pillars stepped on the keelson.

Outboard fittings and details

A very faint waterline is scribed on the hull, giving a depth forward of 17ft 3in and 18ft 3in aft. Each strake of the double mainwales is 1ft 1½in broad, 9in thick and spaced 2ft 0in apart. Simple scarphs are scribed on the wales at intervals of about 24ft 0in. The top side plank is scored to represent individual strakes and is fastened with scattered treenails. In addition, the modeller marked in several thousand more simulated fastenings with what looks like the sharpened end of a metal tube. Several of the broadside features suggest that the model originated from the early eighteenth century. The most prominent is that the gun ports on the upper deck in the waist are fitted with lids, a practice which was totally discontinued after around 1715. Another is the old-fashioned type of chain plate. These are the short curved ones with a single fastening in the lower chainwale in the seventeenth-century fashion, and which disappeared entirely on large ships by about 1720. The channels are braced from above by timber standards – five on the fore channel, six on the main and four on the mizzen. An interesting series of ventilation scuttles are fitted in way of the aft accommodation. Three are at the level of the upper deck,

each with double sliding shutters, and there is one small one with a single shutter at the level of the quarterdeck. A very unusual detail for which no explanation can be given is a series of eight vertical sheaves fitted in the side above the forward end of the main channel. As on many models, the eking of the cat supporter continues round the bow to meet the lower hand rail and coincides with the level of the hawse holes.

Plate 128 *Hull framing at the bows. The simulated fastenings can be seen in the plank between the wales, which are spaced farther apart than usual. One of the scarphs of the lower wale is just forward of the anchor lining. Author.*

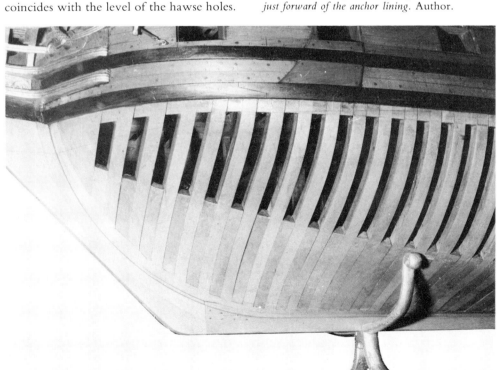

In most cases, the eking is just interrupted and looks somewhat unsatisfactory, but on this model an improvement was made by continuing it across the hawse holes with a pair of moulded arches.

Inboard fittings and details

There is some wonderful work between decks on this model, which is a perfect example of the painstaking attention to detail typical of eighteenth-century craftsmen. To look along the entire length of the lower deck from the stern is a revelation: everything is fitted as it should be, such as the long rows of beautifully turned pillars and hanging knees, transom knees, capstans and ladders, and in the distance, the riding bitts and breast hooks. All is perfectly fitted, and mostly fastened with treenails. The difficult-to-fit hanging knees are particularly impressive, and apart from the ordinary straight ones, there are also raking and cast knees fitted where a beam comes above a gun port. The knees, and the lower edges of the deck beams, have a fine bead worked along the corners. The deck plank at the sides of the upper deck is broader than usual, and extends from the side to the middle of the outer tier of carlings. This saved the modeller some work, as he did not fit any deck ledges below the plank! The capstan arrangement is the one used until the 1730s, ie a single main capstan with a drumhead on the lower deck, and a double jeer capstan with no drumhead or bars on the lower one. A single centrally placed deck pawl is fitted on the upper deck forward of the jeer capstan. The fish davit is rigged out on the port side. The davit is 28ft 3in long, 18in square in the middle, and tapers to 12in square at each end. A pair of span shackles is fitted, one each side of the grating above the galley. The shackles are retained by large eye bolts to allow them to lie flat on the deck when not in use, and their bolts are taken down and fastened through one of the upper deck beams. It should be noted that when there

is a pair of span shackles, the one in use is the farthest from the side on which the davit is employed. The fish hook pendant is taken round a timber head aft of the davit, then leads forward inside the bulwarks to another timber head forward of the davit where it is made up. The single steering wheel is fitted aft of the mizzen mast, and is fairly small at about 4ft 6in diameter at the spoke ends. Directly below the steering rope drum, and against the poop bulkhead, is a glazed companion with a grating in the top through which the steering rope passes. This is one of the very few models where the steering rope is actually fitted and connected with the tiller. The roundhouses at the beak bulkhead are fitted with seats of ease, and have the unusual feature of

small external doors opening out to the beak platform. The area of the latrines extends aft into the forecastle about 3ft 0in where there is a small access door. Aft of this again are small cabins about 5ft 0in square which extend aft almost to the foremost upper deck gun port. Very prominent on the quarterdeck are the side gangways leading to the poop deck. These are rarely seen on eighteenth-century two-deckers, and the length of them, at a scale about 16ft 0in, is extraordinary. The purpose of such long gangways is unknown.

Decoration

The figurehead is a standard type of lion, except that the mane and tail are decorated with oak leaves. The inner cap of the crown and the muzzle of the beast are painted red, and the eyes and eyebrows are picked out in black. An unusual volute, or scroll, is carved on the upper end of the main head rail instead of the normal timber head. The quarter pieces at the stern are Hercules, with his club to port, and Poseidon with a trident to starboard. At each end of the tafferal are crowned medallions containing the A or AR on the port side, and the Admiralty Anchor to starboard. These are painted gold on a blue background and gold on a red background respectively. Outboard of the medallions are Tritons blowing conch shells. In the centre of the tafferal is what appears to be a male bust surrounded by fine carvings decorated with oak leaves. All the carvings and moulded rails are gilt which is unusually brightly burnished. There are four painted friezes at the top of the side towards the stern, all divided by moulded rails. From the upper one, they are painted red, blue, then a design of oak leaves in gold on a black background with the lower one, also in gold on black, being a simple wavy line representing foliage.

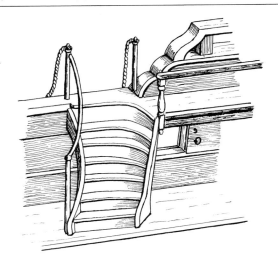

Fig 114 *This is a typical staircase of the early eighteenth century, and its design is quite ingenious, giving access both from over the side and* *from the gangway to the quarterdeck. The ropes attached to the stantions are the 'man ropes' that hang down each side of the boarding steps.*

Colour scheme

Red: Inside of bulwarks; cabins and inboard bulkheads; bitts; capstan; ladders; steering wheel; galley chimney; inside of ports and port lids; inside of stern gallery.

Black: Spirketting on the upper deck; rails at the top of the side; belfry; fish davit; anchors; cat heads; bollards of the head; mainwales.

Gold: All carved work; moulded rails of the head, stern, broadside and inboard bulkheads; outboard edges of plank sheer and fife rails; cheeks of the head.

Gold on black: Friezes of the broadside and beak bulkhead; ship's name on the upper counter; balusters under the breast rail of the stern gallery.

Blue: Beak bulkhead; lower counter.

26. Devonshire, Third Rate of 66 guns 1745

Location: **Kriegstein collection**
Scale: 1/48

Dimensions of ship		Gun ports	
Gun deck	161ft 2in	Lower deck	28
Keel (for tonnage)	130ft 4in	Upper deck	28
Breadth	46ft 0in	Quarterdeck	14
Depth in hold	19ft 4in		—
Tons	1471	Total	70

The *Devonshire* was built at Woolwich Dockyard by J Holland.

Although this model can be classed in the category of 'block models' in that the interior of the hull is completely closed in at the level of the plank sheer, the outboard details are more extensive than on the common ones of this type. The majority of the great many block models that exist are very simple, with the wales, channels, ports, deadeyes and chain plates painted on the hull, but the *Devonshire* is almost as well detailed as any other model. The model has been identified by comparison with a painting by Samuel Scott of the action off Cape Finisterre in 1747, which includes a clear stern view of the *Devonshire*. The quarter and tafferal carvings on the model are very distinctive, and so similar to the painting that there is no doubt it represents the same ship. The painting is in the Tate Gallery, London. Although the *Devonshire* is listed as a ship of 66 guns, the number and arrangement of ports are the same as for the *Culloden*, 1747, the first English 74, and all the later 74s. Like the *Culloden*, the *Devonshire* was originally intended to be a Third Rate of 80 guns on three decks, but was completed as a two-decker, as were several other ships designed as 80s.

General construction

The hull is painted ivory white and scored to represent the seams between the planks, a difficult task which was achieved with some precision. The model is one of the earliest two-deckers to show the fore and main channels in the new raised position on the sheer rail above the upper deck ports. At that time, the mizzen channels normally remained where they were previously, and thus all three channels were at the same level, but on this model they are also raised up one deck to above the quarterdeck ports. The long straight chain plates are painted black and double bolted to the chainwales. The ports on the upper deck in the waist that are not fitted with lids are glazed with glass. An open weave material of some sort is glued on the insides of the glass panes, perhaps to obscure the probably rough interior of the hull. The upper surfaces of the model are covered with a varnished

Plate 130 *The port broadside.* Kriegstein collection.

174

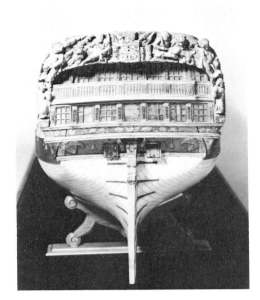

Plate 131 *The stern. The significance of the castle in the centre of the tafferal is unclear, but the flanking figures are an interesting example of classical mythology, apparently showing Hercules engaged in two of his 'Twelve Labours'. To starboard, Hercules is about to slay the Nemean Lion, and to port, the god is depicted with one of the Stymphalian Birds. The full width stern gallery extends round the quarters to form small balconies, a practice that was generally discontinued by the 1750s. Kriegstein collection.*

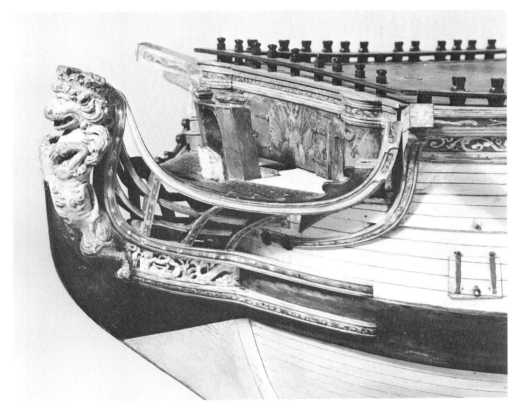

Plate 132 *View of the head. Lion figureheads are seldom seen on models from the 1740s onwards. The seats of ease at each end of the beak bulkhead are two-tier affairs with one above and slightly aft of the other. It does not take much imagination to picture the scene when both were in use at the same time! Kriegstein collection.*

paper which bears the identified London watermark of a mid-eighteenth century paper made by Lubertus van Gerrevink.

Decoration

The decorative work, including the carvings, is painted in soft subdued colours, probably water colour, but it may have been done in egg tempera. Trophies of Arms, on a mid-blue background, decorate the beak bulkhead, upper counter and broad frieze at the top of the side aft. The lower counter is painted in the popular design of draped curtains, with tasselled cords.

Appendices

I. Block Models

Large numbers of block models must have been made in the eighteenth century. At the National Maritime Museum alone there is a huge collection of over sixty, with rather more than half of them dating from between 1700 and 1750. Many of them have the name of the ship painted on the stern or the broadside. Block models appear to be insignificant objects when compared with the familiar detailed ones, and are easy to overlook. But they are very attractive, particularly for their paintwork, and in one respect they may be just as important, or perhaps more so. Why block models were made is uncertain. It is possible they were made as a record of ships that had already been built. On the other hand, they may well have been the ordinary official design models of the time, which were made by shipwrights to submit to the Navy Board for approval before the ship was begun. Design models of the eighteenth century were referred to in contemporary official correspondence as 'solids'. On 4 June 1716, an Order was sent from the Navy Board to the Master Shipwrights of the various Dockyards, requiring them to submit a model, as well as a draught, for ships of all Rates either for a proposed new ship or for the rebuilding of one, 'before the same shall be taken in hand'.[1] The relevant passage reads:

> You are also to prepare and send with your said Draught, a *solid* or Model, shaped exactly by the same, with the Load Water line, the Height of the Decks and Wales, the Channels, Ports, Galleries and Co. *marked* thereon. (Author's italics.)

The reference to a 'solid' and that the details were to be 'marked' on evidently does not mean a fully detailed model, and it is highly probable that a simple block model was all that was intended. The details on block models are not actually 'marked' but painted on.

In an official letter dated 1 July 1717, it appears that Master Shipwright Stacey of Deptford Dockyard had submitted two models as his designs for rebuilding the Fourth Rate *Nottingham*, 60 guns, which was launched in 1719.[2] One was for a ship with a round buttock, the other for a square tuck. Square tucks were probably

uncommon on Fourth Rates by that time, and it is not surprising that the design for a ship with a round buttock won the day. These models were termed 'solids', as was another in the same letter, being a design for the Third Rate *Revenge*, 70 guns, launched in 1718. Among the unidentified block models at Greenwich, there is one of 60 guns and another of 70 guns, both of which are about the right date, and it is quite possible that they are the above models. I have not seen either of these two models, but if the one of 60 guns has a square tuck, it would almost certainly suggest that it is the *Nottingham*, and that block models were the official designs of the eighteenth century.

In another official letter dated 21 December 1739, Master Shipwright Lock of Plymouth was requested by Jacob Ackworth, Surveyor of the Navy, to 'forthwith lay down a body and send a draught and *solid* to the Navy Board'.[3] This was for a design for the Fourth Rate *Exeter*, 60 guns, launched by Lock at Plymouth in 1744. Again there is an unidentified block model of a Fourth Rate 60 in the collection at Greenwich of the right date, although this does not prove anything. About half the identified models in the collection dating from before 1750 are of ships that were rebuilt. It is interesting to note that in the correspondence of 1744 concerning the model for the Admiralty Boardroom – which was obviously an exceptionally detailed one – it is referred to as just that, and there is no mention of its being a 'solid'.

The kind of wood from which block models were made cannot be verified due to the paint, but yellow pine was probably widely used, or some other soft and fine grained variety. Cracks in the paint caused by slight movements in the wood show that the hulls were built up with thick boards, and shaped according to the water-lines in the well known 'lift', or 'bread and butter' method as it is known today. The hull of the Fourth Rate *Centurion*, 1732, is

Plate 133 *A block model of the Fourth Rate Centurion, 1732. The entire broadside details are painted on the hull, including the framing. Like most block models, it is built to a scale of 1/48.* NMM

very heavy and appears to be quite solid.

The remarkable thing about block models is the paintwork. The *Centurion*, illustrated in Plate 133, is a typical example except for the unusual painted hull framing, and the only detail on it that is actually built is the head rails. The entirely flush broadside and stern is curiously painted in suitable colours, with shadows under the channels, chain plates and variously opened port lids, etc, creating a three-dimensional effect. The *Centurion* has quarter galleries fashioned from a single piece of wood, but even this is not shown on some models, and the galleries are painted directly on the side of the hull. These look most odd when viewed from the stern. The hull framing on the *Centurion* is painted in subtly different shades of ochre to distinguish the heels of the top timbers and floors from the futtocks, with the spaces between being black. Cant frames are shown at bow and stern. It would not have been an easy task to mark out and paint the framing on the complex curvature of the hull, but it was achieved with extraordinary precision. The artist had, of course, to paint the framing in the style of a conventionally built model. The figurehead is a square block shaped approximately to the profile of a lion, which is delicately painted on each side, and there is a full frontal view of the beast on the forward side of the figure.

Footnotes

1. The Order is reproduced in an article by W G Perrin, *The Mariner's Mirror*, Vol 5, p56.
2. Public Record Office, Adm 106/3297.
3. *Ibid*, Adm 91/2.

(Both these letters are published in Brian Lavery, *Ship of the Line*, Vol 2 Appendix 1, p164.)

II. Letters concerning a model for the Admiralty Boardroom

(Public Record Office, Adm 106/1021)

Very few official references to models are known to exist, and these letters concerning the actual building of one are of considerable interest. The letters were discovered by Brian Lavery, and I am grateful to him for bringing them to my notice.

Apparently, the Admiralty was becoming impatient at the delay in completing the model, having waited nearly four years for it, and the following letter arrived at the Navy Board from the Officers at Woolwich where it was being built:

> Woolwich 9th February 1744.
> Hon. Sirs
> In return to your honour's Warrent of the 5th inst. to let you know when the Model ordered the 12th June 1740, to be prepared for the Right Honourables the Lords of the Admiraltys Boardroom may be expected, we take leave to acquaint you that her hull is compleated, Japanned and Varnished, and her Masts and Anchors with part of her Rigging and Blocks which are in hand with all the help we can find in this Yard, and as these matters are of a curious nature and tedious to be performed, tis our opinion 'twill be the latter end of June next before she will be ready for placing in their Office, but if we can be assisted by three persons from Deptford that we are informed have been used to such work, presume she may be compleated in May next. We are
> Hon. Sirs
> Your most Obedient Servants
> C. King   J. Holland

It appears that the Navy Board may not have been entirely satisfied with the reply from Woolwich, for another letter in the same vein, and dated two days later, arrived from a Mr Gilbert:

> Hon. Sirs
> Having leave from Commissioner Brown, I have been to inspect into the Works and forwardness of the Model for the Admiralty Boardroom Building at Woolwich, and find her Hull compleat, Guns and Carriages made, Cordage for the Rigging spun; part of the Blocks made and the rest in hand; the Masts and Yards so nearly finished that the Rigging may be begun, therefore Humbly pray Your Honours will be pleased to direct that James Edwards, John Mitchell and Adam Cooper, Shipwrights in his Majesties Yard at Deptford, may be lent to the Woolwich Yard; to Assist in Rigging the said Model, for the quicker dispatch

thereof, as it is very much wanted. I am
> Hon. Sirs
> Your most Obedient Humble
> Servant
> Gilbert
> 11th February 1744
> Hon. Navy Board

Written in a corner are some notes on action to be taken against the letter from Mr Gilbert. Two words are difficult to decipher:

> Acquaint Mr Corbett* in answer to his letter of the instant in what forwardness the Model is in, and that We hope the said be compleated some time in May next. Direct the Officers at Deptford to spare the three Men mentioned in Mr Gilbert's letter to assist in finishing the Model at Woolwich and to cheque them out of Pay 'till their return. Order the Officers at Woolwich to bear them for Wages in that Clas'd and to . . . them the same . . . as is wrought by like Shipwrights there.

An oddity about this correspondence is that the model is referred to as just that, with no indication of the name of the ship, although it was obviously considered an important one to be displayed in the Admiralty Boardroom. A few Third and Fourth Rates of a suitable date exist that meet the requirements of being rigged and fitted with guns and anchors, but it is unlikely that the model was of an ordinary vessel. It all suggests a large and prestigious ship, and one that was launched shortly before the model was commissioned in 1740. We can only speculate on the identity of this mysterious model, but in all probability it was the famous and short-lived First Rate *Victory*, launched at Portsmouth in 1737. The very fine large-scale rigged model of that ship at the National Maritime Museum can be eliminated, not so much because she is traditionally (but not certainly) believed to have been built for the Official Inquiry into the ship's loss in October 1744, but because guns are not fitted.

Although it cannot be substantiated, the prime candidate for the Boardroom model is another superb example of the 1737 *Victory* which is in the possession of the Earl of Cawdor. Built to a scale of 1/48, the model has contemporary rigging and is fully equipped with all guns and anchors. As in so many cases, the origin of the model is unknown, but an ancestor of the present Earl – John Campbell of Cawdor – was a Lord of the Admiralty from 1741, and it is

(*Thomas Corbett, Secretary to the Admiraly, 1742–1751)

presumed that he obtained the model while in Office and carried it up to Cawdor Castle in Scotland, where it remains. (For those wishing to see it, the model is on display in the part of Cawdor Castle open to the general public from May to October inclusive.)

In one small respect, the model follows the draught of the *Victory* more accurately than does the one at Greenwich in that the entry ports are unusually placed in way of the fourth middle deck port from aft, instead of the normal position abreast the main mast. A unique feature of the model is that the upper deck ports are decorated with wreaths in the seventeenth-century fashion.

A number of interesting points are raised in the letters, not least that the hull of the model took almost four years to build, assuming it was begun soon after the commissioning date. The reference to 'all the help we can find in this yard' suggests that several men were engaged on the model before the other three arrived from Deptford. It is surprising that shipwrights were to assist in rigging the model. Being 'used to such work', it is probable that Messrs Edwards, Mitchell and Cooper worked on any one of the finely rigged models dating from around the mid-eighteenth century, perhaps one of them being the beautiful *Royal Oak*, which has rigging dating from about that time.

We can imagine these men – maybe half a dozen of them – in a light and airy workshop at Woolwich, perhaps overlooking the river, painstakingly working on this fine model, and wonder whether they actually completed it by the promised date of May 1744. One certain thing is that model-making, being of a 'curious nature, and tedious to be performed', has not changed a great deal.

The mention of the hull being 'Japanned' appears to refer to the black work of the wales and friezes, etc.

III. Models of Phineas Pett

The earliest certain evidence of English ship models refers to those made in the late sixteenth century by Shipwright Phineas Pett (1570–1647). Pett is also credited as having prepared in 1607 the earliest known model as a preliminary design, for the *Prince Royal*, 1610. This is not to say, however, that it was an uncommon practice at that time, for other shipwrights would almost certainly have made them as well, but with the lack of documentary evidence nothing is known of them, and it is only from the writings of Phineas Pett that we learn anything at all about the earliest models. In his autobiography, Pett makes a number of fascinating references to the models he either made himself or had prepared as designs for the ships he built.[1] Pett was employed by the Master Shipwright Matthew Baker until April 1596, when he was discharged and found work with his brother Joseph, another shipwright, on the rebuilding of the *Triumph* at Woolwich. The earliest mention of a model in the autobiography is from this period, which refers to one made by Pett during the winter of 1596–97:

> ...and was afterwards employed by my brother at Limehouse, upon a small model for the Lord Treasurer, William Cecil, Lord Burghley.

Phineas soon made another model:

> In December this year, 1599, I began a small model, which being perfected and very exquisitely set out and rigged, I presented it to my good friend, Mr John Trevor, who very kindly accepted the same of me.

Although much of the present contents of Burghley House still survive from the time of William Cecil, a small ship model unfortunately does not. But it is quite possible that either of the two earliest models made by Pett still exists. At the Ashmolean Museum, Oxford, there is a small rigged model of a ship of war, which has a length of 24in and a breadth of 5½in. The history of the model is unknown other than that it is recorded as being in the Museum's collection in 1685,[2] but it is reliably believed to date from the first few years of the seventeenth century or a little before, and is therefore, presumably, the earliest surviving model of an English ship, assuming that it is indeed of English origin.[3] It is impossible to identify this model or to suggest who it was made by. On the other hand, the fact that a small rigged model of a suitable date exists, and that Phineas Pett actually made two small models (one of which at least was rigged) at about the same time, means that the Ashmolean model *may* be one of them.

By April, 1607, Phineas Pett was building at Woolwich:

> After my settling at Woolwich, I begun a curious model for the Prince my Master, most part where-off, I wrought with my own hands; which being most fairly garnished with carving and painting, and placed in a frame, arched, covered, and curtained with crimson taffety, was, the 10th day of November by me presented to the Lord High Admiral at his lodging at Whitehall. His Lordship well approving of it, after I had supped with his Honour that night, gave me commandment to carry the same to Richmond, where the Prince, my master, then lay; which was accordingly performed the next day after, being Tuesday, and the 11th day. On Wednesday morning, being the 12th day, having acquainted Sir David Murray with my business, and he delivered the same to his Highness, order was given to have the model brought and placed in a private room in the Long Gallery, where his Highness determined to see it in the afternoon, but my ever honoured old Lord and master, unknown to me, studying by all means to do me good, had acquainted his Majesty with this thing, and the same day, unlooked for of any, procured his Majesty to make a purposed journey from Whitehall to Richmond to see the same model, whither he came in the afternoon, about 3 of the clock, accompanied only with the Prince, the Lord Admiral, and one or two attendants. His Majesty was exceedingly delighted with the sight of the model, and spent some time in questioning me divers material things concerning the same, and demanding whether I would build the Great Ship in all points like to the same, for I will (said his Majesty) compare them together when she shall be finished.

The 'Prince my master' was Henry, son of King James I, then aged 14 and Prince of Wales, and the ship was the *Prince Royal* built by Phineas Pett which was launched at Woolwich in 1610. The appearance of the *Prince* is well known from contemporary portraits of the ship, but whether she turned out 'in all points like to the same' as the model is a matter for conjecture. The model would no doubt have been a wonderful sight in its arched frame, probably with much gilt decoration contrasting with the rich crimson drapes. It seems that the model was made in little more than six months. Whether it was in frame like Pett's later model of the *Royal Sovereign* is not known.

Twenty-seven years later, Pett gives details in the autobiography of the famous plaything made for Prince Charles, then aged four, and later King Charles II:

> The 22nd of June 1634 was finished a little ship, being completely rigged and gilded, and placed upon a carriage with wheels resembling the sea; was enclosed in a great case of deals, and shipped for London in the *Fortune* pink, and was out of her taken into a wherry and carried through bridge to Scotland Yard, and from thence to St. James, where it was placed in the Long Gallery and presented to the Prince, who entertained it with a great deal of joy, being purposely made for him to disport himself withall.

It was argued at one time that the small model at the Ashmolean Museum was this 'little ship'.[4] More recently, the same model has been illustrated and stated as a fact that it was the toy given to Prince Charles by Pett, although there is no clear evidence to support the supposition.[5] The fact that it was crated in a 'great case of deals' and needed a pink and a wherry to transport it to St James Palace makes the connection with a model only 2ft long very difficult indeed to believe. As Pett said, it was a 'little ship' as distinct from a model, and it was probably large enough for young Charles to sit in and be wheeled about.

A few days later, a much more significant event took place:

> The 26th of June, 1634, his Majesty came to Woolwich in his barge to see the frame of the *Leopard*, then half built, and being in the ships hold, his Highness, calling me aside, privately aquainted me with his Princely resolution for the building of a great new ship, which he would have me to undertake, using these words to me, 'You have made many requests to me, and now I will make it my request to you to build this ship,' commanding me to attend his coming to Wanstead, where he would further confer with me about it.
>
> The 29th October, 1634, the model for the great new ship was carried to Hampton Court, and there placed in the Privy Gallery, where after his Majesty had seen and thoughrally perused, he commanded us to carry it back to Whitehall and place it in the Privy Gallery till his Majesty's coming thither; which was accordingly performed.

This model was the design for the 100-gun *Royal Sovereign*, or *Sovereign of the Seas*, 1637, built by Peter Pett under the supervision of his father, Phineas. At the time, the *Sovereign* was the largest and most fantastically decorated ship ever built.

Again we do not know how close she was built to Pett's design, but the model was evidently a very fine one. Some time between 1635 and 1637, a certain Peter Munday travelled to Woolwich and saw the *Sovereign* in building. At the same time, Munday visited Peter Pett's house:

> ...where wee sawe the Moddel or Molde of the said shippe, which was shewne unto his Majestie before he begun her. The said Modele was of admirable Workemanshipp, curiouslye painted and guilte, with azur and gold, soe contrived that every timber in her might be seene and left open and unplanked for that purpose, very neate and delightsome. There were also the moddels of divers other shippes lately built, but nothing to compare with the former.[6]

Although this is the earliest known record of a model built with an open framed hull, there is no reason to suppose, because it is not stated, that Pett's earlier model of the *Prince Royal*, and the others of ships 'lately built', were not constructed in the same way. The framed construction suggests that it was probably quite an elaborate model, despite the very short period of four months in which it was apparently built.

Footnotes

1. *The Autobiography of Phineas Pett,* Edited by W G Perrin, Navy Records Society (1917) Vol 51.
2. Edward Lhuyd, *Ashmolean manuscript catalogue* (1685).
3. For a description of the Ashmolean model and its probable date, see Note by A P McGowan in Arthur MacGregor's *Tradescant's Rarities* (Oxford 1983) p190.
4. Article by R Morton Nance, *The Mariner's Mirror* (1938) Vol 24, p95–100.
5. Christopher Falkus, *The Life and Times of Charles II,* (London 1972) p19.
6. *Travels of Peter Munday,* Hakluyt Society, Second Series, Vol XLV.

IV. Samuel Pepys and Models

Samuel Pepys, the great Naval Administrator, Diarist and Patron of the Arts, formed a large collection of ship models during his long tenure in Office as Clerk of the Acts, and later as Secretary to the Admiralty. At his death in 1703, Pepys bequeathed the collection to his friend and former servant William Hewer, and recommended in his will that they, together with some models owned by Hewer, should be 'Preserved for Publique Benefit'.[1] That they were not is a complete mystery. The collection was seen, apparently intact, a few years after the death of Pepys,[2] but this is the last we know of it, and the models were obviously dispersed, unless they were lost altogether by fire or other catastrophe. If they do still exist, however, it is possible that almost any one of the seventeenth-century models known today originated from Pepys' or Hewer's collections, but they cannot be recognised as such simply because of the lack of any known record as to which models the collections consisted of. But this does not mean that such records do not exist, and it is almost inconceivable that Pepys, who loved neatness and order in everything he did, should not have left at least a catalogue of the models in his own collection, as it is obvious from the Diary that he considered them highly important. The Rawlinson Collection at the Bodleian Library, Oxford, contains a vast amount of Pepys' correspondence and other papers, unsorted, uncatalogued and mostly unpublished, and if any material can be found at all concerning his models, it is probably there. In the famous Diary written in shorthand between 1659 and 1669, Pepys makes numerous interesting references to models, although disappointingly, only one is mentioned as being of a named ship, and no reference at all is made as to the purpose of them. A painting by J Seymour-Lucas at the Victoria and Albert Museum, and a scenic model at the Science Museum, London, depicts King Charles II, the Duke of York, Pepys in his capacity as Clerk of the Acts, and other members of the Navy Board examining a fine model of a proposed new ship. Whether this was normal procedure is uncertain. It is quite likely, but at the same time it is puzzling, and again disappointing, to find that in the whole of the Diary, no mention at all is made of an event as seemingly important as this, although there is much trivial detail concerning the Navy Board affairs. Some of the extracts from the Diary are well known, and have often been quoted, but it is appropriate to include them here in their entirety. The extracts are taken from the full modern transcription of the work.[3]

14 June 1661 (Vol 2, p121)
> I sent to my house, by my Lord's order, his shipp.

'My Lord' was the Earl of Sandwich, Pepys' patron, and the 'shipp' was a model of the Second Rate *Richard*, 1658, 70 guns. The ship was renamed the *Royal James* at the Restoration in 1660. Sandwich lent the model to Pepys.

5 October 1661 (Vol 2, p192)
> ...and so stayed at home all afternoon, putting up my Lord's modell of the *Royal James,* which I borrowed of him long ago to hang in my room.

Nothing more is known of this model, and it is presumably lost.

6 June 1662 (Vol 3, p103)
> At my office all alone all morning, and the smith being with me about other things, did open a chest that hath stood ever since I came to the office, in my office, and there we find the modell of a fine ship – which I long to know whether it be the King's or Mr Turner's.

The only comment that can be made on this model is that it must have been of a date prior to 1660, and that from a later mention of the same model, it was rigged. No rigged model of that period is known, and it too probably no longer exists. Thomas Turner was Clerk General at the Navy Office in the 1650s.

30 July 1662 (Vol 3, p149)
> Up early and to my office where Cooper came to me and begun his lecture upon the body of a ship, which my having a modell in the office is of great use to me.

Richard Cooper was a Sailing Master, whom Pepys employed to teach mathematics and instruct in seamanship.

1 August 1662 (Vol 3, p152)
> Up, my head akeing, [Pepys was the worse for drink], and to my office, where Cooper read me another lecture upon my modell, very pleasant.

It is interesting to note that Pepys now refers to it as 'my model'. Perhaps he had discovered that the model belonged to neither the King nor Mr Turner, and appropriated it for himself.

3rd August 1662 (Vol 3, p154)
Pepys went to Chatham to visit Navy Commissioner and Shipwright Peter Pett:

> And so to his house and had a syllabub and saw his closet, which came short of what I expected, but there were fine modells in it indeed, whose worthe I could not judge of.

The extent of this collection, and what ships the models represented, is completely unknown. Although it is strange that Pepys does not refer to any of these models by name, it is conceivable that they included the design prepared by Peter's father, Phineas Pett, for the *Royal Sovereign* 1637, which was probably still in existence at the time.

7 August 1662 (Vol 3, p158)
Up by 4 o'clock and to my office, and by and by, Mr Cooper comes and to our modell – which pleases me more and more.

9 August 1662 (Vol 3, p160)
Cooper came to the office again:
> . . . fell to work upon our modell, and did a good morning's work upon the rigging.

11 August 1662 (Vol 3, p163)
I to the office, whither cooper came and read his last lecture to me upon my modell, and so bid me god-bwy – he being to go tomorrow to Chatham to take charge of the ship I have got him.

Pepys had probably obtained this position for Cooper as payment for his instruction. On the same day, Pepys had another visitor:

> Mr Deane, the assistant at Woolwich came to me, who I find will discover to me the whole abuse that his Majesty suffers in the measuring of timber, of which I shall be glad. He promises me also a modell of a ship, which will please me exceedingly, for I do want one of my owne.

This was a rather touching remark, and Pepys' longing for a model was soon realised. It was the first time that Pepys had met Deane.

29 September 1662 (Vol 3, p208)
> Went home, where I find Mr Deane of Woolwich hath sent me the modell he had promised me. But it so exceeds my expectations that I am sorry almost, he should make such a present to no greater person; but I am exceedingly glad of it and shall study to do him a favour for it.

This model was probably not a new one specially made for Pepys, but rather one that had been prepared as a design for an

earlier ship, and had served its purpose. Anthony Deane, as Assistant at Woolwich, was presumably under the Master Shipwright Christopher Pett, who was building at that Dockyard in the 1650s and '60s. By 1662, Pett had built three ships at Woolwich – the *Speaker*, 1650, the *Swiftsure*, 1654, and the *Richard*, 1658. Whether Deane made the model himself is not explicit, but with the connection with Pett, it is quite possible it was either the *Speaker* or the *Swiftsure*, the model of the *Richard* being accounted for and still probably in Pepys' house. The model was perhaps given by Deane to Pepys with an ulterior motive, especially as the two had only met in August; it was an age in which when a favour was given, it was expected to be returned, and Pepys, as he said, certainly did this, for on his recommendation, Deane was appointed Master Shipwright at Harwich in 1664 at the tender age of 26.

30 December 1663 (Vol 4, p437)
> . . . and I through the garden to Mr Coventry, where I saw Mr Chr' Pett bring him a modell, and indeed it is a pretty one, for a New Year's gift – but I think the work not better done than mine.

This model too may have been either the *Speaker* or the *Swiftsure*. If Pett had built a model at all, it follows that it would almost certainly have been of a ship he had built himself. As a model (Model No 1) exists that conceivably represents the *Speaker*, it is possible that it is the very same one given to Coventry by Christopher Pett, but the connection is tenuous. William Coventry was Secretary to the Duke of York, and made Commissioner of the Navy in 1662.

19th June 1667 (Vol 8, p279)
> Peter Pett, when charged with the blame for the Medway disaster, and blamed for using of the boats for carrying away his goods instead of carrying up of the great ships, answered: He said he used never a boat till they were all gone but one – and that was to carry away things of great value, and these were his models of ships; which when the Council, some of them, had said they wished that the Dutch had had them instead of the King's ships, he answered, 'He did believe the Dutch would have made more advantage of the models than of the ships, and the King had greater loss thereby,' this they all laughed at.

This entry refers to the daring raid by the Dutch, when they entered the Medway on 12 and 13 June 1667, burnt some of the finest ships in the Navy and towed away the First Rate *Royal Charles* (ex-*Naseby*,

1655). Pett was clapped in the Tower on 18 June, partly for considering his models above the ships, although he was later released. It is not difficult to imagine the scene as Pett loaded the fragile models in his boat, perhaps by night, and we wonder where he took them, and why it was necessary by water. This is the last reference to models in the Diary.

Pepys had proposed to write (but never did) a History of the Navy, and in the 1680s and '90s he made notes for this purpose known as the 'Naval Minutes'.[4] The Navy Minutes were published by the Navy Records Society in 1925, and it contains some interesting comments on various models. The notes are undated.

> *p.186.* Observe the little use, or rather total neglect, of that admirable model of the *Royal James* (I think it is), made and given to Christ's Hospital by Sir A Deane.

If Pepys was correct in that the model was of the First Rate *Royal James*, it may have been either the ship of 1671 or 1675, both built by Deane. As Pepys was not absolutely sure of the name of the model, the only other possibility is that it was the First Rate *Royal Charles*, 1673, the only other three-decker built by Deane.

> *p.222.* Sir A. Deane speaks of a model of the *Royal Charles* shown at a Public House, viz, the Three Pigeons at Ratcliffe.

Although Deane had built the *Royal Charles* at Portsmouth in 1673, the way this is worded suggests that the model had no connection with him, and it is possible that it was actually of the First Rate *Naseby*, 1655, renamed the *Royal Charles* at the Restoration in 1660. Models were apparently made of nearly all the largest ships, and it is quite likely that one of the *Naseby* existed at some time, although if that was the case it is not known to have survived.

> *p.239. Draughts of Ships and Models.* Neither the former, if done in the usual manner upon boards, nor much more the latter, are portable without being exposed to view, as being bulky, and nonesuch therefore could be carried over by Sir A. Deane, without Capt. Fazeby's, and his servants privity, who both are ready to attest of the baggage he carried with him.

Pepys was accused in 1679 of Popery, Piracy and Treachery, and selling to the King of France charts and other Naval secrets, which apparently included models. He obviously wrote this in defence of the charge. The note refers to the occasion in 1675 when

Deane, accompanied by William Hewer, delivered two yachts he had built for the King of France and it seems as though the charts and models were allegedly taken to France at that time. Deane was equally implicated, and both men were committed to the Tower on 22 May 1679, but released on bail for the staggering sum of £30,000 each in July the same year, and later cleared of the charges.

p.246. Monsieur Denise says that to his knowledge, Captain Wentworth did, in the year '71, sell a model of a Fourth Rate ship to Monsieur de Vauvre for 55 guineas.

This is revealing for illustrating the value of a model at that time, as 55 guineas was a considerable sum. A fine seventeenth-century model could still have been purchased for less than £100 as recently as before the last war. Monsieur Denise was a French Merchant and a friend of Pepys.

Footnotes

1. J R Tanner (Ed), *Further Correspondence of Samuel Pepys* (1929) Appendix to Vol 2.
2. John Aubrey, *National History of Surrey* (1719).
3. *The Diary of Samuel Pepys* transcribed and edited by Robert Latham and William Matthews, London, eleven volumes (1970–83).
4. *Samuel Pepys' Naval Minutes* edited by J R Tanner, Navy Records Society (1925) Vol 60.

V. Steering Arrangements

One of the unsolved mysteries of sailing ship development is the date and exact nature of the process whereby the steering wheel was introduced. However, this is one area where a study of Navy Board ship models can suggest at least an outline of that process.

In the seventeenth century the mechanical means for conveying movement to the tiller from the helmsman was the whipstaff. In a short transitional period beginning in approximately 1700, this gave way to a steering wheel linked to the tiller by an arrangement of ropes. Where it has been possible to examine the interiors of models, it appears that the extent of this detailed work hidden below decks is extremely variable from one model to another. Tillers and other details are fairly commonplace on seventeenth-century models, but the whipstaff itself is rarely in place, and in the later period, there is seldom any rope fitted between the wheel and tiller. There are, however, several examples with complete steering systems, and the following is based mainly on the evidence from four models – two with the whipstaff, and two with the wheel. It should be mentioned that in most

Fig 115 *A seventeenth-century whipstaff, as fitted on the Second Rate* Coronation, *1685 (Model No 9) (Drawing by Arnold Kriegstein).*

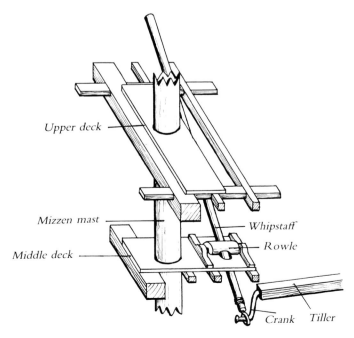

Upper deck

Mizzen mast

Middle deck

Whipstaff

Rowle

Crank   Tiller

cases, any angles and dimensions given are necessarily based on visual estimation, which although approximate, are reasonably accurate for all practical purposes.

The whipstaff

The whipstaff was a long vertical pole which extended up from the tiller to the deck above via a rotating fitting in the deck called a rowle (see Fig 115). From a midship position, the initial movement was side to side by using the whipstaff as a lever, which progressively reverted to a pushing and pulling one by the helmsman as more or fewer degrees of helm were required. The whipstaff was in use on all ships except for those with a single deck, and due to the length of tiller, it was always positioned just abaft the mizzen mast, with the helmsman on the middle deck of three-deckers, and the upper deck of two-deckers. Small seventeenth-century ships with a single deck were steered by tiller on the open quarter-deck, although provision was also made for a tiller below if the occasion arose.[1]

There appears to be no contemporary evidence – either in words or illustration – that specifically refers to the tiller angle obtained by the English whipstaff, and until fairly recently, it was generally believed that only about five degrees was possible. This would have been almost useless for steering a large ship, and the misconception seems to have come about because it was assumed that the whipstaff was fixed in the rowle, whereas in reality, it was a loose sliding fit. This theory was first proposed by Jean Boudriot, when he conclusively demonstrated that the whipstaff in use on French ships was capable of pushing the tiller over to an angle of at least 20 degrees.[2] The whipstaffs as fitted on English models are, of course, utterly reliable evidence of contemporary practice, being the next best thing to a full-sized one, and it is not surprising that they are little different to their French counterparts, except in detail.

The whipstaff from the Second Rate *Coronation*, 1685, illustrated in Fig 115 is exceptionally long – about the equivalent of 14ft or even more – but the side to side movement is severely restricted by carlings on the upper deck which limit the tiller angle to only a few degrees. There would be little point in such a long pole if its length could not be fully employed, and one can assume that the carlings were fitted in error, unless intended to be removable.

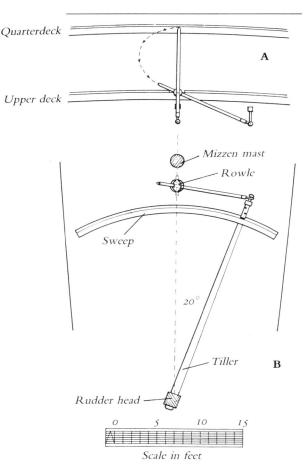

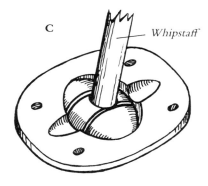

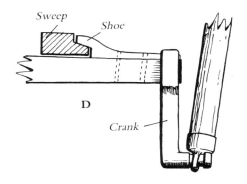

Fig 116 *Details of the whipstaff on the* Hampton Court, *1678 (Model No 6).*

A *Fore and aft view, showing the whipstaff with the tiller in midships and at an angle of 20 degrees. The whipstaff is 12ft 0in long overall, and 4½in in diameter.*

B *Plan view showing the 'sweep' which supported the forward end of the tiller. The tiller is 12in square aft, ½in square forward, and 25ft 0in long from the forward side of the rudder head.*

C *Enlarged detail of the steering rowle. Note the necessary grooves in the surround for the whipstaff when laid over to its fullest extent.*

D *Detail at the tiller end showing the connecting fittings with the whipstaff, and the rabbeted sweep which is bolted to the underside of the upper deck beams. The sliding 'shoe', the 'crank', and the ferrulled eye at the end of the whipstaff are meticulously made from brass. The forward end of the shoe extends beneath the strap of the crank, and is further fastened by two brass bolts through the tiller. The crank is offset from the end of the tiller about 2ft 0in, centre to centre.*

The whipstaff details illustrated in Fig 116 are from the *Hampton Court*, 1678 (see Model No 6). A tiller angle of 20 degrees is achieved by pushing the pole through the rowle to within 2ft of its upper end. A small hole is bored through the upper end, which suggests that it may have been intended for a rope beckett as an aid to pulling the whipstaff back through the rowle. The rowle itself is quite different in construction to that on the *Coronation*, but is typical of those fitted on models dating from the 1690s and early eighteenth century. The pivots at each end of the rowle are presumably let down into recesses in a closely spaced pair of athwartship deck beams, with the surround bolted down to hold it in position. To prevent the whipstaff from jamming in the rowle at extremes of helm, the hole must have been considerably enlarged on its lower side. An alternative way would be to fit the rowle so that its aft end was slightly lower, and by boring the hole vertically, the angle as it turned would tend to follow that of the whipstaff.

Helmsman's companions

Associated with the whipstaff are helmsman's companions. An excellent definition of one is given in a contract-specification for a Third Rate of 1664: 'To make a companion at the aft end of the quarterdeck to lie a convenient height for cutting out of the lights in it to have the better sight of the sails, and likewise to afford length for the whipstaff'.[3] Companions were fitted only on ships with two decks, as they were no use for a helmsman buried deep down on the middle deck of the larger vessels. Their position was always on the quarterdeck just abaft the mizzen mast, and directly above the whipstaff. But companions are not often seen on models, and it appears that they were not standard fittings, at least in the latter half of the seventeenth century, although they may have been more common in earlier times. The *Hampton Court* with the very detailed whipstaff, for example, does not have one, and we can be sure that if one had been intended it would have been fitted on the model. Referring to Fig 116A, it can be seen that a companion was not really necessary, firstly because the whipstaff does not protrude above the quarterdeck, and secondly, a helmsman on a two-decker had no more need to have a 'better sight of the sails' than did his counterpart on a ship with three decks. It is noticeable, too, that when companions *are* fitted, they are not wide enough athwartship to allow any significant increase in the length of the whipstaff due to its swing from side to side (see Fig 117). Of the very few examples of companions noted on models, most are in combination with a steering wheel, and date from the early eighteenth century.

The rope steering system

The rope and wheel steering introduced in around 1700, or perhaps a little before, was an ingenious yet simple device, and a major development. The mechanical advantage over the whipstaff must have been considerable, and the helmsman – still in a position abaft the mizzen mast – had the facility of being on the open quarterdeck. The steering would have been remarkably sensitive. With a tiller length of 24ft 0in, and a 1ft 6in diameter rope drum, for example, a rudder angle of around 5 degrees could be obtained by only half a turn of the wheel. From the time of the first introduction of rope steering, it was possible to obtain a rudder angle limited only by the internal breadth of the ship and the length of the tiller. A greater rudder angle would have been achieved with a short tiller, but a long one was necessary to provide sufficient leverage,

Fig 117 *Helmsman's companion on the Third Rate Boyne, 1692. Unlike on other models, the companion is aft of the poop bulkhead due to its proximity with the mizzen mast position. The grating in the top is presumably for conveying orders to the helmsman below. A steering rowle is fitted in the upper deck directly below the companion, but the whipstaff itself is not in place (Model No 11).*

Fig 118 *Plan of the tiller and steering ropes on a First or Second Rate of about 1702. The pair of angled sheaves on the centre line lead the ropes up to an athwartship windlass on the quarterdeck. The sheaves at the side are fitted in large timber knees. The forward end of the tiller appears to foul the ropes leading to the sheaves on the centre line, but it does not because the sheaves at the side are at a lower level. At the angle shown, the rope system would slacken by about 12in with the tiller put*

and it remained about the same in length as when the whipstaff was in use. Although efficient, there was an inherent defect in the rope steering in that as the helm was put over, the rope became progressively slack. This depended on the angle of the rope to the end of the tiller (see Figs 118 and 119). The amount of slackness can be calculated by measuring the length of rope between the sheaves at the side and the end of the tiller when in midships, and again when the tiller is put over to its maximum extent.

The earliest certain evidence of the arrangement of ropes is confined entirely to one model – a First or Second Rate dating from around 1702, or conceivably a few years before (see Fig 118). Although it is impossible to verify, it may have been the very first experiment made to demonstrate the new fangled steering method. If so, it would not be altogether surprising that the system was not perfected at the first attempt. Superficially, there is an excessive

over to 28 degrees. The absence of a sweep – which would have been similar to the one illustrated in Fig 116 – is an omission by the modeller (Model No 13).

Fig 119 *Plan of the tiller and steering ropes on the Third Rate Royal Oak, date uncertain, but probably not later than 1714. The sheaves at the*

slackness in the rope of about 12in with the helm over at an angle of 28 degrees, and the rope leading from the side to the centre sheaves appears to foul the end of the tiller. Assuming that the tiller would traverse from side to side on a sweep (which is not fitted), at an even distance below the deck beams, the sheaves at the side are not at the same level as might be thought, but about 2ft 0in lower. This seems odd at first, but it was probably deliberate, as the lower level of the sheaves would progressively take up most, if not all, of the slack in the rope, until as the tiller neared its maximum angle, the pull of the rope became ineffective.

It was probably realised quite quickly that the slackening could be minimised by arranging the rope to the tiller end at a more suitable angle. The steering ropes of the *Royal Oak* illustrated in Fig 119 show that there is a slackening of about 3in with the tiller at 25 degrees, and no improvement

side are contained in large blocks fastened below an upper deck beam, and tiller stops are fitted under the next beam aft. The rope leading to the tiller end is at a smaller angle than that shown in Fig 118, and would slacken by about 3in with the helm put over to 25 degrees. No sweep is fitted. (Model No 25).

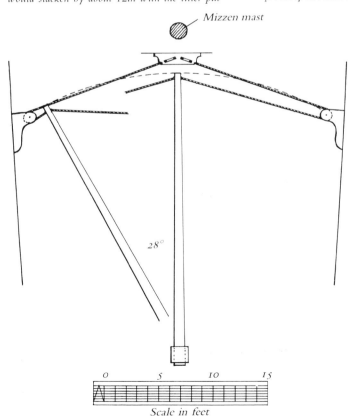

Mizzen mast

28°

0 5 10 15

Scale in feet

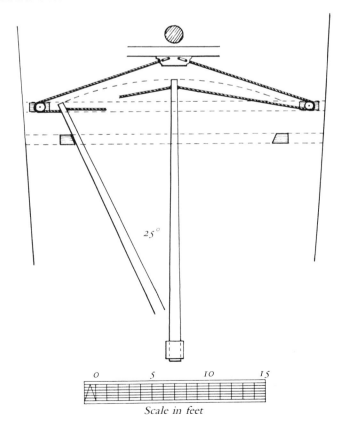

25°

0 5 10 15

Scale in feet

Fig 120 *An athwartship steering windlass as fitted on the First or Second Rate of about 1702. This is one of the very few models where the steering rope is in place and linked to the tiller.*

on this was possible at the time. This was very little, and considering the weight of rope, and its total length (some 70ft 0in on a Third Rate two-decker), it was probably only felt at the steering wheel as being somewhat 'spongy'. But the slack was entirely eliminated at some time in the second half of the eighteenth century, when the rope was taken round the arc of the sweep, and it therefore remained at the

same tension throughout the traverse of the tiller from side to side. In the 1730s and '40s, there was a general tendency to shift the steering wheel to a position forward of the mizzen mast, presumably to allow an increase in the accommodation area on the quarterdeck. This made no difference to the angle of the rope to the end of the tiller, but it might have allowed a small increase in the tiller length, in which case the sheaves at the side would have been shifted forward in turn by the same amount.

Steering wheels

The earliest evidence of a steering wheel, if it can be called that, is found on the model of a First or Second Rate dating from around 1702, and is presumably the only example of its type (see Fig 120). Despite its primitive appearance, it was probably an efficient device for steering a ship, and the sweep of the cranked handles is at least equal to the small diameter spoked wheels which soon followed. But to what extent a windlass of this type was in use on ships, if at all, is unknown. It may be an isolated example, as wheels are not generally seen on models until several years later.

Some early eighteenth-century steering wheels are illustrated in Figs 121, and it is quite remarkable how they suddenly appeared in a form little different from those still in use today on many craft. They are about 4ft 6in in diameter and have eight spokes. On models of the larger ships, the wheel is usually on the forward end of the rope drum, being close to the poop bulkhead, but on smaller ships with a short poop it might be at either end. Over a period of 10 to 15 years beginning around 1735, the wheel generally became a double one positioned forward of the mizzen mast, but examples can be found that are double and still abaft the mast, and single wheels are sometimes seen forward of it. At around the same time, the wheels became larger, at up to 6ft 0in in diameter, and those on the larger ships often have ten spokes.

Footnotes

1. Public Record Office, Adm 106/3070, contract-specification for the Sixth Rate *Penzance*, 1695.
2. Article by Jean Boudriot in *Neptunia*, No 129, winter 1978.
3. Public Record Office, SP 46/136 f227. Specification for a Third Rate dated 1664.

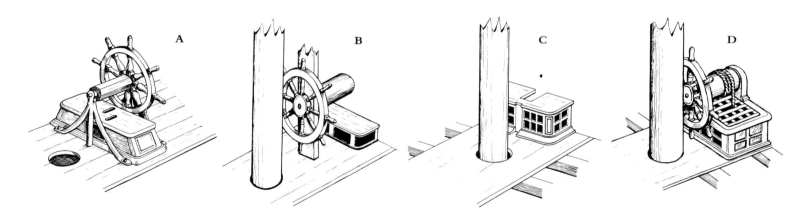

Fig 121 *Early eighteenth-century steering wheels and companions.*

A *Fourth Rate, 1701. The model is the earliest one known to be fitted with a steering wheel. It also has a rowle for the whipstaff on the upper deck directly below the companion. This would be an awkward arrangement, as the ropes leading down from the wheel would coincide with the position of the rowle, and it is possible that the wheel itself was fitted at a later date (Model No 16).*

B *Third Rate of about 1705. The companion is placed against the poop bulkhead, which serves as a support for the aft end of the steering rope drum. There is no whipstaff, and it is uncertain whether there is a rowle for it, but the typical cranked fitting for the whipstaff is in place at the forward end of the tiller (Model No 18).*

C *Third Rate of about 1714. The companion shows evidence of a steering wheel, but it is presumably lost, unless one was intended and not actually fitted. Whether any whipstaff details are fitted is uncertain, but it would be*

improbable at this late date. (Model in the possession of Mr V Montagu).

D *Third Rate Royal Oak. There is no evidence of a whipstaff on this model, and it is possible that companions were retained on some ships as a means of communication between the Captain – whose quarters would be on the upper deck below the steering position – and the helmsman. In full-sized practice, there would have been six or seven turns of rope round the drum instead of only three as shown (Model No 25).*

Index